Gertrude Williams

THE ECONOMICS OF
EVERYDAY LIFE

Third Edition

Penguin Books

Penguin Books Ltd, Harmondsworth, Middlesex, England
Penguin Books, 625 Madison Avenue, New York, New York 10022, U.S.A.
Penguin Books Australia Ltd, Ringwood, Victoria, Australia
Penguin Books Canada Ltd, 2801 John Street, Markham, Ontario, Canada L3R 1B4
Penguin Books (N.Z.) Ltd, 182–190 Wairau Road, Auckland 10, New Zealand

—

First published 1950
Reprinted 1951
Revised and reprinted 1953
Reprinted 1955, 1958, 1961, 1962
Second Edition 1964
Reprinted 1965, 1967, 1968, 1970
Third Edition 1972
Reprinted 1973
Revised and reprinted 1976
Reprinted 1978

—

—

Made and printed in Great Britain
by Hazell Watson & Viney Ltd
Aylesbury, Bucks
Set in Intertype Baskerville

CONTENTS

Foreword   7

Note to the 1976 edition   8

1. Introduction : What is Economics About?   9
2. Price Economy and Planned Economy   18
3. National Wealth and Productivity   40
4. The Structure of Industry   51
5. The Location of Industry   76
6. Markets and Shops   101
7. What is Money?   128
8. Imports and Exports   148
9. Incomes and How We Get Them   199
10. Ups and Downs in Production and Employment   264
11. The Welfare State   290
12. The Meaning and Extent of Poverty   321
13. Conflicting Values   336

Index   357

PELICAN BOOKS

THE ECONOMICS OF EVERYDAY LIFE

Lady Williams has spent her working life (with the exception of some of the war years) as a member of the staff of Bedford College, University of London, where she was Professor of Social Economics. She is now Professor Emeritus of the University of London. She has lectured widely on socio-economic subjects in the West Indies, Denmark, Germany, the U.S.A. and Israel for the Colonial Office, the Foreign Office, the British Council and the Hebrew University of Jerusalem.

She did a considerable amount of work on Government bodies and acted as independent member of several Wages Councils which fix statutory wages for various occupations. She was also a member of the Committee of Enquiry which advised the Government on measures concerned with the treatment of those suffering from occupational diseases.

During recent years she has been primarily concerned with manpower problems, and her researches into the methods of training young people for skilled trades resulted in a book, *Recruitment to Skilled Trades*. Her subsequent book, *Apprenticeship in Europe: The Lessons for Britain*, based on inquiries into methods of training in every industrial country in Europe, included recommendations which were accepted by the Government in its White Paper on Industrial Training which led eventually to the Industrial Training Act, 1964. Since the passing of that Act she has been a member of the Central Training Council (which advises the Minister) and of most of its constituent committees. She has carried out inquiries into preparation for employment in India, Hong Kong, Malaysia and Singapore.

In addition to many articles and pamphlets she has written several books of which the best known are *The State and the Standard of Living: The Price of Social Security* (a study of labour mobility); *Women and Work*; and *The Coming of the Welfare State*.

She was created a C.B.E. in 1953. She was married to Sir William Emrys Williams, C.B.E., formerly Secretary-General of the Arts Council of Great Britain.

FOREWORD

THIS book is intended for the ordinary citizen who is interested in knowing something of the economic issues which lie behind the political problems of the day. Whether we know anything about the principles of economics or not we all find ourselves taking part in discussions on economic questions; e.g. should pubs be nationalized, the dollar gap, are prices too high? should the wages of such and such workers be raised? and so on. But, even more important, we spend our time in making economic decisions which may have wide repercussions. Practically everything we do involves the use of scarce resources. We may think it a matter that affects nobody but ourselves when we decide to buy a woollen shirt instead of a cotton one, to buy a packet of cigarettes or give up smoking, to go to the movies or to take a day off and go fishing. Yet every one of these seemingly simple decisions has innumerable reactions on the whole of our economic organization and, consequently, on other people's lives. We cannot escape this responsibility and, therefore, it is worth while to know something of how our economy works.

This book will not make the reader into an economist; its aim is to give him some idea of the nature of economic problems. One of the most useful results of a study of economic issues is a certain attitude of mind and the realization that there is no simple hundred per cent answer to most economic questions. The same thing may be good in some circumstances and bad in others, and you have to look all round the problem and weigh up the costs involved for what you are going to achieve before you can decide whether it is worth doing or not. Perhaps the most valuable lesson one can learn from a study of economics is distrust of the man with a panacea; you can almost always be sure that the snap answer is the wrong answer.

NOTE TO THE 1976 EDITION

THE economic situation has been changing so rapidly in the last few years that it is impossible to say with certainty that all the figures given in this book are correct at the time of publication. Though a very great effort has been made to update all the facts and figures before going to press, the reader should take this changing situation into account.

G.W.

Chapter 1

INTRODUCTION: WHAT IS
ECONOMICS ABOUT?

ECONOMICS is about the everyday things of life; how we get our living and why sometimes we get more and sometimes less. Nowadays everybody realizes the important part played in their lives by economic factors, because nothing seems to stay put for more than a few weeks on end. Prices are continually changing, generally upwards, and no sooner do we congratulate ourselves on being a bit better off than we seem to lose all we have gained because of having to pay more for everything we want. Industries, such as coal mines and railways, which we have taken for granted as a natural part of the scene, decline in size, and other quite new ones, electronics and plastics and so on, take their place as big fields of employment; and these changes in size directly affect the lives of hundreds of thousands of families.

Those of us who are now middle-aged can recall the shock we had during the war when the scarcity of so many of the goods we needed for our day-to-day living brought vividly home to us how much we depend on the four corners of the world for all the things we normally use without generally giving a moment's thought to their origin.

There was a time when each family actually produced for itself most of the things it needed for its everyday life; it grew its own food and made its own clothes and household equipment. In such circumstances there is an obvious and inescapable connection between the resources of the neighbourhood, the work done by the people who live there, and the kind of life they live; and nobody bothers very much to speculate about the whys and wherefores. If you have little to eat, it is because the land is not fertile, or a storm destroyed the crops, or you have not worked hard enough –

something that is easy to understand. In most of what we call
the Third World, the less developed countries, that kind of
production is still the rule, but it is a long time since it ceased
in this country and, for that matter, it is fast disappearing
all over the world. Apart from growing a few vegetables in
the garden, or knitting a jumper or two, most of us have no
idea how to make the dozens of different things we use in the
course of a day and should not have the slightest conception
how to set about getting them if we could not buy them
at a store. The breakfast table seems a humdrum enough
affair; but if we think of the origin of the goods that were
collected on it this morning it sounds more like the gift of a
fairy godmother. The porridge oats came from Canada or
Scotland, the wheat for the bread from the U.S.A., Argentine,
or, perhaps, England, the bacon from Denmark or Ireland,
the butter or margarine from New Zealand, the tea from
India or Ceylon, the coffee from Brazil, the marmalade was
made from oranges from Spain or California or Israel with
sugar from the West Indies. The tablecloth was made of
cotton grown in Egypt or America or India, and was woven
in Lancashire, the cups and saucers and the knives and forks
were almost certainly manufactured in England. All these
things were bought at a shop and paid for with money
earned by work as a clerk or an engineer or a bus-driver or
punching eyelet holes in shoes, for we specialize in doing one
thing – it may be only a tiny process in the manufacturing
of an article – and with the payment we get for our work
we buy the things we want from others.

In the modern world, therefore, the relationship between
work and wants is much less direct than it used to be, for
most of us spend our time making things for sale and not for
our own use. This specialization, which is the characteristic
of the modern economy, enables us to enjoy things of which
our grandfathers never dreamed, motor-cars and bicycles
and planes, vacuum cleaners and refrigerators, nylon and
plastic clothing, more varied foods, and all sorts of other
goods, but it also makes the world very much more complex.

We make for a market, so that the price we get from what we do, and the prices we have to pay for the things we want to buy, come to be of dominating importance, and anything which alters these prices has an immense influence on our lives. Our whole livelihood may be ruined by something happening in a far corner of the world. The Lancashire cotton weaver, for example, may have found his pay packet smaller because the boll weevil had destroyed the cotton crop in the U.S.A. or because Indians desired national independence. Or the price of coal may go down because scientists find out how to harness water-power to generate electricity in Italy.

The exploitation of natural gas from the North Sea has had an influence on many industries and occupations, and the exploitation of oil, when it really starts flowing, will profoundly change the pattern of world trade. Even as it is, the building of all the necessary installations for the refining of the oil has introduced a whole host of new jobs to the coastal areas of Scotland and, however much some people may dislike the urbanization of beautiful districts, has brought a new prosperity to what was before a rather poor locality.

We are all, in fact, bits of a gigantic jigsaw puzzle, and it is not until we begin to see the pieces fitted together that we get any idea of the general pattern. Who decides what shall be produced in different places and arranges for it to be done? Why does the bacon come from Denmark and the cutlery from Sheffield? Who settles how much each of us has to spend – why do some of us get £30 a week and others £10,000 a year?

The obvious question to ask at this point is, Why bother about the general pattern? Why cannot we content ourselves with doing our work and spending our incomes without bothering our heads about the way in which it fits together? The answer is that we bother because we are not satisfied with it and would like it to be different. We know that there are hundreds of thousands of people living in narrow poverty, that many are perpetually haunted by the fear of the future and the unemployment it may bring, that there is an enormous amount of misery and disease, that thousands live in insanitary, overcrowded houses, and that all sorts of unhappiness might be prevented by different economic conditions.

Need we be poor? Are we producing as efficiently as we could? and if not, why not? and how could we do better? Are we producing the 'right' things? What are the 'right' things? Who ought to decide this, and why? Is specialization always a 'good' method of production? and in what sense 'good'? Might we become too dependent on foreign supplies and does this matter? Is it better to buy goods produced in your own country? 'Better' in what sense? Does it make one richer? or safer? or what? Is monopoly better than competition? always? sometimes? in what circumstances? Why does a factory worker usually earn less than a doctor? and what would happen if you insisted that they should get the same amount? Why does the Government settle some prices and not others? and who settles the price if the Government doesn't?

These are the sort of questions that a study of economics helps us to answer. They are also the kind of questions which underlie the issues on which the ordinary citizen votes at elections, but most people are likely to pay more careful attention to a TV 'Do It Yourself' programme showing you how to make a garden path or mend a leaky tap than to one which attempts a serious analysis of economic problems. If a motor-car breaks down nobody but a fool expects to be able to repair it without some elementary understanding of the mechanism, and the economic system is a good deal more dangerous to tinker with than a car. Unfortunately it is also much more difficult to understand, and there are two main reasons for this.

1. The various bits and pieces of a car are identical in all cars of one pattern, and you know exactly how each bit works in relation to others. But the bits of the economic system are human beings who are not identical and whose actions cannot be precisely calculated or foretold.

2. More important than this variability of human actions is the fact that you cannot separate people's economic activities from the remainder of their lives, and that all sorts of things which are not primarily economic influence the way in which men and women behave in earning and spending their incomes. We are not robots, and there is no such thing as an economic man. We all live in social groups, and the things we value or despise, the kinds of behaviour that we extol or condemn, or simply take for granted as natural, and the ends for which we are ready to make sacrifices, are all products of our cultural codes of behaviour. From our earliest moments we are shaped by the social forces in which we live – even as babies we are kissed for one kind of behaviour and scolded for another – so that by the time we begin to take a place in the wider social groupings, at school, at work, or in the outside world, we have come to respond to certain stimuli and reject others. Our scales of value are not individual ones; they are the personal variations we make on the social evaluations fixed by the community in which we have grown up.

We have only to think of the difference between the U.S.A. and, say, the greater part of China to realize the influence of this on economic activities. In America it is generally accepted that you ought to try and go one better than your father, and the man who, by daring experiment and readiness to break with the past, increases his material wealth is the one on whom the stamp of social approval is set; in China it is exactly the reverse – the palm is given to wisdom of age and there is the strongest urge to follow the traditional path; or at least this was so until very recently and probably still is so in areas that are not very passionately Communist. It is not surprising, therefore, that America and not China is the home of mechanical invention and higher material standards of living.

These two points are worth stressing because it is necessary to realize that economics is a study of a living and working society and not a blueprint for an ideal community. The aim is not to find out how people ought to behave in different circumstances, but how, in fact, they do behave in the circumstances in which they live. By patient observation we try to discover if there are ways of reacting which are so general that we can use them as guides in our attempts to prognosticate the future, and it is to these generalizations, based on observed facts of human behaviour, that we give the name 'economic laws'. Such laws are not, therefore, in the same category as the laws of chemistry or of natural science; we cannot say that, given such and such circumstances, such a result is bound to ensue; all we can say is that it is likely to ensue with the proviso, either implied or explicit, that there may be – will be – innumerable exceptions to the general rule. It is, for example, true in a general sense that the majority of people in an industrialized country such as England are eager to get as good a money return for their work as they can, so that a rise in wages in one industry may be expected to draw larger supplies of workers into it and a fall to cause many workers to withdraw and find other jobs. By and large, and given time for changes in wage rates to become widely known, this is true; but it does not mean that every person always goes to the job that pays best in this way. A man may be attached to a particular kind of work or to the firm that has employed him for some time; he may not want to move from the locality where his friends and family live, may prefer country life to urban (or vice versa), or the 'amenities' that go with one type of work, such as higher social prestige, or greater freedom, or what have you. In a society in which the material equipment of well-being (good furniture, good clothes, the fridge in the kitchen, etc.) is given the highest place in social evaluations changes in wage rates are likely to have a much more direct influence on supplies of labour than in one in which all these other factors play a bigger part. What adds to the difficulty is that the pattern of behaviour is not a static thing but is continually being modified by new circumstances and ideas, and one must be forever on the alert not to assume that the series of economic reactions observed in the past will inevitably repeat itself without modification in the future. There is no doubt, for example, that during the present century both security and leisure have come to play a much bigger part in the economic calculations of the wage-earner than they did in his father's time, and this must be taken into account both in the attempt to explain what has happened in the occupational distribution of the population and in the efforts we make to alter it if we think this necessary.

Blunders are often made, and a good deal of ill temper is engendered, through ignorance of the influence of the cultural pattern on economic behaviour, when two communities of widely differing types of social organization are brought into contact with one another. When the colonization of Africa began, Western businessmen could not understand why native populations were unwilling to work regularly for fixed hours throughout the year when the material rewards they could get for doing so were obviously so much higher than could be made on their own pieces of ground. They found it difficult to accept the fact that many Africans rated freedom from routine, idleness, and occasional ostentatious spending higher than the elaborate equipment of living which takes so high a place in the social evaluations of Western communities; they thought the Africans immoral since they were unwilling to work for the kind of life that the Western wage-earner thinks desirable.

If you remember what kittle cattle human beings are, you will not blame the economist because he is unwilling to make precise and categorical statements about people's actions in getting a living. Almost everything he says must be hedged about with qualifications and modifications if it is to have any relation to truth, for it is no use pretending that men are machines when they are not. But there is another accusation brought against economists on rather different grounds.

What is the use of asking economists for advice, it is asked, when they never agree on what should be done? You find

economists who support free trade and economists in favour
of tariffs; you find some who believe in the planned economy
and others who are just as strongly in support of private
enterprise, and so on. Whatever question you consider, on
which you think the economist could give you an expert
opinion, you are fairly sure to find divided ranks. So why
bother with their views at all? There are two answers to this
criticism. The first is that economics is like every other intellectual discipline; it can develop only by accumulating
more and more knowledge and by more and more careful
experiment in the interpretation of the facts it collects. How
often you find that doctors disagree in the diagnosis and
treatment of a disease; but you do not, therefore, say that
medical science is useless and that it is never of any value to
consult a doctor. The same is true of economics. And moreover there is the added difficulty that the economic body is
perpetually changing and that the economist is compelled to
try to make his analysis while the very thing he is studying is
in process of becoming something else.

But there is a second and more important answer. The
economist is concerned with the production and exchange of
wealth; that is, he is concerned with that as an economist. As
a human being and a citizen he is, of course, as concerned as
anybody else with matters of right and wrong, virtue, duty,
beauty, and the rest. But on these he is no more an expert
than the next man. He can give an expert opinion that, say,
if we insist on growing all our cereals within our own political
boundaries our standard of living is bound to fall and by so
much, but he cannot say that we are wrong to do so, because
man does not live by bread alone, and we may believe that it
is better to eat less, but to have a larger proportion of the
population engaged in agricultural pursuits, or to be less
dependent on foreign supplies in case of war, or put forward
any other objective we value. As getting a living is only part
of a man's life there are practically no questions that are
purely economic in scope, and we have always to balance the
effect of our actions on our wealth with the other non-

economic results they are likely to have. The economist can give an opinion on the economic side of the matter; but he has no more right than anybody else to claim a special hearing on what constitutes the good life or right conduct.

Chapter 2

PRICE ECONOMY AND PLANNED ECONOMY

IF there were enough of everything we wanted we should not need to bother how each of us gets a share; we don't, for instance, count the number of times we breathe, because there is enough air for everybody. But most of the things we want are not free as air and we have to find some way of deciding how much each of us can have. There are two different ways of sharing out goods when the supply is not enough to satisfy everybody, and one of the biggest controversies in the world today centres round the decision of which of these two is the better. In one system we are perfectly free to buy as much of a commodity or service as we like provided we can pay the price asked, and we ration ourselves to the amount we think we can afford; in the other, the Government decides how much of the article shall be made available and what share each of us shall have.

Scarcity is a permanent characteristic of all human society and is the basis of the problem that faces, and always has faced, the human race whatever its form of organization. It springs from the fact that the material resources of the world are limited and that our ability to make use of those resources is even more limited by our ignorance. Everything that we need to satisfy our wants has to be derived finally from two sources – the natural resources that are available and the human ability to make use of them. As our knowledge grows and we increase our skill, we can exploit more and more of the opportunities that nature offers to us. The increase in communications, for example, has brought within our reach the resources of vast areas that were closed to us before; the development in scientific knowledge has made accessible many valuable minerals from depths below the earth's surface that could not be reached by earlier generations. Railways, steamships, and aircraft have vastly extended the 'neighbourhood' on whose resources we can draw, and our increasing skill – both in techniques and in organization – enables us to get more out of what we can reach. But whatever the rate of development may be there is, at any one time, a limit to the total of what can be produced. Here and now, there is only so much of the material resources of the world accessible to us and there are only so many people capable of work and endowed with the capacities and skills that they have developed. We may know that there are immense mineral deposits waiting to be tapped in the Arctic Circle, but, until we find out how to get them, they might as well not exist as far as the satisfaction of our present wants is concerned. No doubt we waste a lot by stupidity; but even if the very best possible use is made of all the resources we can reach, there is still a limit to what can be produced out of them, and it is out of that total that we must satisfy our wants. If our wants were smaller than the amounts we could produce we should not, of course, be faced with any problem of choice and, indeed, in some very simple societies this is the case. Where the pattern of life is both rigid and simple and nature is fairly generous, as was the position in some parts of Africa and the South Seas before the advent of the white man, the adjustment of wants to the wealth available was so much a matter of unchanging custom, often endowed with religious significance, that neither the group nor the individual found it necessary to make a conscious choice. But the moment this unvarying rigidity of pattern is subject to change the problem of choice presents itself, and in the type of civilization with which we are more familiar, in which we are acutely conscious of an unending series of wants clamouring for satisfaction, the problem of choice is only too obvious to us.

Very early in our childhood we are taught that you can't have your cake and eat it, and this is only putting in another way the fact that you can't use the same resources to produce two separate things at the same time. If you want to grow cabbages on a bit of land you cannot also use it for a tennis court; if you spend a couple of hours in a cinema you can't also use them for digging the garden or painting a picture or mending boots. You have to choose which of the many possible uses to which you could put the same materials or the same time is the one you prefer, in the knowledge that the price you pay consists of all the other alternatives you have thereby given up.

This inescapable fact has nothing to do with any particular form of economic or social organization; it is part of human experience. As far as we can judge, there is no limit to wants; in fact, the growth of civilization is largely the development of new wants or new kinds and varieties of old wants – physical, intellectual, emotional, aesthetic, spiritual. Our desire for any one object may be quickly satisfied – even the heartiest trencherman finds that his stomach's capacity is limited – but for wants as a whole there seems no end. We get more choosy and want more different kinds of satisfaction, greater varieties of food; houses with rooms for specialized purposes such as sleeping, washing, cooking, playing, reading; clothes suitable for various occasions; music, pictures, books, churches, tennis racquets, and golf clubs and all the rest of the paraphernalia for recreation; or more leisure to sit and stare. All these different wants are jostling for preference and competing for the limited productive resources available. Whatever we do – or don't do, for doing nothing uses up time and wears out clothes and tables and chairs – has to come out of the wealth whose total is fixed by our resources and effort. Some method has to be evolved to decide the order of priority in satisfying these many wants – whose wants shall be satisfied first, which wants shall be satisfied first, how much of one want shall be satisfied before starting on supplying another, and so on – and it is principally in the different methods that have emerged for this purpose that the main differences between present-day economic societies consist. Two rival ways of doing the job have developed; in one the decision is made by State regulation, i.e. the planned economy, in the other it is left to the pull of individual choices, i.e. the price economy. During this century the conflict between these two methods of cutting our coat according to our cloth has become one of the most crucial of all the issues on which we have to make up our minds, so it is worth while to examine them a little more closely to see what is involved in them.

In a price economy the things that are produced are those for which consumers are willing to pay enough to make it worth somebody else's while to put them on the market. It is assumed that the amount we are ready to pay is an indication of the value we put on a thing, so that the more important it is to us the more we are willing to pay. We have, of course, to learn by experience and we may make mistakes, but most of us are sufficiently alert to our own interests not to go on buying something that we don't like or to pay more for it than we have found it to be worth. The prices we are ready to pay for different things do not remain the same for ever, but as our desire for them changes, so too do the prices we are willing to pay, and we can thus make known our individual idiosyncrasies. If I decide that I should like to be vegetarian during the summer months, I can use the money I save on meat to buy more butter and eggs than I do in the winter and then change back again when the warm weather is over. If I bother to give careful attention to my budgeting I can make sure that I never spend a few pence on, say, going to the cinema that would have given me more pleasure if I had spent it on something else, e.g. a few cigarettes, or an ice, or put it towards my savings for a new radio or the needs of old age; and in that way I can get from my income the maximum amount of the kinds of satisfaction that appeal to my particular needs and tastes. It is true that there are certain things that figure in practically everybody's expenditure because they are part of the customary way of living in the country in which one lives, but there are almost as many variations on the theme as there are individuals in the community. Some people get a lot of pleasure from being well-dressed, some from having seen the latest film, some from food, or the evening drink at the local, or having a bit on the dogs, some from the sense of security that comes from adding to the nest egg, or from the knowledge that the family is well provided for; and the price system allows each person to lay out his income according to his fancy by buying more of one thing and less of another.

If you think of your own experience as a consumer you will realize that I have over-simplified the buying process. We don't, as a matter of fact, ever think of the various lines of expenditure as being in direct competition with one another. We don't think of saying to ourselves, 'I prefer modish dressing to food, so I'll live on bread and water and put all my money into clothes.' It is rather, 'I won't buy chicken if it is expensive, but eat mutton stew instead and spend the money I save in that way on an extra pair of stockings.' As with all our purchases we are always considering the little more or less. If the price of something we like goes up we don't stop buying altogether, but we buy a little less than we did before; and if the price goes down we buy a little more. But the 'little more or less' is not always the same. The more important a thing is to us the more difficult we find it to cut down our consumption and the less effect do changes in its price have on the amount we buy. Such demands which respond only slightly to changes in price are called 'inelastic'. During the last thirty years the price of tobacco has multiplied by about three times, but the amount bought has not fallen much, for the habit of smoking has become so ingrained that many people find it easier to sacrifice other things that they used to buy, in order to have enough money left for cigarettes or a pipe. There are other things, however, that you buy gladly if you can get them at a low price, for example, peaches or books, but you cut down your purchases without a pang if the price rises even a little. Such demands are said to be 'elastic' because they stretch out or shrink greatly when the price alters.

I have purposely chosen these particular commodities for

my illustration because of another point on which it is important to be clear. Many people think of inelastic demands as being associated specially with 'necessities' and elastic demands with 'luxuries'. This is not true unless we remember that the term 'necessity' itself requires definition. What is essential to one person is a luxury to another and a matter of no concern at all to a third. How we value an article depends on (a) the customs of the country; (b) the stage of social and economic development; (c) our own income; and (d) our personal tastes. All these can be better appreciated by illustration.

(a) In this country bread, made of wheat, is one of the staple foods, but in India and China rice, not wheat, is the prime necessity. We groan if the price of bread goes up but do without rice pudding with equanimity; in the East it is the other way round. Changes in the price of tea matter much more in England than in France, where coffee has pride of place. In England wine is considered a luxury for the rich, in France it is the normal drink of the roadmender and peasant.

(b) The customary pattern of living is not fixed once and for all, but it changes as circumstances and new techniques bring different goods within the scope of the more modest incomes, so that articles of consumption which were once thought of as the greatest luxuries for the rich, or which were not known at all, come to be looked upon as the basic necessities of life. We have only to compare our present-day diet with the budget of a typical working-class family of the early part of the century to realize how rapidly and widely the constituents of the category 'necessities of life' change from one generation to another. Or think of clothing; the introduction of mass production methods in the clothing industry and of new man-made fibres have reduced the cost of looking well-dressed to such an extent that working girls now follow fashion as quickly as the society debutante. Mini, midi, and maxi skirts, knee-high boots and all the other things that are part of being 'with-it', 'switched-on', or 'trendy' become customary expenditure throughout the younger female population. And now the same tendencies are fast becoming similarly part of almost obligatory spending amongst young men.

Television, radio, cinema, tobacco, beer, motor transport, and such amenities cannot be claimed as physiological necessities, lack of which would lead to disease or death, but they have certainly grown to be conventional necessities which play so large a part in the way of living accepted as usual by the majority of the community that any appreciable reduction in their consumption involves a more radical alteration of habit than most people are prepared to make without suffering and protest. Hence the demand for all of them is highly inelastic.

(c) and (d) On the basis of these two common factors we introduce our own personal variations due to our income and our own tastes. To the rich man a house of a particular type or size, conforming to recognized standards in its furnishing and equipment, is considered as much a necessity as are the washing machine in the kitchen and the TV in the living-room by a person of more modest means. Earlier in this century when the standard of living of wage earners was much lower than it is today, butter and meat, which were considered necessities by the rich, were luxuries to be enjoyed only on Sundays. If their prices went up, the rich continued to buy almost as much as before, whilst the poorer people substituted margarine and cheese. And within each income range individual tastes and idiosyncrasies have to reckoned with. The student will go without dinner rather than without books; the ordinary reader won't.

We can put the whole thing briefly by saying that the easier we find it to discover a substitute for something, the less essential do we consider it to be and, therefore, the more elastic will be our demand for it. There are some types of goods which we look upon as substitutes for one another, but the group of which they form a part seems to be essential. For example, we may not mind whether the Sunday joint is beef or mutton but would feel badly done by if there were no joint at all and we had to make do with fish or cheese. We would not rate either beef or mutton as 'necessities' but we would put 'meat' in this class. Or we might think of gas and electricity as equally pleasant and convenient ways of heating the house, so that whilst neither could be considered as a necessity by itself, some easily manoeuvred means of heating would be. Or whilst we feel the need for some form of recreation outside the home we ring the changes between a bingo session, the cinema, or a dance at the local discotheque. So for each of these the demand is more elastic than for 'entertainment in company' as a whole.

So far we have been considering prices simply from the point of view of the consumer who has so much money to spend and is thinking of how he might get the best value. But prices have an additional job to do; they are an indication to the producer how best to allocate productive resources. If more men decide that they prefer woollen shirts to cotton the price of the former goes up and of the latter comes down. Woollen-shirt manufacturers need more wool, more workers – spinners, weavers, and makers – more machinery, building-space, more packers and distributors, more transport; in fact, more of everything that is included in the making and disposal of their goods and, because they expect to get bigger sales than before, they are prepared to compete against other industries wanting similar factors of production by offering higher prices for them. As a result more of all these are taken up in their industry and others have to cut down their use of them. Who decides which uses shall be curtailed? Nobody and everybody. Thousands of separate persons make their independent assessment of the demand there is likely to be for the things they make and settle in their own minds how far they can profitably go in bidding for the resources they require for their products. They are not, of course, completely in the dark in making their guesses; they have the experience of the past to guide them, and there are collections of facts which act as pointers to them in making their decisions. But finally they have to guess; for goods have to be produced in anticipation of a market (since production takes time) and the producers cannot know for certain that purchasers will, in fact, buy the goods when they have been made. One of the most important functions of the 'businessman' in a price economy is just this, of estimating consumers' demands for the thousands of different things that could be produced at varying prices so as to ensure that productive resources go into the channels where they are likely to be used to make the things the public want, and are prepared to buy, in the proportions they want them and will pay for them.

It is very unfortunate that the chances of conversational terminology have come to apply the term 'unplanned' to the economy in which this important work is done. The term 'planned economy' has come to have a very special significance, denoting not simply that plans are made for the production and distribution of wealth, but that the machinery for making such plans is of a particular type; and 'unplanned' naturally came to be used for other kinds of organization. But, because of the associations of the word, many people have fallen into the mistake of thinking of the price economy as completely haphazard and find it difficult to understand that there may be very efficient organization, even if there is no Supreme Command to which one can point as the 'brains' of the system. The businessman, who knows from experience that his livelihood depends on the skill with which he anticipates and meets the wishes of consumers, is well aware that his work involves planning and management of a very high order. As is explained more fully later (see the chapter on the structure of industry) the measure of the skill with which he provides the public with what it wants, where it wants it, when it wants it (as shown by the willingness to buy what he offers) is brought home to him very sharply by the amount of profit he makes on the job, and he is inclined to think somewhat ruefully of the use of the word 'unplanned' for an activity which demands so much foresight, calculation, and good judgement.

In a planned economy, on the other hand, using the term in its modern accepted sense, the decision on what shall be produced – and, therefore, the order of priority of wants to be satisfied – is made by authority. The planning authority may make its decisions in any way it thinks good. It may, for example, try to arrange that the things produced are just the ones that people would have bought if left free to spend their incomes as they liked; but this is improbable, because there would be little point in deliberately planning a scheme of production if the aim is to make it exactly as it would have been if no planning had been introduced. The more usual aim of a planned economy is to use the productive resources to make a rather different pattern from the one that would have resulted from the pull of prices, that is, to produce certain things, or to produce them in larger quantities than individual purchasers would have been willing to pay for, and, consequently, to cut down the production of other things that consumers would have bought if they had been free to do as they wished. A corollary of this control is the necessity for the authority to determine what share of the amount it has decided to produce shall be the share of any individual. This does not mean that the individual gets his share without any payment (though this may be so, as is the case, for example, with the education of children under sixteen) but that the size of the share does not depend, as it does in a price economy, on the price one is prepared to pay, nor does the amount produced depend on the total that consumers are willing to buy. A rich man has to pay for the education of his son at the university (since there is a means test for university awards) but the amount he pays or would be prepared to pay has no effect on the total number of university places available, nor on his son's chance of getting one of them allotted to him. This depends on the decision of the Government as to how many universities shall be established and what size each of them shall be.

During the Second World War the area of planning increased enormously, for there were certain things that had to be produced in immense quantities and with no avoidable waste of time, if the war was to be waged successfully – tanks, aircraft, guns, fighting forces and their equipment, ships, civil defence, etc. – and all these, like everything else, could be produced only out of the total supply of natural resources, human effort, and ingenuity. They could be made only if there were a proportionate reduction in many of the kinds of production in which those resources had been used in peace-time and, hence, a similar cutting down of consumption. Unless the smaller amount available for consumption had been allocated by Government rationing, only the richest people would have been able to get a share of these goods. In the more 'normal' times before the war a rise in the price of an article induced increased production and thus tended to get rid of both the high price and the scarcity that had caused it; whereas in war-time no price, however it rose, could have made the slightest difference to the amount produced, as the Government was using the resources that would have been needed for the increase for other purposes.

In some countries, e.g. Soviet Russia, the Government exercises this control as a part of its normal routine and not simply as a war-time measure. It decides what shall be produced and in what quantities and does not allow the amount of production to be determined by the preferences of consumers, as shown by the prices they will pay for different amounts. And even in Britain, long before the great expansion of Government planning for war purposes, we did not leave everything to the control of prices. Some things were undertaken by the State and supplied to us without consideration of how much we were willing to pay. For example, schools and hospitals, libraries and roads and parks, and many other things are provided by public authorities and we may make what use we like of them. Of course, we pay for them out of rates and taxes, but the amount of our rates and taxes does not depend on the use that we, as individuals, make of these things. We still pay the same amount in rates, even though we have no children to go to the schools, or

play in the parks, provided by the local authority. So the
contrast between us and Russia is largely one of degree. On
the whole, we leave the greater part of our production to be
determined by price movements but have a big and growing
section in which the State makes the decisions without regard to prices, whereas in Soviet Russia the emphasis is the
other way round.

When we try to compare the two systems we have to remember that the issues are not purely economic; they also
involve our ideas of what constitutes a 'good society', and it
is in determining what we mean by 'fair' and 'reasonable'
and 'just' that the main difficulties arise. The following
section is an attempt to state some of the considerations that
must be taken into account in deciding which of the two we
prefer.

1. At first sight it seems that the price system ensures that
goods are distributed most economically because they go to
the people who want them most. The keener you are to have
a thing, the more you are prepared to pay to get it, and as
the more you pay the more likely you are to be able to buy it,
scarce goods presumably will get into the hands of those who
really want them. But one of the greatest bothers about this
is that the same price means such different things to all of us;
it depends on the size of our income and the number of
people dependent on us. For example, a bachelor with
£5,000 a year can lightheartedly spend £1 on a whim whereas a man with £40 a week and a wife and three children to
keep must consider carefully before he spends half that
amount on something as necessary as the midday dinner. To
the manufacturer who is trying to estimate the market for
his goods, it does not matter that one man's 50p represents
more sacrifice than another's £1; he cannot know this. So if
we leave everything to prices the rich man's whims will be
attended to before the more urgent wants of the man with a
smaller income. The building industry, for example, will
find it more profitable to build weekend cottages for the
rich man who has already got one or two houses to live in

than homes for the worker who has nowhere to live.

2. On the other hand, one has to remember that what may seem to be strictly equal treatment (as, for example, when each person has a ration allotted to him) may be just as unfair as the effect of prices just discussed. In order to ensure that the quantity allowed to each person by a quantitative ration is available, the production of other commodities has to be curtailed. Suppose that I dislike meat and bacon, and would prefer, if left free to choose, to spend my money on Cheshire cheese and oranges. Under the rationing system I seem to be getting as fair a share of food supplies as anybody else but, in fact, I get the same weight of food but it represents less satisfaction to me than it does to those who happen to like these foods best. Or take another example. During the severe fuel crisis of 1963 people were urged to cut down their consumption of gas and electricity. There is no doubt that the most effective way of doing this would have been to raise the price of both of them very sharply, so that those who insisted upon having a fire during breakfast (one of the peak periods) would have realized how much it cost. Opinion was opposed to such rationing by price, because it was thought wrong that the sick or the aged, or those with young children, should be prevented from getting necessary warmth on account of the heavy cost. The result was that careless people, or those with less sensitive consciences, wasted a lot of fuel because it was cheap, but during the almost daily breakdowns in the service which were the consequence of this extravagance, the sick and aged had to leave their much more urgent wants unsatisfied, not because they could not afford the price but because the supply was turned off at the mains. This is not an argument for abandoning all rationing or for conserving fuel by raising prices; it is merely a warning against the danger of being taken in by appearances. What seems to be absolutely equal treatment may turn out on further examination to have the same faults as the admittedly unequal method of sharing through the medium of prices.

3. But another point. Is it really fair to say, as I have done here, that sharing through the medium of prices is 'admittedly unequal'? The inequality is not due to the fact that we get our share by buying it, but to the fact that we have unequal money incomes. If we all had the same amount of money to spend nobody would think it unfair that some of us were prepared to pay more for beef and others more for mutton. All that the price system does is to translate our unequal money incomes into unequal shares of consumable goods and what we are, in fact, complaining about is not the price system but the inequality of incomes. But, as was pointed out above, our judgements about our economic organizations are not based on purely economic grounds, and we often criticize part of our economic set-up for social rather than economic reasons. Even if we don't want complete equality we shrink from allowing differences in income to have their full effect on the life of the individual citizen. There has never been any time in the modern world when the person who had no income at all was left to starve; and in the last half-century or so, a larger and larger part of the wealth of the community has been shared out amongst its members on the basis of their common citizenship, rather than according to the size of their incomes. Education, health services, housing, and many other common services fall into this category; and the more accustomed we become to getting a share of goods and services on this civic basis, the readier we grow to criticize the price system for not doing something that it was never intended to do, i.e. share everything out equally amongst us all.

4. Some people argue in favour of a planned economy that, as our productive resources are limited, we should use them first on necessities for all before we have any luxuries. The problem here is to decide what is a luxury and what is a necessity (see the earlier section on elastic demands). How does tobacco rate in this? To the non-smoker or the man who has an occasional cigarette, cutting out smoking seems not only an obvious way to release resources for more important

needs but also a positive contribution to better health because it reduces danger of lung cancer; but to the millions of
habitual smokers tobacco is as essential as basic foods, despite the risk involved. Moralists have always complained
that a good deal of poverty is due to wasteful expenditure and
that persons of small income have only themselves to blame
for their condition, if they do not concentrate their buying
on the most important elements of healthy living. Others
might answer that nobody can go on working unless he has
some fun out of it and that a glass of beer, or 10p on
the pools or the dogs, may be a psychological necessity. Even
though life could be maintained in one's body without these
pleasures, would there be any incentive to work if one could
never let go for a moment? 'One man's meat is another
man's poison' remains as true as ever, and we all feel rather
superior when we think how our neighbours waste their
time and money.

5. But many people will still insist that there is nevertheless a fairly general consensus of opinion about the importance of certain things for healthy living (as is evidenced by
the general agreement on the commodities that should be
rationed during the war scarcities) and that it would be best
to make sure that these were produced in sufficient quantities
without bothering about prices, even if there were wide
differences of opinion on the relative importance of all the
rest. There are some foods which the dieticians have shown
to be necessary to health; there are certain standards of
housing and clothing which custom has decreed as the
minimum acceptable to the community. Here at once you
have an enormous area in which personal assessments of
necessity and luxury are irrelevant and which could, therefore, be produced without regard to price. But here too there
is the problem of the 'little more or less'. Everybody would
agree that playing tennis is not a necessity as bread is. Ought
we then to dig up all our tennis courts in order to grow
wheat on them and bake millions more loaves? Every extra
batch of loaves is less and less a necessity; every tennis court

dug up leaves less and less opportunity for healthy exercise and relaxation. Which loaf ceases to be a necessity and which tennis court becomes one?

6. There is another difficulty. Suppose we agree that bread is a necessity and must be produced in 'adequate' quantities without bothering to define too carefully what we mean by 'adequate'. Digging up the tennis court is not the only way to increase the bread supplies. I might prefer to keep the tennis courts and have fewer rose gardens, or cabbages, or factory sites, or what have you.

The great advantage of a price system is that it enables each person to make his own individual assessment of the relative 'essentialness' of things to him, to judge for himself which of his comparative luxuries he would prefer to give up, and how much of each he would prefer to give up, in order to get for himself more of the things he values more highly.

That is the difficulty of giving up the price mechanism. Faulty as it is, we have not yet discovered any other method of measuring relative values more accurately. A planning authority has, in fact, to guess and to hope that it guesses in a way that, on the whole, satisfies the ideas of the majority of the people. But every bit you take out of the price mechanism and put into State planning, the more difficult guessing becomes, because you have fewer indicated preferences to act as guide. Moreover a 'guess' made by the State has much wider repercussions than the decisions made by individuals. If 10,000 independent producers attempt to guess the public likes and dislikes each one may guess wide of the mark, but it is unlikely that they will all go wrong in the same direction, so that on balance the total may not be far out; if a Government official, even with more information available to him than any one of the 10,000, guesses wrong, there is no other wrong guess that can possibly compensate, and his wrong judgement may direct productive resources into a more wasteful channel than they would have gone into, if left alone.

7. Is it true that we get the best out of our money if we are left to spend as we like? Do we really make these delicate assessments so carefully that we always get the greatest possible amount of satisfaction from our incomes? We have to admit that some people are better managers than others and we all know the remarkable difference in standards of living that seem to be enjoyed by families who have the same income. (Remember there is danger in such judgements, for we may be imposing our particular views of what constitutes a good standard and assuming that everybody must accept the same valuation. Mrs Smith may be an excellent housewife who gets the most amazing value out of her husband's wages, while Mrs Jones, whose husband earns the same amount, does not find it worth while to spend so much time and energy on bargain hunting, but prefers to play with the children and laugh at her husband's jokes. Who is to say, except their respective families, which is the better manager?) But, allowing for differences of judgement about what is worth having, we know from our own experience – if we are honest enough to admit it – that we often buy from habit, and that we are both too conservative and too lazy to change, even though it would be to our advantage to do so. This is particularly true when the sacrifice we have to make (in the form of the price paid) is immediate, whereas the benefit accrues over a long period, as is the case with education or health facilities. Could we be certain that every child would get an education, if the choice was left to its parents and the fees had to be paid regularly, to cover the cost of schools and equipment and teachers' salaries? We have to agree that in many ways the State can spend our money in a way that is more conducive to our welfare than we could do it ourselves. The problem here is to know where to draw the line. When the welfare of children is in question the matter is not so difficult, for we can argue that, as the child cannot make its own decisions and must trust to some adult, it is the duty of the Government to protect those who might suffer through being in the charge of an ignorant or careless or

selfish person. But an adult is in a very different position. I might be convinced that Mr X is wasting his money on silly pleasures that do him no good and a great deal of harm, but what right have I, or anybody else, to impose my ideas on Mr X? There is no more insidious vice than that of interfering with one's fellow man in the guise of 'doing him good', and we have to be careful not to become dictators with the best intentions. One of the freedoms for which most of us would be prepared to die in the last ditch is the right to go to the devil in our own way, rather than to Paradise by Government direction. It is very difficult to reconcile the liberty of the individual to go on in his own crass, muddle-headed way – but a way which pleases himself and does no harm to anybody else – with the wish to see every member of the community living a healthy, efficient life.

The B.B.C. is a good illustration of this problem of reconciling the likes and dislikes of the individual with what other people think is good for him. If we paid for each TV or radio programme as we tuned in to it, as we do when we go to the cinema or the theatre, the ups and downs of the market would determine the proportions of symphonies and pop singers offered to us or the number of westerns and whodunits in proportion to discussions on the Common Market. But, as it is, the B.B.C. has to make up its mind, as a matter of policy or planning, whether to give us an opera or a variety show or a talk on international affairs, or anything else that can be transmitted by radio or TV, and, in consequence, angry letters pour daily into Broadcasting House complaining that too much time is given to talks, to light music, to classical music, to highbrow plays, to comics, and to everything else. One set of people argue that they don't pay their licence fees for nonsense and noise, but they want to be educated and elevated; another insists equally warmly that they have a right to be entertained and don't want to be 'improved'. One has only to remember the storm of criticism which greeted the White Paper on *Broadcasting in the Seventies* to realize the widely differing views of what should be offered to us. The B.B.C. (I think sensibly but you may take the opposite view) takes a middle course between the extremes. It takes the line that grown-up people have a right to use their leisure as they like, so it provides for all kinds of taste more or less in the proportion that its Research Department shows to exist – highbrow, low-brow, and mezzo and all the grades in between. But at the same time it accepts its responsibilities as a public service of being just a little, but not too far, ahead of public tastes and interests by experimenting with plays and music and discuss-sions that listeners would not have asked for themselves, but which they may gradually learn to appreciate.

8. There are many things which are of benefit to the com-munity as a whole but which it would be impracticable for us to pay for individually as we make use of them – for example, the defence services or roads. Moreover there would be a danger in leaving the provision of these to the stimulus of individual preferences as shown by prices, be-cause we should not have the permanent basic organization which is essential to further development in case of need.

A warning is necessary here. In this chapter I have been dealing only with the methods of deciding how scarce pro-ductive resources shall be distributed amongst the many uses to which they might be put, i.e. how the choice shall be made of which wants and whose wants shall get priority. I have not been concerned with the organization of produc-tion. There are many people who argue that a publicly-constituted body can organize production more efficiently and more economically than a number of privately-owned and competing firms. This is a matter of 'techniques' and is discussed in a later chapter on the structure of industry; but the fact that an enterprise is publicly owned or controlled does not, of itself, mean that it has contracted out of the price mechanism, though to assume that this is so is a mistake that it is very easy to make. Experience in the past showed that there were many advantages to be gained by having the tramways or buses or gas supply provided by the local authority, but this did not mean that they did not conform to the price mechanism, just as if they were owned by shareholders. It all depended on how they were run. The local authority might be anxious to persuade people to live in the country away from the congested industrial part of the town and might decide to run bus services at a loss and make up the losses out of the rates. In this case it would be determining the production of transport by other criteria than the price consumers were prepared to offer, and would thus be 'planning' the allocation of productive resources in the sense defined above. But if it provided bus and tram routes only if they paid their way by the fares charged to those who used them it would still be part of the price economy. The point is that the fact of public ownership does not of itself constitute planning or take production out of the price mechanism; it depends on the policy of the publicly-owned concern.

How difficult it is to keep this distinction clear in one's mind can be seen by the controversy over the railways. When coal, transport, gas, and electricity were nationalized the Acts which brought the new structures into existence laid a statutory obligation on their governing bodies to follow a policy which would enable them to earn sufficient revenue to cover their costs over a period of time – that is, taking good and bad years together. This means that the nationalized industries were deliberately placed, by law, inside the price economy and instructed to produce goods and services of the types, and in the quantities, demanded by the public as shown by their willingness to pay the prices necessary to keep them going without loss. In fact, however, the deficit on the railways has grown from year to year and it was for this reason that Dr Beeching was appointed Chairman of the British Transport Commission in 1961 and asked to consider the means by which the railways might be made to fulfil their statutory obligation.

His analysis showed that a very large part of the railway system was very little used so that there were very heavy expenses incurred in maintaining the permanent way, the

stations, and safety devices, and paying for all the personnel
required for a tiny amount of traffic. In fact, at the time of
his investigation half of the lines between them carried 95
per cent of the freight traffic and 96 per cent of passenger
traffic. Moreover the greater part of the under-employed
mileage was identical for both kinds of traffic so that if
freight and passenger had been combined we could see that
half of all the railway mileage dealt with only 8 per cent of
the total traffic and the other half dealt with 92 per cent of it.
In such circumstances what is the right policy? How far,
and for what reasons, should the country decide to keep
open lines and stations which are very little used.

Dr Beeching was perfectly justified in recommending that
uneconomic functions should be cut out. In fact, that is
what was required by statute in the Act which nationalized
the railways; and it was foolish to stigmatize him, as so
many people did, as an anti-social hard-hearted man for
doing exactly what the Government that appointed him
had asked him to do. Since he reported there has been a
great deal of discussion about what should be the policy to
be pursued. If we judge by the power to pay their way – as
a price economy does, and as the British Transport Commission was instructed to do by the Act which brought it
into existence – many lines and stations would have to be
closed; and unless bus routes were immediately established
many people living in villages and small towns would suddenly find themselves virtually cut off from communication
with the rest of the community. It is true that many more
families now have a car than used to; in fact, the latest calculation is that a car is owned by more than half the households in the country. But not only does the other half depend
on public transport but even the family which does own a car
must also rely largely on public transport. If the husband
goes off to work for the day in the car, how does the wife
do the shopping, get the children to and from school, pay
visits to the dentist, or take part in social activities? How far
are we, as taxpayers, willing to subsidize uneconomic sections

of the railway network in order to provide these valuable
social advantages to those who otherwise would be deprived
of them? If we decide that it is necessary, for whatever social
reasons we consider important, to keep the non-economic
lines in action we must do so as a matter of policy with our
eyes open, on the grounds that this is a social service, like
free education or the health services, and is not part of the
price mechanism. This is, indeed, what we have done but it
is doubtful if many of those who felt so bitter against Dr
Beeching realize how much they are paying in taxation for
this purpose.

Chapter 3

NATIONAL WEALTH AND PRODUCTIVITY

WHAT do we mean when we say that one country is richer than another? Or that we are better off now than we were fifty years ago? How far is it possible to make accurate and precise statements about these things? It is much easier to say what we don't mean than what we do. We certainly don't mean that a richer country is necessarily happier or 'better' or lives a nobler or more satisfactory life than the poorer one, for these are things that we cannot define or measure. When we talk about wealth – or economic welfare – we are referring only to those goods and services which are customarily exchanged for money. It is important to be clear about this point, because confusion here leads to a good deal of discussion at cross purposes. When two people disagree about whether there has been progress in the world or not you may find that one is talking about food and clothes and houses and the other is talking about happiness and virtue. Whether we consider we are better or worse off than our grandfathers depends upon what we believe to constitute the 'good life': it is a matter for qualitative judgement. But the question of whether we have made economic progress in the sense of being richer than our grandfathers is rather a matter for measurement. You may believe that civilization has taken the wrong turning and that life in Merrie England was happier and more worth while than in the crowded streets of the highly specialized urban cities of today; but this does not invalidate the fact that we are richer now than we were then, and that standards of living have risen.

Unfortunately, when we try to make our quantitative comparisons a little more precise we find all sorts of difficulties. The goods and services which are customarily exchanged for money include hundreds of thousands of different items, which vary enormously in different parts of the world. How can we compare the sugar and bananas of Jamaica with the textiles and ships of Britain? Obviously the only way out of the difficulty is to take their common denominator, i.e. money values, the prices they fetch in the market, and this means that we cannot help but exclude from the totals many things which are of the same type as those bought and sold, but which ordinarily do not have money values attached to them. The biggest item in this excluded group is the extensive and valuable service done by women as mothers, wives, nurses, and housekeepers for their own families. If all housewives went on strike and refused to do their work unless they received regular rates of remuneration for it, their pay would be added to the total money value produced by the community. It would look as if we had suddenly become richer, but in fact we should be producing just the same amount as before. Similarly, we do not take account of the jobs that people do for themselves or their households, but for which payment would be made if they were done by strangers; the work done by fathers in growing backyard vegetables or mending the children's shoes, for example, because it is not possible to estimate the amount of work of this type done by millions of separate households. In ordinary times this does not amount to very much in an industrialized community such as this, though there is no doubt that in times of stress it may add considerably to national wealth. During the Second World War, for instance, there was an appreciable contribution to total production made in this way.

There is a similar difficulty in estimating the production of such countries as India and China where the majority of the population live in economically self-sufficing households, whose main products are for their own use and not for the market, but as they mostly work on a traditional and uniform pattern it is possible to get a fairly good idea of the value of the work they do.

If we base our comparisons solely on money values we have to remember to take into account the fact that these values do not remain constant. They differ from one country to another, and from one period to another in the same country.

Most people in Britain now receive very much bigger money incomes than they did ten or twenty years ago but until we calculate the increase in prices over the same period we cannot judge whether they are richer or not. Ever since the beginning of the Second World War, and even more since the end of it, there has been an inflationary tendency; that is, the general level of prices has been going up. During the sixties and seventies the rate at which this has been happening has increased very rapidly and incomes and prices have been chasing one another in a bewildering way.

The price level does not move at exactly the same rate or even in the same direction in all countries at the same time so that just as we cannot compare the wealth of one country at two different periods unless we take account of changes in prices so too we cannot compare the wealth of two separate countries unless we take account of the differences in the prices they pay for the things on which incomes are spent. In the U.S.A. for example, money incomes are higher than they are in this country but so too are prices and a comparison simply of the amounts of money that an American and an Englishman receive for the same kind of work has no meaning until we know what the difference in prices is.

Everybody would agree that America is richer than China, but this does not mean that every person in China is poorer than every person in America. In all countries there are inequalities of wealth, and there are thousands of people in China who are much richer than hundreds of thousands in America. Nor do we mean that the total produced in one country is bigger than the total produced in another. As countries are all of different sizes this would not have much meaning. Denmark is richer than China, but you would not expect to find that its 4¾ million of population could pro-

duce more than China's 700 million. So that the only fair
basis of comparison is to measure the amount of wealth produced by each person, i.e. to divide the total produced in the
country by the number of people of working age who have
contributed to it. Many will actually receive larger incomes
than this and many smaller, but this gives an idea of the
average output of that community, and is thus a measure of
its economic productivity.

If you think of all these difficulties you will realize that it
is not possible to get a completely accurate comparison of the
economic position of different countries; but statisticians
have worked out methods which act as a very fair indication
of their relative wealth. In the thirties, just before the Second
World War, Mr Colin Clark made an estimate of real income in most countries of the world by expressing them all
in terms of goods and services that these incomes could
have bought in the U.S.A. over a certain period of time. This
calculation showed that more than half the world, including
all India and China, had an average weekly income of less
than 4 dollars (80p). The richest ten per cent of the world's
population, living in the U.S.A., Australia, New Zealand,
Argentina, Great Britain, and Switzerland, had an average
of 20 dollars (£4) or more per breadwinner, and the next
richest 9 per cent, living in the principal industrial countries
of Europe, had an average varying between 10 and 20 dollars (£2–£4).

Even, then, before the wholesale destruction and dis-
organization caused by the war, the world was an extremely
poor place as a whole and its wealth was very unevenly distributed. Nearly half of the total economic output of the
world was produced in four countries (U.S.A., Great Britain, Germany, and France), which contained between them
only thirteen per cent of the world's population.

Recently the United Nations has estimated the wealth of
each country in relation to the size of its population, and this
enables one to make comparisons by showing the amount
produced for each person in that community. This does not

mean, of course, that each person produces that amount, for young children and old people must be provided for out of what is produced by those able to work; but it does allow one to get some idea of relative levels of wealth and productivity.

Such a calculation made in 1968 for instance shows that whilst the U.S.A. produced the value of 3,552 dollars a head India produced only 71, Burma 60, Brazil 197, and Jamaica 412. In Europe the richest countries were Sweden, with 2,822 dollars a head and Switzerland, with 2,295. The United Kingdom, France, Denmark, West Germany, and the Netherlands fell into the next richest group.

How are these vast differences in economic productivity to be accounted for? There is no short answer to this question, for there are so many factors which must be taken into account. We can say definitely that there are certain things which play a part, but we do not know how much relative emphasis we should put on each of them.

1. Natural resources are not, of course, distributed evenly all over the world's surface. Some places are well endowed with easily worked minerals, some have particularly fertile soil or a climate suitable to certain crops, or perhaps a coastline that provides good harbours and facilitates sea communications, or an interior that may offer opportunities for rapid inland transport of men and goods. Italy's lovely golden sunlight and Switzerland's scenery give those countries obvious advantages in developing a tourist trade, just as the fact that Britain's coal and iron deposits were placed so conveniently for cheap transport was a major factor in enabling her to become the first industrial society.

All the same, the incidence of natural resources alone is not enough to explain such big differences in economic productivity, for nature has not been guilty of such favouritism as these wide divergences might suggest, and it is in the skill, persistence, and ingenuity with which the resources are exploited that the chief differences are to be found. There is no human society, however primitive, which has not discovered the use of tools, even if these consist of nothing more than sharpened pieces of stone and wood with which to kill animals for food, or to dig the soil for crops. But communities differ enormously in the extent to which they have evolved tools of more complex design, and there is little in common between the digging stick of the South Sea islander and the motor tractor of the American farmer. Probably the size and suitability of the technical equipment (or capital) is the one most important determinant of differences of productivity. In a calculation made recently it was estimated that the output per head in manufacturing industries in this country was only half that in the United States, largely because American industry is so much more highly mechanized than British – the mechanical horse-power used per worker is twice as great in U.S. factories as in British.

2. As tools themselves have to be produced, the resources they embody form part of the total which sets the limit to the satisfaction of all wants of whatever kind they may be; so that the wealthier and more productive a society is, the greater are its possibilities of adding still further to the ingenuity and number of its mechanical aids, for the wider is the margin between productivity and the wants that people wish to satisfy now. The community which lives close to the subsistence level, i.e. which produces only enough to keep itself alive, cannot afford to devote any of its resources to making tools or training capacities for the future, even if its members realize that better equipment would give them a higher standard of living later on. But as soon as there is a slight improvement, by a lucky chance for instance, we can choose whether we shall satisfy present wants more fully, or turn the increased resources to constructive purposes, by making them into technical equipment which will add to our productive efficiency in the future. The remarkable improvements in machinery which raised standards of living in so revolutionary a way during the nineteenth century would not have been possible had it not been for the fact that it was customary for owners to put back into their businesses a considerable proportion of their profits, instead of using

them to live as expensively as their incomes would have permitted. In this case the choice of the proportion of present resources to be devoted to technical equipment was left to individuals, who decided how much they thought could be profitably used in that way. In the U.S.S.R., which similarly tried to develop its resources to a higher level of productivity after the Russian Revolution, the choice was made by the State. The First Five Year Plan was mainly concerned to reduce consumption in order to leave a wider margin of resources for the formation of capital, and the higher standard of productivity of the late thirties was the result.

3. The degree to which people are willing to tighten their belts now in the hope of letting out the notches later on depends, of course, primarily on the mental outlook of the community – though, perhaps, in a planned economy it is the mental outlook of those in control, rather than that of the whole community, which matters most. But whether the choice is left to the individual or imposed from above, it is determined largely by the current scale of values. There are some people whose temperament leads them to live more in the present than in the future; taking pleasure in good things when they can get them and doing without them when they can't. There are others who have developed more of the telescopic faculty. A society which measures social success by the amount of wealth people possess is more likely to be ready to make sacrifices for the sake of the future than one in which other qualities take precedence. There are some communities who value old ways and who are content so long as they can continue along traditional paths; there are others for whom past achievements merely provide the standard by which to measure the greater successes of the future. The whole pattern of behaviour – the complex of social values, of what is considered the right way to act, of what constitutes success or earns the applause of one's fellow men – is a determinant of the amount of capital that is produced to equip the worker in the effort to produce the goods needed to satisfy wants.

4. But the amount of capital depends also on circumstances. There is no doubt that one of the most important reasons for the economic backwardness of the East is to be found in the enormous supplies of labour available. Men usually do not think unless they are compelled to do so, and the existence of an immense reservoir of workers makes it unnecessary to think out ways of lessening human effort by devising tools. When American industries were first establishing themselves there were available large tracts of fertile land, to be had for the asking, and manufacturing firms had to compete for workers against the attractions of independent farming. Only high wages could offer sufficient incentive, and from the first, therefore, American industrialists were bound to turn their inventive genius into the provision of first-rate technical equipment, so as to economize in their use of expensive labour. How important this factor is can be seen also by the extraordinarily rapid strides made by technological experiment in this country during two wars. There is no truer proverb than that Necessity is the Mother of Invention.

5. Quantity of capital is not the whole of the story; its suitability for its purpose and the skill shown in its use are equally important. For these, ceaseless experiment is necessary, and here again the attitude of mind is one of the chief factors in determining the level of wealth. It is probable that America's predominant position is due as much as anything else to the fact that her industrialists are inclined to assume that last year's methods are out of date and that there must be something better, if only they can find it, whereas, on the whole, England is more prone to think that old methods are good methods unless there are definite proofs to the contrary. Rapidity of change can, of course, be carried too far, and novelty may become an expensive fetish. It is always a question of whether the outlay of resources and labour involved in introducing new methods and the new tools they require is justified by the resultant increase in productivity. The new method may be better technically, and yet not so

much better in its effects on output as to justify scrapping the old machinery and skills, and using labour and material to make the new. Both extremes, whether of conservation or of novelty-worshipping, are wasteful; but a country which is eager to try out new methods is much more likely to increase its average productivity even if it sometimes scraps techniques and their equipment too easily.

So far I have been discussing differences in the average productivity of different communities, but this is not the only factor which accounts for differences in the standards of living. There is no country in which the total produced is divided into absolutely equal portions amongst the population, and the individual is concerned as much, if not more, with the share he gets as with the amount produced as a whole. During the present century the standard of living in this country has been very much influenced by changes in the distribution of the national income as well as by increases in the total. This matter will be discussed more fully in the chapter on the ways in which people get their incomes; here it is enough to point out that it is much more difficult to measure changes in the standards of living of individuals than it is to measure changes in average productivity, because the things on which we spend our incomes change in content and relative importance from time to time. There are now very few wage-earning families who do not possess a radio and TV or go occasionally to the cinema; but none of these pleasures was enjoyed by their counterparts of fifty years ago, not because of poverty but because they did not exist.

It is generally accepted that the greater variety of consumption which the development of scientific knowledge made possible represents a rise in the general standard of living, but it would not be possible to represent it by numerical comparison of the living conditions of two persons living at different periods. We have to admit that we cannot do more than get an indication of changes by restricting our comparisons to a much narrower scope. What we can do is to calculate the proportion of the community who are living in poverty at one time, and compare it with the proportion in that condition at another, because it is reasonable to assume that a decrease in such a proportion will indicate a general rise in the standard of the masses of the population as a whole. However, 'poverty' itself is a relative term and requires further definition before it can be used as a measuring rod. For this purpose it is taken as being the condition in which the individual's income is insufficient to buy him the bare necessities of life, and if we calculate, on the one hand, the amount needed for this purpose at ruling prices and, on the other, the actual incomes earned by the people in the community (taking into account, of course, the number of persons they must maintain out of their earnings) we can get a fairly good idea of the proportion of the population living in poverty.

Unfortunately even this is not as accurate a measure as it may appear at first sight. The term 'necessities of life' is a relative one, and what we, in this country, would include in the bare minimum would, undoubtably, seem like unheard-of luxury to an Indian peasant. Our interpretation of 'necessity' is largely conventional, so that a poverty line is drawn in some relation to the standards of consumption of the period and of the country. But if we are concerned primarily with measuring changes of standard in one country and the periods of time are not too far removed, so that customs and manners have not altered too radically, the poverty line gives us a pretty good indication of changes in standard as they affect individuals rather than averages.

A number of well-known investigations have been made on these lines, but in only three instances do we possess information with regard to conditions in the same district at two different times : one of London done by Charles Booth in 1889–1903 and again by the *New Survey of Life and Labour in London* in 1928–30; the second by Seebohm Rowntree into the conditions in York in 1899 and again in 1936; and the third, much narrower in scope, into the econo-

mic conditions of working-class households in five towns
(Northampton, Warrington, Reading, Stanley, and Bolton)
in 1913 and again in 1924. In 1890 the percentage of persons
in London working-class families containing children who
were living in poverty was 37·3; in 1929 it was 10·7, and
even this figure was too high for the actual conditions. In
1929 the Great Depression was beginning and the amount of
unemployment was exceptional; if the inquiry had been
made when this serious unemployment had not been in existence but all other conditions had remained the same the proportion would have been only 5·1 per cent. In York there
were 15·6 per cent of the working-class population living in
the worst poverty in 1899 and only 6·8 per cent in 1936. In
the five towns the 1913 percentage was 11, but by 1924 it was
6·5 per cent in the actual week of the inquiry and would have
been only 3·6 had unemployment at the time been normal.

These remarkable changes, due both to increases in
average productivity and changes in distribution, give one a
good idea of the rise in the standard of living during the
present century.

Chapter 4

THE STRUCTURE OF INDUSTRY

You probably buy your daily vegetables at the little shop at the corner, which is kept by a man who does all the work himself with the help of his wife and a boy to run errands; but if you wanted to get new furniture for the dining-room you would be more likely to go to a big store in the centre of the town where you would be served by a salesman in the employ of the firm who own the shop. Or perhaps you are a member of a Consumers' Co-operative Society and get most of your goods from one of the shops that you, as a member of the Society, own yourself. In your own job the probability is that you work with hundreds or even thousands of others who are all employed by a company composed of numbers of shareholders. Your wife can choose the shop at which she buys the food for the family, but she cannot choose from which company she will get the water to drink with it, for it will be provided by either the municipality or a firm which has the sole right to serve your locality. Your radio programme, on the other hand, comes to you from a public corporation which serves the whole country, or one which is for your region alone.

Here we have some examples of the large number of different kinds of productive enterprises which make up our economic world. They differ from one another in size, in structure, in their ownership and control and in the degree to which they are able to control their market.

LARGE AND SMALL SCALE

Let us take size first. There is a popular idea that large-scale production is always cheaper than small and that it is only a matter of time before all the small firms are swallowed up.

This is a complete fallacy. What are the advantages of the big firm?

1. It can divide up the processes of manufacture so that each can be done by labour and equipment specially adapted to the purpose. This applies to managerial and technical functions as well as the more routine processes. It is not worth while putting in highly specialized machines or a highly specialized official unless the output is large enough to keep it or him in pretty constant use.

2. Packing and transport can be cheapened by standardization.

3. By buying its raw materials in bulk it can get better terms.

4. It can maintain its own research department and can afford to experiment with new methods.

5. Overhead charges, such as factory buildings, power, managerial organization, etc., do not increase proportionately with output, so that these costs per unit are less if the firm is big.

But it is foolish to have a plant which can produce an enormous number of an article, however low the cost, unless there is an equally large market for it. You might be able to manufacture boot buttons very cheaply in a gigantic factory, but as boot buttons are out of fashion there would not be sufficient demand for the product to make it worth while. Now markets vary enormously in size, and for all sorts of reasons. Sometimes transport difficulties are the main problem; with bulky or heavy or perishable articles the cost of transport to reach outlying regions might outweigh the advantages of concentrated production. Sometimes it is a question of political factors; the manufacturers of the United States have been able to grow very big because of the enormous area of free trade, which offered them a huge market, whereas European countries have had to be sure that the economies of large-scale production would be enough to compensate for the tariffs they would have to surmount in selling to foreign markets. This will be discussed further in the chapter on international trade and the Common Market. In other cases it is a matter of convenience; the housewife prefers to buy her everyday groceries near by, instead of taking a bus ride into the centre of the town – so you have a large number of fairly small retail shops instead of one big central store. Sometimes it is a matter of individual taste; we don't mind having overalls of a standard pattern but we object to wearing the exact replica of a neighbour's dress – so overalls are more suitably produced by mass production methods than are evening dresses. In some things fashions change very rapidly, and it would be wasteful to establish a large plant designed to produce cheaply something for which there is a big, but ephemeral demand, unless the equipment could be quickly adapted to make the next thing wanted by a fickle market. Sometimes there is a comparatively small section of the public which wants the article; a learned treatise is published in a much smaller edition than a popular novel.

There is another consideration which may limit the size of a business. Every increase in the scale of production puts a bit more strain on the capacity of the men who are in control at the top. Not only does direction become more difficult, but any mistake in judgement is more expensive and more disastrous. Where the technical problems have been pretty well overcome and methods are fairly standardized this may not be a serious difficulty; but where techniques are continually changing or where the conditions in which production is carried on do not remain stable for any length of time, a big firm is too unwieldy to be efficient. In the textile industry, for example, there is a great difference between the size of spinning firms and those engaged in weaving. Spinners can produce standard thicknesses of yarn to be used in an immense variety of materials, so they can take advantage of all the economies of mass methods, but weavers must take account of the vagaries of fashion, and the firms must be small enough to move rapidly from one type of product to another.

Perhaps the best example is to be found in agriculture. A farmer in this country cannot plan all the details of the work on his farm for three months ahead and arrange the jobs to be done by each worker. The climate changes so bewilderingly and so abruptly that he must be prepared to scrap his plans and issue new instructions literally from hour to hour; he could not do this for a thousand workers, and so a farm must be kept sufficiently small for the person in charge to be able to envisage it as a whole, and yet be fully and continuously in touch with what is being done in each section. This problem can be seen in an extreme form in agriculture, but it is always present; for in no industry do conditions remain completely stable, and this means that businesses often decide not to expand to the size which would be economical on purely technological grounds, for fear of becoming too unwieldy and inflexible for good management.

During the present century the size of businesses has, on the whole, increased greatly, mainly for two reasons. (1) The rapid development in cheap and quick communications has enabled firms to reach wider markets. Goods can be distributed easily from one centre; purchasers can move about more freely. The woman in the country is no longer dependent on the village dressmaker but enjoys the shopping outing to the big stores in the near-by town; and the larger the area served, the greater the chance of finding enough people of like tastes to justify producing in bulk the things they want. (2) The rise in the standard of living has extended the range of articles that have come to be considered as conventional necessities, or the 'standard equipment' of life. This is especially obvious in such things as women's clothes, but it is equally true, if less obvious, in our demand for house equipment, and for such leisure-time amenities as bicycles, games, camping kit, etc. One interesting example of this is seen in the Holiday Camps, which have introduced the large-scale firm into the provision of hotel accommodation as the result of the expanded demand for holidays resulting from higher wages and 'holidays with pay'.

Or perhaps even more striking is the development of the 'package holiday' whether it consists of the coach tour in the United Kingdom complete with visits to famous cathedrals and 'stately homes' or the all-in tour to some Continental tourist area when air fares, hotel accommodation and food and courier service are all included in one initial payment. As a result of this development hundreds of thousands of people now consider a foreign holiday once a year as an essential part of their way of life.

The rise in the standard of living has a dual effect on the size of businesses. On the one hand it increases the number of articles of common consumption for which there is, consequently, a big settled market; on the other it widens the margin of our income in which we can allow our individual preferences more sway. The smaller the income on which we live the greater the proportion of it that must be spent on sheer necessities; but as it increases there is a bigger and bigger area in which we can exercise real choice and, unless we all grow strictly to pattern, that means that more of our choices will differ from our neighbours' and therefore be less amenable to production on a large scale.

The problem discussed in this section is very pertinent to our plans for the future. Most of us have in our pockets a blueprint of the world we hope for, and it is very easy to assume that all kinds of enterprises can be run efficiently on more or less the same pattern. But this is not true, and we must be careful not to plan a world which ignores necessary variation in industrial structure. It is worth while to discuss, for example, what bearing these factors which determine efficient scale in manufacture and distribution might have on the choice of industries to be nationalized; or how far the choice before us might be between standardized consumption on the one hand, and, on the other, a greater opportunity for varied individual choice, though at a higher cost.

WHO OWNS? WHO CONTROLS?

In the little shop at which I supposed you buy your vegetables there is somebody whom you recognize as the owner.
In the big department store, or in the works where you earn
your living, there is no person to whom you can point in
this way, because the business is owned by a large group of
people – the shareholders of the company. Here are illustrated the two chief types of modern production – the private business and the joint stock company. A private business is owned and controlled by one individual (or a few
partners) who takes the risks connected with it. He has
probably got a little capital of his own that he has put into
the stock and has possibly borrowed some more from relatives and friends. He has to pay interest on all the capital
he borrows, for, of course, we must pay for the use of capital
just as we pay for the hire of a car, and that interest is part
of the costs of production which he must meet out of the
prices he receives for the goods he sells. In starting out as a
businessman on his own in this way he is certainly taking a
risk. He has to pay his rent, as well as the interest on borrowed capital, meet the wholesalers' bills for the goods supplied, pay his assistants and delivery men their weekly
wages, and all these charges must come out of the receipts
for his goods. There is no guarantee that he himself will
get anything at all for all the work he is doing; what he gets
is the difference between his costs and his receipts, and it
depends on how good a businessman he is whether he makes
any income at all. If he has made a good guess at what his
customers want, always has the kinds and quantities of the
things they like, knows where to buy, sees that his shop is
well organized so that people are served quickly and cour-
teously, can prevent bad debts from piling up and so on,
he will make a good profit – not necessarily by being able
to charge higher prices (if he does that too obviously his
customers will probably transfer their custom to the shop in
the next street) but by a quicker and larger turnover. If, on

the other hand, he is a poor businessman or perhaps has bad luck, then the margin between costs and receipts will be squeezed narrower and narrower, until it becomes so small that he will begin to question whether the amount he gets is enough to pay him for all the work he does in running the shop and all the anxiety it involves. If he decides it does not, he will give up the shop and perhaps take a job somewhere else as a salesman, where he has neither the responsibility nor the risk.

This simple description shows the chief characteristics of all firms which are run as private businesses (though they are certainly not all on this small scale). The owners are not guaranteed any payment for all the work they do and they know that anything they make depends on their skill in finding out what customers want, organizing its supply, and persuading people to buy it.

In the joint stock company the business belongs to all the shareholders who between them have contributed the capital, and there may be many thousands of these scattered all over the country or, indeed, in other countries too. Some of them may have only a few hundred shares in the business and others may have several thousands. It is obvious that such a scattered body of persons cannot do the day-to-day work of organization involved in running a business. Most of them know very little of the technical and commercial problems that have to be solved and, even if they do, they are too far from the scene of operations to take any part in it; moreover, they have their own jobs to do at which they earn their living. So the sort of work that in a private business is done by the proprietor has to be done, in a joint stock company, by salaried officials working under the direction of a committee of management called the Board of Directors, who receive fees for their trouble. In theory, the Board of Directors is under the control of the whole body of shareholders, who can call them to account if they disagree with the way in which they run the business; but as the shareholders are not an organized body of people it is understandable that this ultimate control is not very important in practice and shareholders rarely question the work of the Board of Directors. This is particularly true if the company is making good profits; if there are losses the questioning may be more serious, for, as the shareholders have no guarantee of receiving any return on the capital they have contributed to the business, the dividends they get depend on the amount of the profit the company has made. If it has been a good year shareholders may get 15, 20, or 30 per cent on their shares, but if it has been a bad year they may get as little as 1 or 2 per cent or even nothing.

There are some people who do not like to take as much risk as this, and, for them, two other types of share have been devised. (1) The preference shareholders are a privileged group. In common with the ordinary shareholders they have no guarantee that they will receive any dividends, but they have the right to have the first dip into the profits, if there are any. But as they do not take as much risk as the ordinary shareholders they do not get as much chance of the big profits when they occur, and the amount of dividend they receive is limited, while that on ordinary shares is not. (2) The debenture shareholder takes even less risk than this; he lends his money to the company for an agreed interest, neither more nor less, and the payment of this interest is as much a charge on the firm as the rent of its building or the wages of its employees. In fact, the use of the term shareholder here leads to confusion, for the debenture holders are not part owners of the concern, as are the preference and ordinary shareholders, but simply creditors. The difference in their position is shown by the fact that they do not have even the nominal control exercised by the others, as they have no voting rights at the meetings of the company.

In both the private business and the joint stock company then, it is the owners of the firm who take the risk, but in the private business the owner is the man who actually controls the day-to-day work and probably does a great deal of it himself, while he may have put up only a small proportion of the capital out of his own pocket; whereas in the joint stock company the owners are those who have provided the capital, but they take little or no share in the running of the business.

The outstanding advantage of the joint stock company is that it allows the mobilization for productive purposes of a vast amount of capital that would otherwise have little chance of being used. Most of us do our best to put aside a part of our income for a rainy day or for use in the future. Generally we have not enough to set up in business for ourselves, and, even if we have, we may not want to give up our own way of earning a living for something for which we have neither skill or liking. By buying shares in a company we become part owners without the necessity of giving up our own job. There is the added attraction that, as shares can be bought in small amounts, we can divide our savings amongst a number of companies, and this reduces the overall risk. If it is a wet summer the firm making macintoshes will find good markets, if there is a heat wave there will be a specially big demand for bathing suits. If we have shares in both we need not feel unduly anxious about the weather, for what we lose on the swings we shall gain on the roundabouts.

The fact that shares are negotiable – they can be bought and sold on the Stock Exchange – gives joint stock companies a further advantage in attracting capital. If we save money for an emergency we want to know that we can put our hands on it easily when the need arises and, by having our capital in shares, we have this assurance. Of course, we can't always be sure of getting back exactly the same amount of money as we paid for the shares. People will not be eager to buy them unless the company is doing fairly well or is expected to do well in the near future. If you want to sell your shares just when the company has been through a bad patch you will have to accept a lower price for them than you paid; but on the other hand, if the firm has been doing well and paying high dividends, and is expected to continue doing so, purchasers will be so anxious to buy your shares you may get very much more than they cost you.

This method of collecting capital from many people, each of whom may have only a comparitively small amount, gives a joint stock company the use of a much larger total than can easily be collected by a private business which must depend on what the proprietor possesses or can borrow. And this means that wherever large-scale production is particularly advantageous there is a likelihood that the business will be organized on the joint stock pattern.

But don't assume that all small firms are private businesses and all large ones joint stock companies. Many firms can start small and, as they grow larger by successful trading, they get the extra capital they need by ploughing back their own profits without borrowing from anybody or asking the public to buy shares. In this way many private businesses grow bigger than a moderate-sized joint stock company. But if an enterprise is such that it cannot begin on a small scale and gradually expand, but is bound to start big, it must be organized on a joint stock basis. For example, a railway needs a great deal of equipment before it can function at all – a furniture factory doesn't.

Both joint stock companies and private businesses are examples of private enterprise, and between them they account for more than three-quarters of all production, but there are certain other kinds of structure which must be mentioned. In any form of private enterprise the decision to produce is taken by certain individuals who accept the responsibility for their decision. In public enterprise, on the contrary, the decision is taken by some public authority and the responsibility for failure is borne by a public body. But just as private enterprise takes different forms, so too there are varied forms of public enterprise.

Until comparatively recently the Post Office was a department of Government but it was also a gigantic productive organization involving millions of capital and employing thousands of workers. Usually the prices charged for its services were enough to cover its total costs – and even leave a little over – but it was not run primarily as a profit-making concern, and any losses which might have occurred were met by the taxpayer. Its policy was determined by the Government.

This was the first large experiment in State business, and it was copied on a smaller scale by certain kinds of municipal activity in the provision of such public utilities as gas and water and transport. Many of these public utilities have now been nationalized, so that the most usual form of public enterprise nowadays is to be found in the Public Corporation. This is a body composed of experts appointed by the Government, whose general policy is under Government control, but which possesses independence in detailed administration. Examples of this kind of structure are to be found in the B.B.C., the National Coal Board, the British Electricity Authority, the British Transport Commission, and some others. The Post Office has recently joined this group. In one way these corporations are like joint stock companies, since the work has to be done by a group of people acting as a Board and receiving payment for their services. But they differ from a joint stock company in two important respects. (1) They are bound to pay an agreed rate of interest on all their capital. All their borrowed capital, in fact, is in the same position as the debenture shares of the joint stock company, so that no owner of the capital has any controlling voice in the affairs of the business. (2) They can be called to account for their policy by Parliament, though it must be admitted that the means by which this can be done is still very obscure, and, indeed, is proving to be one of the most hotly debated issues connected with nationalization.

Between private and public enterprise there is a type of productive structure which does not fit into either of these two categories, the Consumers' Co-operative Societies. Their enormous capital, for they are among the largest businesses in the country, is provided by their members (nearly ten millions of them) who are also, in general, the purchasers of their products. Unlike the owners of a joint stock company, the amount of control exercised does not depend on the amount of capital one has contributed. Each member has one vote, and one only, and the profits made by the Society are divided, not amongst the capital owners, but amongst the purchasers of the goods in proportion to the amount of the purchases made. In so far, then, as the Society is controlled by its owners and not by Government authority, it is a form of private enterprise; this is also true of its relationship to its work-people, for, although it has the reputation of being a good employer, its position in regard to those employed by it is essentially the same as that of any joint stock company. But in so far as it is run primarily in the interests of those who consume its products, and not as a profit-making concern (since all the profits that do, in fact, accrue are distributed amongst the purchasers), it is more in the nature of public enterprise.

COMPETITION AND MONOPOLY

When you decide where to buy your daily or weekly provisions you have a choice between several shops selling more or less the same type of goods and you pick the one that you think will suit you best. It may be that the shop is close at hand, or is prepared to deliver the goods to your home, or perhaps you like the assistants or your prefer the free and leisurely choice you can make when you wander round a supermarket; or maybe you have always dealt at a particular shop and see no reason to change. So although all these shops are in competition with one another it is easy to see that their rivalry includes so many aspects of trading that comparison is by no means simple. I would rather pay a bit more for a thing – particularly if I don't buy it very frequently – if I can get it at a shop I pass on my way to work than waste time and temper in snooping about the side streets on the chance of getting it a penny cheaper. But if I needed a lot of the article I should probably find it worth

while to change my route so as to go by the cheaper shop.
Competition, then, does not work slickly and automatically;
in fact, perfect competition can hardly be said to exist at all,
because we can't bother to spend so much of our time finding out all the possibilities before making our choice. This
is especially true, of course, of the individual consumer, because we buy such hundreds of different articles that we
rarely take a great deal of trouble over any of them, and we
are too ignorant of the details of most things to be able to
make really sound comparisons. (How many of us can
choose a car or a radio with knowledge?) But it is also true
of the manufacturer and trader. Theoretically one might expect them to explore every possibility before deciding, since
a difference of a penny will have a real influence on profits,
when goods are bought in thousands; but, in practice, firms
continue to trade with those with whom they have long-
standing connections without troubling very much to discover alternatives. It is sound business to establish mutual
relations of confidence and respect in this way; you are
likely to get an early delivery of something scarce or better
credit terms than the casual purchaser. So that even when
you have businesses ostensibly in competition with one another, it is, as the economists say, only 'imperfect competition', which means that all sorts of things, such as habit
and ignorance and social relationships, prevent it from
working very rapidly or with the sharpness of a razor blade.

Even this imperfect competition is not found over the
whole of the productive field. If you want to cook the dinner
in a gas cooker you have no choice about the company
from which you order the gas, you must get it from the
only source of gas supply in your area. The same thing applies to the water you use or the electricity or the bus on
which you travel to work. All these things which we call
'public utilities' are monopolies, i.e. only one company supplies each one of them in one locality, and this was true even
before nationalization of transport, electricity, and gas. Why
is this?

If you examine these industries you will find that they have certain characteristics in common. They all need an exceptionally large amount of fixed capital which does not vary much for different amounts of output. (For example, you would need to run your water main or gas pipes along a street whether you wanted to supply every house or only occasional ones.) Again, they all have a local market the size of which is not connected primarily with their efficiency, but depends on other factors over which the concern has no influence. (It is not likely that people would remove to a town simply because they could get their gas cheaper.) So if there were more than one company supplying the locality each would have to incur the same heavy overhead charges but would have only a share of the market, and consequently each unit supplied would have to bear a proportionately heavier part of the overheads. Only by providing for the whole demand from one source can you effectively economize the capital equipment and provide the service at the lowest cost. There are, of course, many other reasons in favour of such unified control. Imagine the general upset and confusion if half a dozen rival gas companies were continually taking up the streets to lay their gas pipes, or the traffic congestion if several bus companies plied over the same routes. And would the rural districts get any transport at all? A company which has the monopoly of the busy streets can afford to accept the condition that it must also serve the less populated and therefore less paying areas.

All such services as gas, water, electricity, local transport, etc., which have had to become monopolies for economical running, play such a large part in the life of the community that they have been either publicly owned or publicly controlled for some time. It must not be thought, however, that these form a clearly defined group about which there can be no dispute. In fact, it has taken a long time for what is sometimes called 'gas and water socialism' to develop and there is always a lot of difference of opinion as to where the boundaries should be drawn. One of the strongest arguments used by those who wished to bring about coal nationalization was that the industry had reached a stage in its development when the economical use of its capital equipment necessitated unified control of the whole, and again with transport many insisted that it could not be run efficiently, and at low cost, unless all forms of long-distance transport – motors, railways, and canals – were combined under one control, so that each type of traffic could supplement the other instead of competing with it. But in both cases there were many who disagreed and who strongly opposed the Acts which nationalized these industries.

These illustrations are given merely to draw attention to the fact that the principles discussed in this section must be continuously applied to changing circumstances. One cannot say with finality, 'These are industries which must be run as monopolies if they are to be efficient, and the others are not.'

But not all monopolies are public utilities. The elimination of competition can be brought about for other reasons, and by other means, and the results are much less obvious to the consumer, because they are brought about by groups of people acting voluntarily and in their own interests. The forms taken by such agreement are so numerous that it is not possible to list them in this short account. They vary from the unwritten understanding amongst a small local group of dealers not to lower their prices without consultation with one another to a highly integrated amalgamation of businesses covering a whole area of productive activity. Broadly speaking, they fall into two categories :

1. Associations of firms dealing in the same commodity, who jointly settle the amount to be put on the market and the minimum prices at which it will be sold, but who for all other purposes (i.e. the processes of manufacture and marketing) remain separate and competing firms.

2. Amalgamation of firms which give up completely their individual identity and become welded together under a joint control which governs the whole of their functioning.

It would be difficult nowadays to find any part of the productive sphere that did not show some amount of agreement among firms of one or other of these types, but the extent and authority of such agreements vary enormously. The size of the industrial unit has a good deal of influence – it is more difficult to get a working agreement amongst a thousand small firms scattered all over the country than between half a dozen big businesses which share an industry between them. The amount of foreign competition is another important factor, for the exclusion of foreign goods allows greater power of control to the firms inside the country dealing in that particular commodity. The two world wars did much to increase monopoly development, not only by cutting down foreign competition but because most industries were compelled to organize themselves, so as to have a representative body capable of negotiating with the Government on such questions as the rationing of raw materials. Although it was not the intention of such government action to encourage monopoly organization, this was, in fact, the result, for firms which were brought together for certain government purposes took the opportunity of retaining their joint machinery for their own interests.

To most of us the term 'monopoly' has somewhat sinister associations and we are inclined to lump all types together as anti-social attempts to exploit the consumer. Yet the fact that few of us would denounce trade unions as bodies that ought not to be allowed to exist (though we might not necessarily be in sympathy with all their policy and action) should make us realize that there may be occasions upon which agreements among traders may have much to commend them. For a trade union is, of course, no different in principle from any other price association in which the members agree to maintain a minimum selling price for their products. Too much instability in the price of an article may have undesirable social repercussions and it may be worth while – even from the point of view of the consumer and much more so from that of the producer – to have slightly higher prices than there would be with competition, in order to have less fluctuation. Such agreements as those made by price associations attempt to introduce a certain degree of stability into the market.

It is when we come to consider amalgamations, however, that we find the most important opportunities for greater economy in production than is possible in competing firms. When firms are in competition with one another the offer of a great variety of designs, differing both from one another and from those of rival firms, is one of the chief ways in which they catch the attention of the purchaser. If they amalgamate they can cut out unnecessary variations and concentrate on a smaller number of designs, each of which is produced an enormous number of times. This makes it possible for each machine to have a long run without resetting and reduces the quantities of spare parts that are needed, as well as enabling component processes to be carried out in bulk. (It is perhaps worth while here to emphasize that there is no intention of suggesting that all variations in design are wasteful and unnecessary. On the contrary. The more highly developed we are as individuals, the more do we dislike a dreary uniformity in the things in which we express our different personal tastes. But that does not mean that we have to differ from everybody else in every point of behaviour. I should dislike to have to wear the same clothes as my neighbour, but to cook in the same shape of saucepan does not make me feel a regimented robot; so that pans provide a more likely opportunity for the elimination of redundant designs than clothes.)

There are many other ways in which joint control can cheapen production : e.g. by the pooling of technical knowledge and in the abolition of cross-transport charges, so that goods can be sent to their destination from the nearest plant. Again there is a tendency for the plants of competing firms to outrun the demand for the product. It is not only that each firm hopes to increase its own sales and expand its scale in the desire to cheapen unit costs but that it is afraid of losing its customers if it is unable to promise quick delivery. Particularly in industries where the demand is highly fluctuating, this results in the establishment of plant by each competitor which is far in excess of its average needs. When the firms unite, production can be concentrated on the most efficient plants and the remainder closed down, with a great saving in both unit and overall costs.

In fact, so great are the improvements that can be effected only if all firms are working under agreement that the Government was continually urging a greater degree of such unified control on all the depressed industries during the difficult years between the two wars; and, in some instances, it used compulsion to bring this about. Under the Coal Mines Act, 1930, for example, a council representative of the coal owners of all districts was set up to fix the total output of the industry and the minimum prices to be charged for each class of coal, and fines were exacted for any breach of these regulations. At the same time the Act established a Reorganization Commission with the task of encouraging and, if necessary, compelling amalgamations between colliery undertakings. And this, it must be remembered, took place before the nationalization of the coal industry. Similarly the Agricultural Marketing Acts, 1931 and 1933, provided that a majority of producers of an agricultural product might compel a minority to observe uniform conditions of marketing by means of a statutory scheme controlled by the producers themselves, and milk, potatoes, hops, pigs, and bacon were important products whose sale was controlled in this way.

Many of these schemes have aroused a good deal of criticism, for the real problem is to ensure that joint control is used for constructive purposes and not simply to exploit the consumer. To say that the amalgamation of firms allows of more economical and efficient production is not the same as to say that this will inevitably be the result. In fact, very often it is not; for the united organization, finding it no longer has to fear the competition of rivals, often loses whatever stimulus its constituent firms had to improve their methods and cut their costs. This is the dilemma with which we are likely to be increasingly faced. If businesses remain in competition with one another they retain a real stimulus to improvement and they are prevented from crude exploitation of the consumer; but the very fact of competition prevents them from effecting some of the most important economies. If, on the other hand, they amalgamate they find it much easier and simpler to raise prices than to reorganize their methods of production. The consumer loses on both counts.

In some industries the problem is more social than economic, that is, what is feared is the effect that a powerful combine may have on people's lives rather than on their purses. This was the fear behind the criticism of the purchase by some very big companies owning newspapers and periodicals, of a large number of their competitors. The amalgamation could certainly lead to more economical production and there was not much risk of prices being unduly raised, because most papers aim at a very wide circulation in order to increase their advertising revenue. But newspapers and magazines have great influence in moulding the opinions and prejudices of their readers, not only by their editorials, but by the way in which news items are selected and presented, and even by the kind of advertisement to which they find it profitable to give prominence. A concentration of ownership may lead to an unhealthy control of public opinion, particularly if the owners impose any conditions on the editorial policy of the individual papers. When, as has happened since the introduction of ITV, newspaper firms extend their control to TV channels, the social impact is incalculable.

The difficulty is to know what to do about it. In the United States there have been many attempts at what is known as 'trustbusting' legislation, but with only limited success. The trouble is to define the thing that you want to stop in such a way that you leave the agreements that work in the public interest and cramp the style of those who use their joint power in their own interest. During the inter-war years when the markets for many of our products were rapidly and disastrously shrinking, it was the possibility of saving industries from complete extinction by some degree of control that took the dominant place in people's minds, and the dangers were ignored or discounted – hence the effort made by the Government to encourage what was euphemistically called 'rationalization' or 'orderly market-ing' so as to rid it of the unpleasant associations recalled by the word 'monopoly'. But at the present time the situation is very different and there is a general fear that monopoly control may result in all the disadvantages of private enter-prise without its compensating advantages.

A good deal of effort has been made since the Second World War to find ways of preventing agreements amongst producers from acting against the interests of consumers. The first step taken was the passing in 1948 of the Mono-poly (Inquiry and Control) Act through which a Monopolies Commission was set up to investigate any industry referred to it by the Board of Trade and decide whether it did, in fact, operate against the public interest. The Act, that is, did not assume that monopoly was 'good' or 'bad' in itself; it provided machinery for discovering the facts on which such a judgement might be made.

In the years immediately following the passing of the Act about twenty industries were investigated and reports on them published. The Monopolies Commission had two separate duties to perform in these reports : the first was to find out the facts, the second was to judge as accurately and as impartially as possible whether the methods employed could be said to be against the public interest. It may be, for example, that their agreements lead to higher prices than would be charged if there were no such collective arrange-ment; or that competition was kept down by restricting supplies of raw materials to new entrants to the industry, or that technical innovation was prevented in order to main-

tain the value of existing capital. To find the facts is a difficult and lengthy process, for the Commission must act with
the most scrupulous fairness; but as it has very wide powers
to examine the books of firms and to call for evidence, this
is far from impossible. What is much more difficult is to
judge in what ways the methods affect the public interest,
for this depends on where you think the balance of public
interest lies. For example, which is more important – that
the consumer buys the goods at low prices, or that the profits
are high enough to attract new capital into the industry or
to provide funds for improved working conditions? Or is it
more in the public interest to have agreements amongst
producers which restrict competition but which allow complete interchange of technical information, or for firms to
hoard their new processes because they are in competition
with one another.

Whatever its judgement may be the Commission has no
power to compel firms to abandon any of the practices they
condemn. This is something which only the Government
can do, because it requires legislation; and, in fact, it has
not usually taken any such action. This does not mean, however, that the Commission has had no effect. Far from it.
In many cases, the publicity itself has been enough to bring
about a change, and various types of restrictive practice have
been voluntarily given up by agreement between the Board
of Trade and the industry concerned, without any need to
resort to compulsory powers.

Most of the reports of the Monopolies Commission have
dealt with particular industries which have been referred to
it for investigation, but one report dealt with practices that
were general over a wide area of industry; in particular,
that of Resale Price Maintenance. This is the name used
when a retailer is compelled to sell at a price fixed by
the manufacturer instead of choosing for himself how much
to add on to the wholesale price he pays for his supplies.
This practice is associated with the sale of 'branded' goods,
which now form a very considerable proportion of consumers'

purchases, and it has led to a great deal of controversy.

Most such articles are packed and advertised by the manufacturer, who tries to create a special 'image' in the minds of possible purchasers – an image made up of the look of the article, its use, its price, and everything else which might lead purchasers to ask for that brand rather than any other. If a retailer is allowed to charge any price he likes he may find it worth while to sell one brand at 'cut' prices even though this involves a loss, because he hopes to attract customers to the shop, where they may be persuaded to buy many other types of goods at higher prices. The manufacturer of the brand that has been 'cut' fears that the retailer may be tempted to reduce the service on this article; but, even if he does not, there is a danger that the customer becomes unsettled and is unwilling to pay the 'standard' price of the article because he feels he may be being 'done'. This may, and indeed often does, affect the reputation of the manufacturer and lose him his market in the long run.

It is sometimes said also that the housewife – who is the principal buyer of most of these goods – prefers a fixed price because she knows where she is and is saved the bother of going from shop to shop in search of lower prices. If one shop cut all the prices of its branded goods she would undoubtedly have an advantage in shopping there. But this does not happen. A store usually lowers the price of one or two articles which act as a decoy and makes up its losses on others, and changes the cut-price articles from week to week so as to attract different groups of customers. And so the housewife may feel rather guilty if she does not spend time tracking down the cheaper goods. How far this is true is a matter of temperament and it is impossible to estimate what proportion of purchasers prefer a price that they can rely on wherever they choose to buy and what proportion enjoy the challenge involved in finding the store that offers them a bargain.

Those who oppose Resale Price Maintenance, on the other

hand, point out that there are now a great many different channels of distribution – chain stores, department stores, Co-operative stores, independent or unit shops, super-markets, mail order houses, and so on. It would be absurd to assume that all of them have exactly the same cost to meet in stocking and selling their goods so why should they all sell at the same price? If they were allowed to choose for themselves, the more efficient retailers would sell at low prices and consumers would benefit. Where prices are fixed, the retail price must be sufficient to cover costs of the less efficient avenues of distribution and this means the others make a bigger profit than necessary at the expense of the public. The supporters of the fixed price argue that this is only half the story. The efficient trader can still compete without lowering his prices. He can offer better service – long credit, or quick delivery or a pleasant shop décor or helpful assistants – and can do this without imperilling the long-term interests of the manufacturer.

Definite action was taken in 1964 when Resale Price Maintenance was made illegal. Since that date firms can state what they believe to be the 'recommended price' but retailers can do what they like about it and this means that housewives – who are the main purchasers of retail goods – must use their own gumption about the store from which they make their purchases.

But although opinion was divided on the rights and wrongs of Resale Price Maintenance when a particular branded article was in question, it was certainly not divided when the attempt to impose restrictions on the retailer was made by groups of manufacturers making similar but not identical goods. And this distinction is made clear in the Restrictive Trade Practices Act passed in 1965. By this Act whilst an individual manufacturer was still permitted to fix the price at which his goods might be retailed it became definitely illegal for a group of manufacturers to do the same thing.

Despite the Act it does not mean that all such practices

on the part of a group of firms have been brought to an end although, in theory, they are illegal. In some cases the members of a trade association have made individual agreements with retailers (as this is within the law) but take care that all these agreements have a strong family resemblance; in others where one big firm has a dominant share of the market it can impose its own conditions of sale knowing that its small competitors find it easier to follow its lead than to attempt to undersell it. But it does now mean that it is much harder than it was before for a group of manufacturers to cut out all competition and share the market between them.

Price fixing is not the only way in which competition can be prevented, and the Act takes account of this. A large number of different kinds of agreement which may have the effect of reducing competition must now be registered and a Restrictive Practices Court has been set up to determine whether these are in the public interest or not. Most of the decisions have been given against the agreements (which then become illegal) and a very large number of those registered have been voluntarily abandoned because it was thought that they would be legally condemned if they were brought before the Court.

But not all such agreements are condemned by the Court; if an agreement can be shown to be in the public interest it can be maintained. One of the most interesting of such decisions concerns the agreements made by publishers not to supply booksellers unless these agree to sell the books at list prices. After a very long hearing the Court ruled that this restriction was not against the public interest on account of the special circumstances of book publishing and selling. The production of books is highly speculative; in fact, practically every publication is something of a gamble, and publishers rely on the profits they make on the books that have a large and steady sale to finance those which may be slow starters or never sell enough to repay their costs. Similarly reputable booksellers must hold a very large stock of different books, many of which may be on their shelves for years. If booksellers could charge what price they liked, those for whom books are only a side-line – such as news-agents, supermarkets, Woolworths, etc., would sell only those which have a very quick turnover, such as paperbacks, the more popular fiction, and so on, and nobody would be able to hold the stocks or gamble on the more expensive and slower-selling books, to the great detriment both of the reading public and of authors and publishers.

Since the passing of the Act of 1965 the Monopolies Commission has been given a more restricted function. It continues to operate but now it deals only with single-firm monopolies that can be shown to supply at least one third of the total output of a particular commodity whilst the Restrictive Practices Court deals with possible monopoly action by groups of traders. So many problems of definition arise in this work and so much time is required to investigate the ramifications of a firm and its share of the market, quite apart from then deciding whether its operations are or are not against the public interest, that there has been little positive development since the reconstitution of the Commission.

Chapter 5

THE LOCATION OF INDUSTRY

I F you want a job in the cotton industry you know that you must go to Lancashire; if you want employment in making cutlery you look for work in Sheffield. In wool you would have rather more choice – the West Country and Scotland as well as Yorkshire – and in motor-car manufacture you would be able to choose even more widely, though you would probably be wise to look first somewhere in, or near, the Midlands. If, on the other hand, you wanted to be a builder or a shop assistant or a clerk or a hairdresser or a schoolteacher you would probably be able to get employment in practically any locality in the country. What determines the siting of businesses? Why are some occupations concentrated in a few areas whilst others are found all over? And what has made the concentrated ones choose their particular spots out of all the possible ones?

Let us take first the type of jobs that you find all over the country. There are some occupations that provide the day-to-day services for individuals and households and, as they must be done on the spot, they are necessarily as dispersed as the population. Personal services are included in this category, for such work as domestic service or hairdressing cannot be done by remote control. The same is obviously true of the work done by doctors or lawyers or teachers or the churches. With retail distribution, however, it is rather different. Goods could be, and often are, sent by post to households from a large central warehouse but, as most people prefer to choose their own purchases after inspection and don't want to go long distances for everyday shopping, the retail shops, and all their attendant occupations, are widely dispersed. All the amenities for recreation are similarly spread out – restaurants, cinemas, theatres, football grounds, and so on – because the communities they exist to serve are scattered.

Until about twenty-five years ago one would confidently have classed the building industry in this way, for houses built of brick or concrete must necessarily be erected on the site they are to occupy; but experience has now shown that it is not difficult to prefabricate houses in one locality for erection in another. Immediately after the end of the Second World War the acute shortage of houses due to the devastation of many areas through bombing led to experiments in prefabricated houses which were intended to be only temporary until the ordinary building industry could expand to make up the ravages of war. But since then there have been big developments in what is now called 'industrialized building'. Schools, factories, and even blocks of flats are made in factories and later assembled in the locality they are to occupy when in use; and every newspaper carries advertisements of simply constructed 'extra rooms' which the householder can buy and bolt together himself to add to the accommodation of his home. With these developments one might, therefore, find a concentrated building industry in the future.

Even so, however, the amount of building labour required to prepare the site, assemble the structure, connect water and drainage, build roads, etc. must be locally established so that even if the prefabrication of the building itself became much more usual than it is at present the building industry would still be more scattered than most manufactures.

If you examine these occupations you will see that they fall into two categories : either (1) they require close contact between producer and purchaser, which is true of domestic service and dentistry and house repairs and retail distribution : or (2) the cost of transporting the product is so high that the compensating advantages of producing it in one area, and distributing it over the whole country, would have to be enormous to make it worth doing, which is generally true of building.

But there are a great many industries, possibly the majority, in which neither of these two factors is outstandingly important and in which it is quite possible to produce the article in one place and distribute it over a large area. As we have seen in considering the size of businesses, the increase in communications has extended the size of the market that can be served by one plant, so that wherever large-scale production is advantageous, one might expect to find manufacturers serving as far afield as they can reach. But this does not explain why a large number of factories producing the same thing congregate in one region and what makes them choose that area rather than another.

CHOOSING A SITE

At first thought it seems natural that such regional specialization should be closely allied to its particular natural resources, and, indeed, this has often been the case. You can expect to find a mining industry where there are coal deposits to be worked, and shipbuilding where coal and iron and a good harbour are in close proximity. But this does not get one very far, for it does not explain why the cotton industry came to be concentrated in Lancashire, which is about 3,000 miles from most of its basic raw material, or the pottery industry in Staffordshire, to which county most of its original materials had to be carried from Cornwall.

Modern industries need a great many things in addition to their prime raw materials – machinery of different types, power and labour to work them, and transport to get the finished products to market, and it may quite well happen that it pays to carry the raw materials over long distances in order to avoid transporting machinery or fuel or workers. The businessman wants to produce his goods as economically as he can, and get them to the purchaser in the cheapest and most convenient way, and it would be a very remarkable coincidence if he found a particular spot which is most advantageous from every point of view – basic materials, power, transport, labour, and markets. He has to balance advantage against disadvantage and make up his mind whether, for example, it is better to have the expense of carrying his raw materials a long way in order to be near his market for the finished goods or save the carriage on raw materials but have to meet the extra cost of transporting his finished goods. As circumstances change, so do different factors take the determining place in this calculation. In the early years of this century there would have been some excuse for confusing a map of the coalfields with one showing industrial concentrations, for the two were so closely connected. Nowadays, however, such confusion would be unlikely, for the emphasis of industrial development has changed greatly. Until the First World War the large majority of manufacturing industries relied on steam for their power, and this made heavy demands on coal. As coal is a bulky article and expensive to carry, it generally paid to settle the factory on or near the coalfields and bring all the other necessary materials there, rather than the other way round. When, however, electricity began to replace steam as the chief motive force, this concentration on the coalfields was no longer so essential for, although electricity is usually generated from coal in this country, it can be carried long distances with comparative ease and cheapness. This allowed industries to give greater weight to other factors when deciding their location, and it happens that the type of goods with which our manufacturing industries are now mainly concerned induces producers to gravitate to other areas than the coalfields, if their power can be equally well provided. The outstanding development of modern production is that of mass-produced consumption goods – the sign of a general rise in standards of living. In all kinds of clothing, house equipment, radios, electrical gadgets, bicycles, gramophones, motor-cars, and their fittings, etc., technical improvements had so cheapened production in the thirties that huge new markets had been created for these things amongst the whole population – markets which had become so large that, even though the goods were produced by mass-production methods, it was possible to offer a large variety of designs and alternatives. In such circumstances, producers were eager to be as closely in touch with their markets as possible, so as to be quickly aware of any changes in taste and fashion that might affect the size of the demand; and London, as the greatest and wealthiest centre of consumption, acted as a magnet, drawing more and more of these new consumption industries within its orbit. Had manufacturing industry still depended on steam power, this would probably not have happened, for the cost of carrying coal would most likely have been enough to outweigh the advantage of being so close to the market; but as electricity was almost universally employed this difficulty had not to be overcome.

A striking illustration of this can be seen in a comparison of the growth of population in different areas. Between 1921 and 1938 the population of Britain went up by 3,430,000, and 86 per cent of this growth was concentrated in the Midlands and South-East. In that period Great Britain's population increased 8 per cent but, whereas the South-East's numbers grew by 18·1 per cent, the Midlands' by 11·6 per cent and the West Riding's (the only other area to show an appreciable increase) by 6 per cent, South Wales's fell by 8 per cent. This was not due to any great regional differences in birth and death rates but to the migration of young people in search of work, as the old export industries (coal and cotton and shipbuilding) declined and the new industries which took their place (motors, electrical apparatus, entertainment, furniture, etc.) were concentrated in the areas near to their richest markets.

There was another factor which influenced the development of the new industries in the Home Counties and the Midlands. Mass production methods do not usually require many skilled workers. A small nucleus of highly-skilled workers to set the machines and supervise those who operate them is enough; but the greater part of the work consists of repetitive processes which can be done by men and women who have had no more than a few days' or a few weeks' training. In the suburbs of London and the Midland towns, there were large numbers of inexperienced women and young girls who were ready to enter these new factories. As a general thing the supply of labour has not been as important a determinant of the site of an industry as the costs of transporting materials, or nearness to markets, because people have usually been ready to congregate in districts where there were chances of good work. Occasionally some small industries have established themselves in areas where the existence of a much larger one would assure them of the particular type of workers they wanted. For instance, sometimes a factory might choose to settle near the docks because it knew that the families of the men working there (the docks being an entirely male occupation) would offer a field of recruitment for jobs depending on female labour.

During the thirties when mass unemployment was chronic, this was not often a major determinant in a firm's decision but with the full – or even over-full – employment of the post-war years, it often became the most important factor. Experience has shown that it is only a minority of people who are prepared to move their homes if they can find jobs at what they consider reasonable wages in the neighbourhood, and many firms have found it wiser to find out first where there are pockets of unemployed people available and establish their businesses there even though, from other points of view, they would have chosen a different locality.

It would be foolish to pretend that the position of every industry is the result of careful rational calculation; in many instances it is due to nothing more than chance. An industry does not come into existence en masse; it begins when one or two firms try out a new idea for producing something that has not been done before or for doing an old thing in a new way. If they are successful other firms copy them and gradually an industry develops. There is a very strong likelihood that the originator of the new idea or method carries on his business wherever he happens to be, particularly if the scale of the firm is not very large. If it is the kind that must begin as a large unit and millions of pounds of capital are involved, it is probable that a careful survey will be made of the rival attractions of different districts, and there are, of course, instances in which even the owner of a small firm makes similar careful inquiries before coming to a decision. But most industries start from small beginnings and the man who has the new idea is much more likely to start where he is, provided it is not a wildly unsuitable place. There are some good reasons for doing so apart from personal convenience. He knows the district and people know him; he is more likely to persuade those he knows to give him a trial order and the firms from whom he buys his materials and equipment are generally more willing to give him credit. Then again, there are his personal ties which hold him to the place he is used to : he does not want to leave his family and friends unless he is forced to do so. Later on, he may find that another site would, in fact, have been more advantageous; but by that time moving is more difficult and expensive, for it entails giving up the buildings, fixed capital, contacts and organization he has built up, so that it will not be worth his while to do so unless the extra advantages of the other site are outstanding. This does sometimes happen. New firms, with more knowledge at their command before they begin, settle in the more favourable position and expand at the expense of those in the old area, so that gradually the main emphasis of the industry comes to be settled in the new district. This was the case with the cotton industry which had been started in several localities during the late eighteenth century but which was concentrated in Lancashire by the middle of the nineteenth. But it is not always so, and there are many areas today whose specialization is due more to the chance that it was the home of the founders of its main industry than to anything more fundamental.

ADVANTAGE AND DISADVANTAGE
OF CONCENTRATION

Whatever the reasons that account for the establishment of the nucleus of an industry in one locality, there are very strong reasons for the tendency of other firms carrying on the same work to locate themselves near by, for the economies of concentration, apart from those deriving from the locality, can be considerable. Here are some that are worth mentioning.

1. Firms specialize in particular processes, thus gaining all the advantages of long runs on their machines.

2. Subsidiary industries grow up to provide the necessary specialized tools or to do repair and maintenance work or to make use of the by-products of the main industry. If the industry were widely dispersed it would be too expensive to maintain contact, and to collect and despatch materials, for these subsidiary processes to be worth while.

3. Markets for the benefit of all can be organized more efficiently, whether it is for raw materials, for disposing of the finished product, or for the different types of skill needed.

4. Packing, handling, and transport facilities, specially designed for the products, can be provided. They could not be kept fully employed unless the firms needing them were near to one another.

5. The industry comes to be part of the common interest and concern of the locality. Research centres can be set up from which all can gain; local authorities find it worth while to arrange technical institutes in which young people can learn something of the industry; ideas are more easily discussed and new methods more rapidly disseminated when a large number of people have these interests in common. These advantages are large and positive, but there is another

side to the matter. A high degree of specialization may, at times, bring disaster to a region, if the whole population comes to depend for its living on the prosperity of only one or two industries, whose fortunes may suffer a serious reverse. Such was, indeed, the case in the period between the two wars, when the export industries, coal, cotton, and ship-building, were extremely depressed. All these industries were highly concentrated and, as they declined, they dragged all the other occupations associated with them into poverty. It was not only their own subsidiary industries that were affected but also the trades that had grown up to meet the needs of people employed in them. In some localities a third of the workers were unemployed and the rest living in constant fear that they would be overtaken by the same fate, because there was so little demand for all the things that people could possibly do without – such as new clothes and houses and furniture, cars and cycles and radios, restaurants and holidays and entertainments, and so on – with the result that firms that were very prosperous in other parts of the country, where the main industries were expanding, were hard put to it to keep their heads above water in the areas surrounding the shrinking export trades. Thus was created the problem of the Depressed or Special Areas, which proved such a tough nut to crack throughout the inter-war years and which finally led to the demand that industrial location should be controlled in order to prevent a recurrence of such a disaster.

The repercussions of such a wholesale decline in prosperity are wider than are seen at first sight. As has been pointed out earlier, the expanding industries catered principally for those with money to spend on a higher standard of living, so that manufacturers of such commodities as electrical gadgets, furniture, or household equipment naturally enough did not choose to settle in areas where purchasing power was exceptionally low. Again, owners of factory and other buildings were not encouraged to put money into repairs and rebuilding, and local authorities hesitated to spend the rates on general amenities, when there might be a danger of having no demand for them. So these districts took on a neglected and rather derelict appearance, which acted as a further deterrent to those who might otherwise have been persuaded to start their new businesses there. It must not be forgotten also that manufacturers have wives and families to think of and it is not surprising that most of these threw their influence on the side of life in one of the bright new suburbs, rather than in the depressing atmosphere of a district that seemed to be going steadily downhill.

As a result of all this, there were no alternative occupations into which the unemployed workers of the declining industries might be absorbed, unless they moved away to the localities in which the new industries were establishing themselves, and thousands of them did so move, as is shown by the population figures quoted above.

But who are the people who are most likely to move in such circumstances? Not the older people, who have got their roots deep in their home towns, nor the young married men with families, who dread the insuperable difficulties of finding accommodation in towns where, as strangers, their names would be low down on the waiting lists for vacant houses and rooms. The groups who found it easiest to move were the unmarried men and women who were old enough to fend for themselves but had not yet undertaken serious family responsibilities. Many thousands of these moved away from their homes in search of work, leaving behind them the very young, the middle-aged, and the old, with the unfortunate consequence that both the communities they left and the ones they went to became rather lopsided. The old locality was left with more than its proportion of people in need of care and assistance, while the new one, in which the young people married and reared their families, had more than its share of the young and virile section of the population, who would be the breadwinners of the future. During the inter-wars years – between 1921 and 1938 – the numbers of men and women between 25 and 44 (the strongest section of the working population) increased three times as much in the South and Midlands as it did in the rest of the country (North, Scotland, and Wales).

Such a transference of population as took place when the export industries declined is, therefore, cumulative in its effects. New industries do not choose to settle down in areas where their markets are dwindling and where the most vigorous part of the community, the young men and women who can readily adapt themselves to the unfamiliar conditions of new types of work, are moving away. And just because the new industries do stay away, the market goes on shrinking even more quickly, and, moreover, it shrinks lopsidedly.

Since the end of the Second World War the changes in industrial location which were so marked a characteristic of the thirties have continued to develop and many people have become alarmed by the 'drift to the South'. Between 1951 and 1969, for example, the insured population (wage and salary earners) rose by 2,373,000 but more than half this increase, 1,493,000, was to be found in the region known as South-East and East Anglia, i.e. the whole complex based on London. The West Midlands, with Birmingham as the magnet, had the next biggest increase, with 283,000, and the South-West came close after it. So whilst the South-East and East Anglia had increased during this period by 2.8 per cent the North-West region had dropped by 1.5 per cent and the North, the West and Scotland had similarly decreased though not quite to the same extent.

Until 1975 unemployment as a whole was very slight – even in late 1971 when the rise began to cause grave concern the figure for Great Britain was only 3.5 per cent. But the incidence remains uneven and the same regions as in the thirties are most seriously affected though on a much lower level. For example, when the proportion out of work in Greater London was 1.7 per cent the following table shows the different fate of some other areas :

Region	Percentage of insured population unemployed
South-Western	3·4
Northern	7·1
Scottish	6·3
Welsh	5·0
Yorkshire Coalfield	4·3
Northern Ireland	8·7

This has proved one of the most worrying problems of the present century and there are a great many factors to be taken into consideration.

1. The size of many industries is now so much greater than it used to be that an immense amount of suffering is involved in the decay of an occupation that has employed hundreds of thousands of workers. The difference in degree is so great as to constitute a difference in kind. When a few hundred people are squeezed out of an industry their suffering is no doubt severe (for most of us are too conservative to welcome change of occupation) but it has not generally been found difficult for such a number to be absorbed fairly quickly into other types of work. But when a quarter of a million men, from one industry alone, become redundant within the short space of a couple of years (as happened in coalmining in the early twenties) it is a very different matter.

There has been no structural change of such dimensions in recent years, but the reduction in shipbuilding, a highly localized industry, has threatened hundreds of men with unemployment in areas where there are few alternative openings for skilled men; and the reorganization of the railways is dreaded because of the repercussions on the demand for men who make the locomotives and who run the railways.

2. Industry now requires an enormous amount of fixed capital which cannot be moved to another district if the industry for which it was intended declines and nothing else takes its place.

3. There may also be a loss of social capital. Nowadays a great deal of collective provision is made for any sizeable group of people in order to ensure the kind of life that is considered necessary in a modern community – roads, drainage and sewerage, water, gas, and electricity supplies, transport, schools, public libraries, municipal washhouses and baths, etc. If a large proportion of the population for whom these amenities are provided have to move away in search of jobs these things cannot be transferred with them. They become a dead loss before their term of usefulness is over and similar provision has to be made anew in the locality to which the people move.

Much stress was laid on this last factor in the thirties but it is doubtful if it is really of much importance. Many of the old towns which grew up before there was much idea of town planning are so badly laid out, with narrow grim streets, inadequate housing, gloomy ill-equipped schools, public libraries, and other communal facilities that they almost defy any effort at real improvement and there is a lot to be said for starting again where one is not hampered by the legacy of the past. Indeed, one of the reasons why so many new firms decide to establish themselves in the South rather than in the old industrial areas is that the managers and their families snatch at the opportunity to get away from such dismal surroundings to the bright clean new towns and suburbs with modern housing and roads, good school buildings, and so on. And firms in the new areas find it much easier to recruit the scientific and technical personnel on whom modern industry now depends so largely. So if new industries are to be attracted to the older industrial localities, most of this social capital would have to be written off and gigantic new investment undertaken.

4. There is, however, another kind of social capital where the loss involved in the movement of people cannot be made good so easily as in the building of houses and schools, and that is the intricate network of personal and communal relationships that plays so important a part in our lives. People

don't usually leave their old towns as a group but as isolated individuals – one person goes here, a few there, all trying to squeeze themselves in, wherever they can find accommodation and work. If small numbers go to old-established centres of population they can soon find a place for themselves within its social life, but when new areas are becoming populated (as has happened in the Home Counties with the establishment of so many new industries) there are thousands of people drifting together but there is no existing social framework into which they can fit. This is so new a problem that we have only recently begun to realize how important it is. In an old town there are dozens of invisible ties between people that give a sense of belonging to one another; the church where generations of the same families have worshipped, the Mothers' Meeting, Sunday School, the local at which the same group has been meeting for years, the trade union branch where you know all the other members, the Boy Scouts and Girl Guides for the children, the choir and the darts club – in fact, all the little or big interests and activities that make up everyday life. And even if you are not a member of many such definite groups there are other things that lift the sense of solitude. You know the neighbours will come in and help if there is illness in the house; the shops where you usually deal will be ready to give you credit if you strike a bad patch; you know the topics of conversation and even the customary slang.

But in the new place there is none of this feeling of being part of the place itself; and, often enough, newcomers have found that, despite their well-built new houses and clean roads, they felt starved for lack of social vitamins. Nowadays, very great efforts are made to get over this difficulty and to build up, deliberately and carefully, a social life and sense of community. But such things do not grow quickly and it is a great advantage to be able to earn a living without being forced to tear the fabric of social life.

It is not only the family that migrates that suffers from this disruption; as it is generally the younger people who move, the older members of the family are left behind, and it is much more difficult for people to get and to give the informal help that is of such importance in time of trouble. Family feeling is still very strong; and in localities where parents and children, and sisters and brothers live within easy distance of one another, there is a two-way traffic in kindness. Grandparents, particularly grandmothers, help their daughters with young children and in their turn get a lot of care and support when they are too ill or grow too old to be able to do everything for themselves. When the young family has moved in search of work, both groups suffer; the young mother is often very isolated and the grandparents have to come to depend on organized social services to do the jobs – shopping, cooking, nursing, etc. – that their families would gladly have done had they been nearer to them.

The individual business of moderate size cannot be expected to take all these 'imponderables' into account when it is balancing the advantages and disadvantages of alternative sites. In the case of the rare firm that employs twenty or thirty thousand workers – the size of quite a large town if you count in their families – one can expect that a sense of social responsibility will allow these factors to have some weight; but the more numerous average-sized firms, reasonably enough, take the social background for granted and make their decision on more purely economic grounds. It is only society, acting as a whole, that can include these social repercussions in the debit and credit sides of the calculations, and there has, consequently, arisen a demand for positive planning of the location of industry. The aim is to ensure that regions do not develop as one-sidedly in the future as they did in the past, but that there should be such a variety of occupations that a depression in one would not spell disaster to the area as a whole.

Though employment problems were the first to rouse public concern, other considerations have come to lend support to this demand. As more and more firms try and squeeze themselves into the favoured areas the cost of land

and buildings rises and there is a tendency for the centre of the towns to be devoted to offices and banks whilst factories, which require more space, establish themselves on the outer circles and the residential suburbs stretch farther out into the country. This results in a great increase in the time and money spent on travelling to work and congestion of traffic in the streets during the hours when most people are trying to get to their jobs or back to their homes. In London this might add two or three hours to the length of the working day, not to mention the expense of travel, and also the nervous wear and tear associated with pushing one's way into crowded trains and buses or driving through jammed roads.

The suffering is not confined to those who actually have to travel. The spread of buildings means more pressure on the countryside and open spaces, rising property values which make it more difficult for people to get homes at rents or prices they can afford, and longer and more tiring journeys to reach the fresh air during leisure hours.

How far is planning possible? Could the Government direct any industry to go wherever it thought proper or are there any limitations on its powers? This is not the sort of question to which it is possible to answer a firm 'yes' or 'no', for the position is different with different types of industry.

1. In extractive industry, for example, you have obviously not a great deal of choice of site. You can't decide to put a coal industry in an area in which nature has failed to do her part of the job, and even though a coalfield may extend over a fairly large area, the site of the pitshaft and surface workings must be determined primarily by technical factors. But as far as such things as building stone, or clay, or sand and gravel are concerned there is very much more opportunity to choose, for all these things are available in a great many places. As all of them, however, are bulky and costly to transport, the choice is not quite as free as it seems at first sight. For social reasons, you may want to work in one place, though the houses are to be built in another, and the

heavy transport charges involved push up the cost of the housing. How much higher rent are you prepared to pay for so much social advantage?

2. We have to remember that the past has already happened and we can't undo it any more than we can unscramble eggs. There are many industries which, given modern knowledge and scientific ingenuity, could easily have been sited somewhere else than their present places; but if the industry is a heavy one, with immense quantities of capital equipment built on to a particular site, there is no possibility of moving it without incalculable loss. During the war an American shipbuilder showed that it was no longer essential to build ships near to the sea but that they could be prefabricated in inland factories and merely assembled on the water. If this system were further developed there would be much freer choice for the location of shipyards than there has been in the past, but the advantages of building in this way would have to be fantastically high before it paid to move the existing shipyards from their present positions.

Other industries are similarly rooted because of their long association with a certain area and the resultant growth of many interrelated parts which could not be easily transferred. Such industries as cotton and wool, cutlery and pottery, have been intimately connected with particular regions over so long a period that a new firm, starting up away from the rest, is a little bit out in the cold and rightly fears the losses that it may incur through its lack of contact with the main centre.

3. In some instances, an industry which so far as its technical processes are concerned could be equally efficient in any one of a number of districts, finds its choice limited because of its close attachment to other industries that it exists to serve. This is true of such things as the manufacture of packing-materials and boxes or of the finishing processes of textiles. In others, the industry depends on a dozen or more specialist types of production which have grown up in the

area to provide component processes. This is true of many of the miscellaneous industries which flourish in the Midlands.

When this problem became acute in the thirties the conclusion was reached that the number of industries in which we have freedom in the choice of location is severely restricted and that only one big section of production offered reasonable chances of success – that is, the section making light consumption goods. As these are almost all made by mass-production methods there is not a great deal of difference between the styles of building and common services they need for efficient work and, provided that there are cheap and quick transport facilities, adequate supplies of workers willing to man the machines, and a good market near by, almost any place will do as well as any other. It was in this section, therefore, that control of location seemed to offer most opportunities; and as the new expanding industries were found predominantly in this section, it offered considerable scope for exercising a fair amount of public control over future industrial development.

More recently, the attempt to influence location has cast its net more widely. One very big works, for example a motor manufacturer such as Fords, or a steel works, might by itself make all the difference between stagnation and prosperity to an area, because in addition to the jobs available in its own employment there are all the other developments – building, shops, recreational facilities, and so on – that are corollary to an increasing population with good wages to spend.

WAYS OF CONTROLLING LOCATION

How can control be exercised? It depends on whether the general organization of economic activities is part of a planned economy or whether it is predominantly unplanned, in the sense given to those terms in the second chapter. If the allocation of resources and the order of priority of wants is determined by authority it is, of course, a simple matter (and, indeed, an obvious and essential part of the

functions of those in control) to decide the location of all productive work, whatever the reasons for which the choice
might be made. The governing body may wish to have a
diversified group of industries in each locality or to ensure the
provision of certain facilities in time of war, or to establish a
particular balance of town and country life; but, whatever
the determining considerations, it is not forced to take the
'profit and loss' factor into account, unless it wishes to do
so. But, in an economy which is based on private enterprise, the situation is very different, for the decision regard-
ing the uses to which the resources shall be put, the kind of
goods to be produced, and the techniques to be employed in
their production are left to individuals who must calculate, as
carefully as they can, whether the prices they are likely to
get for their goods will repay the expenses they incur in getting them to market. No business is free to do exactly what
it wants, for factory and public health laws build a legal
framework within which it is necessary to keep; but most
Government control of independent businesses (i.e. businesses that are owned by individuals or companies and not
by public authorities) is negative in character. Factory
legislation, for example, does not say what methods shall be
employed but only what shall not be done; it does not direct
employers to employ work-people for so many hours but only
that they must not employ them for more than the maximum permitted. Nobody need build factories to employ
workers if they don't want to, but, if they do choose to do
these things, they must comply with the regulations laid
down for safety, health, protection of minors, and so on.

With regard to the location of industry it is a much simpler
matter to prevent firms from settling where you don't want
them, than to get them to establish themselves where you do
want them. If you prohibit businesses from putting their
plant in a particular spot you leave them the choice of (a)
whether they will have a factory at all anywhere and (b)
where in all the non-prohibited places they will decide to
have it; and if they do, in fact, decide to set it up some-

where, they have, presumably, made their necessary calculations and judged that it was likely to be worth while. If later events prove the calculations to have been wrong and that losses rather than profits are made, the firm has nobody but itself to blame. But, if the Government goes a step further and prescribes the place in which the factory must be established, it takes away the choice from the firm which owns it and leaves it to bear the losses that may result, if the position turns out to be disadvantageous. This is the chief difficulty about positive planning of location when the majority of businesses are run, as they still are, at private risk; and it is on this account that the control of location, in common with other forms of Government control, remains negative. It can stop further industrial development in some places by putting them, so to speak, out of bounds, but it can only get businesses where it wants them by persuasion.

Immediate post-war developments in State control of location followed the lines laid down in the recommendations of the Royal Commission on the Geographical Distribution of the Industrial Population, whose report (the Barlow Report, published in 1940) urged the importance of preventing further industrial congestion in Greater London and the need for encouraging a greater diversity of occupations in areas that had become too highly specialized. Towards the end of the war the Government, in a White Paper on Employment Policy, publicly accepted the responsibility for maintaining a high, stable level of employment by (amongst other measures) 'so influencing the location of new enterprises as to diversify the industrial composition of areas which are particularly vulnerable to unemployment', and the Distribution of Industry Act 1945 was the result. The main part of this Act related to the Development Areas (the new and more hopeful name for what used to be called the Special Areas and, earlier still, the Depressed Areas), and gave the Government power to encourage and assist the growth of new industries in these localities. Such basic services as transport, power, housing, and health might be provided, derelict land might be reclaimed so as to improve the general amenities of the district, factories might be built and financial assistance given, either to individual businesses proposing to set up or to industrial estate companies (the new name for trading estates) providing industrial premises for new firms.

The Act came into force at a moment which was peculiarly favourable to its operations. With the conversion from a war to a peace economy there was an acute shortage of factory buildings and little material and labour available to overcome this shortage. As no new building could be undertaken without a licence, the Government was able to ensure that the large majority of new premises were built in Development Areas and there was, consequently, a much greater amount of industrial building in these districts than in the rest of the country. This accentuated a trend which was already noticeable during the war years. Most of these areas had been judged fairly safe from air raids and, partly for this reason and partly because there were large supplies of qualified labour available, many of the Government war factories had been established there, and the expansion of these war industries had provided a profitable market for a big increase in the service and consumption trades. The reduction in armaments freed a great amount of factory space and many firms were ready to settle in those areas simply so as to have buildings ready for them for immediate civilian production.

As acute shortages disappeared these influences on location lost their force, but another more permanent influence took their place. The Town and Country Planning Act, which was passed in 1947, places on the local planning authority the duty of ensuring that new factories are well sited from the point of view of health and appearance, but any firm applying for permission to erect a building of more than a very modest size must be able to attach to its application a Board of Trade certificate stating that the development in question can be carried out consistently with the proper distribution of industry. This power to prevent factory building where it is feared that it may exaggerate indus-

trial congestion still further has already proved its efficacy in
the case of Greater London and the most congested part of
the Midlands. Between 1932 and 1938 Greater London and
the Midlands had 57 per cent of all the new industrial development, whereas a comparable figure for the post-war years
would be 26 per cent. Although, therefore, the Government
cannot dictate to independent firms carrying on business at
their own risk exactly where they shall be situated, it can
weight the dice whilst the choice is being made; and the developments since the war show that this power, negative as
it may be, may have very positive results.

The purpose of the Town and Country Planning Act was
not primarily to prevent or alleviate unemployment. Like
the New Towns Act 1946, under which eighteen new
towns have been built, it was concerned to reduce urban
congestion by providing employment opportunities in areas
of less dense population. But there was further legislation
following the lines of the Distribution of Industry Act 1945,
directly aimed at inducing industry to settle in localities
where unemployment had already shown itself or seemed
likely to do so in the near future. The original policy was to
offer financial incentives to firms willing to establish manufacturing businesses in areas scheduled as Development
Areas but the later development of this policy instead allowed the Board of Trade, through the Local Employment
Act 1960, to give assistance to firms in any area in which
the rate of unemployment averaged $4\frac{1}{2}$ per cent or more
over a year or seemed likely to do so.

During the sixties it began to be realized that the conception of special Development Areas in which efforts should be
made to induce industry to settle was much too narrow, because there are wide localities, comprising perhaps a whole
region, in which growth was taking place at a much slower
rate than in the more prosperous areas. When a firm is considering where to site its business it is looking for an environment which, as a whole, is conducive to economic
growth and not simply considering the facilities available on

the spot. More and more the greater proportion of employees are now skilled and managerial (the increase in mechanization and automation reduces the demand for unskilled workers, not for the skilled) and unless the district has the range of social, educational and cultural facilities – schools, shops, hospitals, and opportunities for further education – the employer is unlikely to attract the calibre of worker he needs. A financial incentive to a firm is not likely, therefore, to have the desired effect unless a great deal of effort is put into the task of rehabilitating the whole region and this means new well-planned housing, roads, schools, shopping precincts, cinemas and other facilities for leisure-time occupation, colleges and everything else, together with the wholesale removal of derelict streets and depressing housing, factories and commercial premises. All this needs an immense amount of money as well as thought and effort.

The question is how to decide which areas are worth such an amount of expenditure. Unemployment is one obvious criterion : during the sixties the unemployment figure in the Scottish Development Area, South Wales and in the North-East was just about twice the level of the national average, and even more important, the duration of the unemployment was very much longer, and consisted to a greater degree than the average of unskilled men.

Experience has shown that one of the most potent facts in inducing firms to choose one area rather than another is the availability of a suitable labour force and the fact that so large a proportion of those unemployed in these localities is unskilled works against rather than for a choice of a siting of a firm in these areas. In order to overcome this difficulty the Government has made special grants for training but nobody can compel a man to take training or ensure that he has the capacity to make use of it. There has been a large expansion of Government Training Centres particularly in the areas of high unemployment, and fairly generous financial inducements to men to take advantage of them. Moreover the men who do complete the training are quickly placed in employment but there remains a large number who refuse this step to jobs.

The problem with all our schemes for controlling location is that we know so little of the effects of what we do. If we had tried to prevent the great movements of population and industrial development which took place in the last century it is fairly certain that we should now have a much lower standard of living than we enjoy at present and there is no reason to assume that the geographical distribution of people and industry that has grown up in the mid twentieth century should be regarded as sacrosanct and fixed for all time. Undoubtedly there is a good deal of suffering involved in the decline of some industries and the expansion of others but we have no means of measuring even the economic losses and gains consequent on insisting on particular locations for development, and very much less of measuring the social ones. There is a danger therefore that 'Take work to the worker' may become simply a parrot cry and lead to the assumption that it is invariably the duty of somebody – industry or the Government – to provide jobs for the people wherever they happen to live, however uneconomic the locality might be for the expanding types of production. Both wage rates and site rents are very much higher in the new industrial areas and labour more difficult to get; so if firms are still anxious to settle their works there it seems likely that they calculate that other advantages are outstanding. We need to be very sure of the compensating social benefits to be gained before exercising too much pressure on them to go to another locality, chosen by the Government because of political pressure or for any other reason.

In recent years a new problem has begun to make itself felt. As a result of the increase in motor transport (more than half the households in the country own a car) there is much more inducement for large numbers of people to move to the outer suburbs of large towns. Many industries have done the same, to take advantage of lower ground rents. The result of this is that to an ever increasing extent the centres of big towns are no longer industrial but concentrate mainly on commercial and service occupations.

This poses many problems for the local authorities who have to decide what proportion of their resources to devote to the rehabilitation of decaying areas, for many workers have to live near their jobs; for example, post office workers or railway workers who cannot live in the suburbs and travel long distances to report for their shift of work. If little or nothing is done to improve the areas in which they are forced to live, the standard of their housing or the schools which their children attend is lower than in other localities and often falls below an acceptable standard.

Chapter 6

MARKETS AND SHOPS

MOST towns and even many villages have a Market Place or a Market Street which marks the spot to which people from round about used, in earlier days, to bring the goods they had produced, in order to sell them direct to those who wanted them. Such direct sale still goes on and, often enough, in the same place. Farmers bring their sheep and cattle and their butter and cheese and eggs to the country town and strike their bargains with people wanting them; but this direct contact between producer and consumer is no longer the rule. As a general thing we do not buy our goods from the firm that has made them but from a dealer or middleman. This is a natural result of the development of specialization, both functional and geographical. As enormous quantities of particular goods are produced by firms, or even by whole areas, which concentrate on one type of manufacture, it is necessary to establish connecting links between them and the masses of individuals who are scattered all over the country and, perhaps, all over the world, who want to buy what they make. This is the work of the distributor, and this chapter deals with the ways in which these connecting links are made.

There are many kinds of commodities which cost as much to sell as to make, and there are even some, particularly new kinds of manufacture, which cost more. How important a part of our economic system this job of distribution has become can be judged from the fact that about twelve and a half per cent of the whole working population is engaged in it. Not all of these are employees, for there is an exceptionally large proportion of small businesses in this group of trades; but altogether more than two and a quarter million people are occupied in getting goods from the producer to the consumer.

Let us begin with the end of this with which most of us are familiar – the retail shop. This may be anything from the little village sweet shop with its few bottles of coloured sweets displayed in the parlour window, to the gigantic department store which caters for practically every human need under one roof. The first Census of Distribution was taken by the Board of Trade in 1951 and a short report on the result was published a year later. This showed that there were more than half a million shops operating, which means more than one shop for every hundred persons – men, women, and children – in the community.

This total seems so huge that there are many people who insist that we are over-served in this respect and that a great deal of effort is wasted in distributing goods that could be better employed in making more of them to be distributed. They point to the duplication of small shops selling almost identical goods in neighbouring streets and argue that the consumer would gain if he got into the habit of making all his purchases in a central store which supplied a whole neighbourhood. Before we can judge in this matter we must get some idea of what a retailer does.

WHAT THE SHOPKEEPER DOES

If you think of the things we use during the course of a week or so you will realize what an enormous variety of goods we need to buy in quite a short space of time – many different kinds of food and household equipment, a reel of cotton, a collar stud, some tacks and screws, cigarettes, a bottle of beer, notepaper and envelopes – it is impossible to begin to list the hundreds of things we might include as ordinary day-to-day buying. Most of us have not the slightest idea where these things are made and even if we had we should have neither time nor means to get into touch with their manufacturers. The tiny amount we require of each article would not be worth considering by a maker who is turning out thousands of them every day and he could not spare time to send out innumerable small parcels to the thousands of individuals who want his products. Very often we don't really know just what it is we want; we have a vague idea of the kind of article that might meet our need, but we want to see many different kinds of goods displayed so that we can choose the one that we think will suit. We need somebody to advise us about the qualities and types and uses of unfamiliar products and show us how to make the best of them. We want to be able to buy the amount we need when we need it and not have the bother and expense of storing a large supply; and we want to have goods delivered to our homes at convenient times. These are the wants that the retailer satisfies, and sometimes one is more important and sometimes another. Sometimes, all sorts of extra services and amenities are thrown in in addition.

It is simplest to consider all these functions one by one.

1. We don't usually give our orders for goods in advance, but expect to be able to buy them when we want them. The retailer must, therefore, take the risk of anticipating our wants and buying in advance the goods he thinks will satisfy us. In addition to the risk he runs that we may not, in fact, want the goods, or not in the quantities he has calculated, he has to meet the cost of storage (which covers the loss of interest on the capital embodied in the goods, as well as the provision of physical space) and the danger of spoiling. The cost, both of risk and storage, varies of course with different kinds of goods. A piano shop must provide a lot of space and correct temperature but doesn't generally need to fear rapid changes in demand; a model hat shop needs small storage space but knows that fashion may change so suddenly that its stock may have to be drastically marked down. A flower shop has to reckon on the possibility that bad weather may delay the visits of its customers until the flowers have lost their first valuable bloom; a greengrocer may be able to judge the demand for potatoes and cauliflowers but

not be so sure of the tastes of his neighbourhood when he introduces something unfamiliar, such as pomegranates or corn on the cob; a crockery and glass shop is likely to have a bigger bill for damage and breakages during storage than a shoe shop.

2. The retailer buys in bulk and sells to customers in small quantities, so he has a lot of work to do in dividing up the goods he buys, sorting and grading them, and packing them into parcels that are convenient to us. In some types of goods this work has been taken out of his hands and the products reach him graded, packed, labelled, and priced, and ready for immediate sale to the customer. This is true of most cigarettes and chocolates, of many kinds of food, and household articles such as soap and cleaning materials, and it is likely to develop further. But there are still an enormous number of things in which the knowledge and skill of the retailer are required, whether in cutting a sheep into joints that are suitable for the family dinner, or dividing a roll of cloth into lengths to suit the customer's requirements. In some shops this sorting and grading of goods has to be done many times over because of their high degree of perishability. Soft fruit, for example, must be continually picked over and regraded, and this adds to the cost of the retailer's work.

3. Very few of us have expert knowledge of many of the things we buy, so we depend on the advice and information the shopkeeper can give us. The importance of this function varies enormously from one type of commodity to another. Some shops try to eliminate this part of the retailer's job altogether. In such stores as Woolworths or Marks and Spencers, for example, all the available goods are displayed on the counters and the customer makes his choice without any help from the sales assistant, whose job consists solely of packing the customer's choice and receiving payment. Whilst this is still the exception it is a practice which has grown enormously in recent years. The self-service store is found most commonly in grocery and provision shops be-

cause nowadays the large majority of goods they sell are pre-packed and labelled by the manufacturer or wholesaler ready for sale. There are very few grocers who still blend tea or grind freshly roasted coffee to the customer's individual taste, and with the prevalence of the calculating machine the grocery shop assistant no longer needs any special know-ledge or ability – not even the capacity to do mental arith-metic quickly. The same thing is spreading to the sale of other types of goods. A large number of stores, for example, now have 'hat-bars' or 'shoe-bars' – particularly for their less expensive lines – where the customer does all the work of selection for herself and meets the assistant only when the point of packing and paying is reached.

But there are many people who like to have the help of the salesman in comparing qualities or by calling their attention to other goods, even when buying familiar articles of food and clothing and household equipment, and with less usual purchases we all rely greatly on his assistance. A bookshop would soon lose its customers if the shop assistant had no knowledge of the insides of books and could not suggest a suitable present for a boy of ten or an old lady of seventy. When a woman buys a hat or dress for a special occasion she expects the saleswoman to help her to pick the one that be-comes her, and is quite ready to pay the higher price that such service involves. Most new articles would never be tried at all if there were not expert sales-people available to explain and demonstrate their uses. This is particularly true of such things as vacuum cleaners, electric washers, television sets, pressure cookers, etc., but in a lesser degree it is true of all but the most usual and familiar kinds of goods.

Apart from the help given by the salesman to the indi-vidual customer the shopkeeper finds it necessary to provide a great deal of information for the use of his customers in general. Catalogues make known what is available and, though a good deal of the lavish presentation may be adver-tisement (of which more will be said later), some indication of what can be provided, particularly of new varieties of goods or of seasonable commodities, is necessary to enable the customer to make his selection. A similar part is played by advertisements in periodicals and window displays, both of which are partly a means of giving essential information and partly a means of attracting the notice of potential customers.

4. Even though most things are bought in small amounts a number of them together may prove too heavy or bulky a burden for the shopper to carry home, so delivery must be provided by the shopkeeper. In some instances, as, for example, furniture, this is absolutely essential, but even if the weight is not very great, delivery is a convenience for which the customer is usually prepared to pay. Sometimes the buyer is given a choice and a small extra charge is made for home delivery; this is often the case with newspapers and groceries, but more often it is assumed that a fairly large proportion of buyers will expect it and the cost of maintaining an errand boy or a fleet of motor vans has to be included in the prices of the goods sold. In some districts, where the retailer knows that low price is more important to his customer than convenience, 'cash and carry' is the rule, and the customer is served on the understanding that he pays on the nail and takes his purchases away himself. In other instances, the other extreme is reached, for the retailer sends not only the purchases but the whole shop to the door of the customer by means of motor vans stocked with all the different types of goods he has for sale. This is naturally more usual in country districts than in the town, but it is not unknown in urban areas in the sale of certain types of commodity, e.g. household brushes and similar things.

5. Mention of 'cash and carry' introduces another function performed by most retailers – the readiness to give a certain amount of credit. Sometimes this may represent a very appreciable cost to the retailer; for example, the months or even years of credit given by a high-class tailor, or the periods allowed by firms to customers who pay their accounts monthly or quarterly. Nowadays, however, the majority of

purchases are made on a cash basis or the period of credit
is so short – a week – that it does not add much to the retailer's costs, except in so far as it increases the amount of
book-keeping he must do.

6. In addition to these essentials there are certain amenities
which cannot be said to be an integral part of the work of
the retailer but which the customer has come to expect and
the absence of which he would resent. The shop must be pleasantly and tastefully decorated, goods must be well displayed, the assistants are expected to give courteous and
unrushed service. If the shop is large, lifts and escalators, a
restaurant or tea room, an information counter, and other
such trimmings are looked for. Some part of this may be
simply advertisement, to persuade customers to choose one
shop rather than another; but a good deal represents the
kind of environmental conditions in which purchasers in a
modern community expect to be able to do their shopping.

BIG AND LITTLE SHOPS

Although all retail shops perform most of these listed functions to some extent, they vary greatly in size and structure.
Six principal kinds can be distinguished: (1) unit shops
(2) supermarkets (3) department stores (4) multiple or
chain stores (5) Co-operative Societies (6) mail-order firms.
There are a good many other ways through which goods
reach the consumer, for example, automatic machines, street
hawkers, hotels and public-houses (for cigarettes, popular
medicines, cosmetics, etc.), but these six account for far and
away the largest part of retail distribution. It was mentioned
earlier that we cannot be certain of the total number of retail
outlets and therefore we are equally ignorant of the precise
proportions of the trade done by each of these six; but an
estimate made in 1930 calculated that over 90 per cent of the
total outlets consisted of the unit shop – the independent
tradesman owning and managing a single shop, usually on a
fairly small scale – and although the average turnover was

not very large, this group accounted for about two-thirds of the whole retail turnover. The average annual turnover of the department store was seven or eight times that of the unit shop, but as there were only about a thousand such stores their total was only about 15 per cent of that of the former group. Since that date the role of the unit shops has declined with the growth of the multiples and supermarkets, but in 1971 they still accounted for 70 per cent of the total of retail establishments though their turnover had dropped to around 40 per cent of the total.

Why has the small shop such a tenacious hold on life when at first sight the advantages seem to be so greatly on the side of the big store? Far and away the most important advantage offered by the unit shop is the convenience that derives from its ubiquitousness. This can be seen if we consider the types of shop that are the most frequent. In a street of about a hundred houses (a usual size in most towns) we find that there is nearly always a grocer and a clothing shop; for every two streets there is a butcher; for every three a sweet shop, a paper shop, and a greengrocer. These all sell things we need to buy almost every day and we should not be willing to go any distance to get them. Even if we realize that we can get a larger variety of greens and groceries at a big store we prefer to buy from the shop at the corner and save a long walk or bus ride. Children can safely run out to do the errands when the shop is close by, or the odd purchases can be made by the man on his way to and from his work. When people have a strongly entrenched liking for something as, for example, smokers have for a particular brand of cigarette or tobacco, they will go to great lengths to get what they want. This was shown during the post-war shortage when purchasers stood in queues or snooped from street to street to get a supply. But would the habit ever have become so firmly fixed if such quests had been necessary from the beginning, instead of being able to buy a packet of cigarettes every few yards along the road?

In the poorest districts of most towns there are large numbers of small general shops which 'cash in' on this desire to be able to buy a variety of goods in small quantities whenever we happen to think of them. Many of these do so small a trade that it would not be worth while for a large concern to open a branch there, but it forms a useful sideline to a family whose main living is earned in another field. The wife can combine the care of the shop with her domestic duties and the profits make a welcome addition to her husband's wages.

The majority of unit shops are not, of course, of this 'sideline' variety, but provide a reasonable living for the proprietor and are often large enough to make it necessary for him to employ a considerable number of assistants.

It is not only its nearness to one's home that gives the unit shop an advantage. There are many people who prefer the single shop because they believe that they get more personal attention than at the branch of a multiple store. There is a pleasant feeling in being greeted by name and in the opportunity for the exchange of a little local chat. The manager of a branch may be just as anxious to bind his customers to him by friendly attentions, but he probably does not live in the area (for the managers of multiple shops get moved about for experience, and on promotion) and has not the same interest in its affairs.

In some branches of retail trade the single shop gains by its ability to build up a reputation for knowledge and taste. This applies particularly to such goods as antiques or jewellery or old books, where the customer learns to rely on the advice of the salesman; he would not usually be offered such expert assistance in a larger department store with dozens of different sections. The same thing is true of fashionable dress shops, where articles are designed to suit the individual purchaser and where the price charged includes the payment for the expert taste of the saleswoman.

At one time most luxury articles – flowers or gloves or beautifully packed chocolates – were sold by unit shops because of a certain degree of snobbishness amongst some customers who prided themselves on the fastidiousness of their demands; but nowadays, although this is still true to some extent, more and more of this class of merchandise is included in department stores.

Whilst the unit shop still comprises the largest number of individual outlets it has lost a great deal of its trade to the self-service store and supermarket which is one of the outstanding developments in retail trade of the last few years. In 1972 there were about 8,000 such stores and they were responsible for close on two-thirds of retail sales in groceries and food generally. More recently they have been diversifying to a marked extent and about 25 per cent of their trade is now done in non-food articles such as cosmetics, records, household equipment, books, and so on. Much careful planning and consumer research goes into the form and position of display of the various goods. Bright lights and colours and background music give the housewife the illusion that she is enjoying some social occasion rather than trudging through a domestic chore. Trolley baskets are designed with a place to park the baby so that perambulation all round the shop is easy. Sheer necessities that every housewife will buy – such as meat – are put in the part of the store that requires the purchaser to walk past shelves of tempting goods that she would not have thought of for herself, and practically everything needed for the day-to-day running of a home can be bought in one great buying spree under one roof. The difficulty is in getting the stuff home, because these stores do not usually arrange for delivery. But the increase in the number of households with cars, and homes equipped with refrigerators and store cupboards, makes it worth while – particularly if the wife is also in a job which leaves little leisure for shopping – to have a once-a-week expedition to the supermarket.

The great advantage of these stores to the shopper lies in the wealth of choice she is offered. Everything is displayed, clearly marked in price, and the purchaser can take as long as she likes to make up her mind. Even such things as meat and cheese have been cut, weighed, and packed behind the scenes so that the housewife can buy exactly the weight she wants or can afford instead of being compelled to take the two or three ounces more than she asked for that the salesman has cut to her order and that she does not want to pay for. From the point of view of the retailer the advantage is in the lower wages bill, for whilst the sales analysts, display organizers, and packers behind the scenes are highly skilled, with appropriate pay, the shop staff can be reduced both in number and quality. This is specially important when it is remembered that the shop staff must be maintained for long periods when there is hardly anybody in the shop, whilst the staff behind the scenes are at work throughout the working day. In addition, there is a much quicker turnover of stock, and the sale of hardware and cosmetics is helped by displaying it under the same roof as the shelves of food. Perhaps the success of these stores is also due in part to the higher money incomes of large sections of the population whose choices, of necessity, used to be extremely limited. To them the supermarket offers a wide variety of goods they would never have dreamed of asking for at a unit shop if they had not seen them displayed before them, in part because of ignorance and in part through diffidence in asking the sales assistant for something unfamiliar.

A further development of the supermarket has already taken place in the United States and it is likely that the example will be followed in this country. This is the out-of-town regional shopping centre. This has been defined by the Urban Land Institute as a minimum site of at least 40 acres with parking facilities for 4,000 cars and containing at least one department store. It is based on the idea that shoppers prefer to get most of their purchasing done at one time and that they can be persuaded to take the trouble to drive a short distance from the town where they live if they are certain of being able to park. At first this may seem too arid and impersonal a method of getting one's supplies but one can see how it could be developed to offer a pleasant coffee shop and restaurant, a hairdresser and beautician, a nursery where young children could be safely left while the parents are going the rounds and so on. But such a development requires a population of at least 200,000 and so far there has not been much similar development in this country.

A less ambitious development has been that of the super-store which has appeared both in America and some European countries. Although the store is sited out of town it does not offer the same range of goods as the Regional Shopping Centre. It is more like the supermarket with which we are familiar but on a larger scale. Both take advantage of the lower ground rents which are usual outside an urban area and depend on the fact that a large proportion of households now own a car and are prepared to take advantage of this to get a large choice and perhaps lower prices than they are offered in the supermarket in the High Street. So far only one firm, Woolworths, has taken this step in this country but as, according to their chairman, the trading performance has so far outstripped expectations it is likely that their example will be followed, though those who know most about retail trading do not believe that there will be more than a dozen or so similiar stores between now and the 1980s.

But there are many shoppers who prefer the intimacy of the unit shop because they enjoy being recognized and ad-dressed as individuals or because they are glad to have an opportunity to ask for advice about rival brands; or it may be they simply dislike the hard glitter and impersonality of a bit of their day-to-day business which used to have something of a social relationship about it. There are two ways in which the unit shop can hope to compete successfully with the supermarket and with the chain store, even in groceries and other foodstuffs. One is to specialize in things which do not have a mass market but for which there is a sufficient clien-tele in the neighbourhood to provide a reasonable turnover, the slightly more exotic foods, for example, or the higher-priced preserves, or the type of article one finds in a delica-tessen shop, and so on. The other, and it is one which is developing rapidly, is to join with other shops to institute bulk buying whilst remaining independent as sellers. Almost a quarter of the 148,000 grocers in Britain are linked up in groups or chains for this purpose whilst carrying on their own businesses independently in every other aspect of their work.

The object of a department store is to offer such a wide variety of choice that it is worth while for the customer to make the journey to the place where the store is situated. The earliest such stores specialized mainly in drapery and fashion goods, in which wide choice is particularly desired, but they have gradually added everything else from foreign travel to funerals. They reckon on the fact that one department helps to sell another. When a customer comes in to buy a dress, she may find it convenient to buy other things at the same time, or her attention may be caught by goods she sees on her way from the entrance to the dress section and for which she would not have come specially. It is, therefore, important for them to inveigle people into the store to have a look round; and to attract potential customers they often turn themselves into enjoyable social centres. A good many of the amenities they offer are really in the nature of bait, 'Meet your friends in —— Cafe' or '——'s Inquiry Office is at your service', and so on. The well-planned buildings, the lights and decorations, the lavish window displays, the rest rooms and restaurants, the uniformed lift attendants, the numerous attractively dressed saleswomen, are all part of the outlay necessary to make a visit to the store such an enjoyable outing that women (who form the large majority of retail shoppers) will look forward to their visit and deliberately postpone their purchases of as many things as possible until they are able to make the journey.

The increase in quick communications by bus and electric railway has added greatly to the potential market of the department stores. Thousands of women in the suburbs and small country towns look forward enormously to the weekly or fortnightly visit to the nearest big town where they can do their shopping, have their hair dressed, and meet their friends for meals in much more glamorous surroundings than are offered by the little shops near their homes.

Apart from its social attractions the department store has many of the advantages already discussed in connection with large-scale manufacture. By extending its market it can spread its overheads so that costs are proportionately less and it can give better value for money than the small concern. Its expert buyers can acquire a comprehensive knowledge of sources of supply and know where they are likely to find goods that will attract customers. Its trade in most of its departments is sufficient to justify the employment of staffs with specialist experience and to stock a variety of goods that would be beyond the resources of most unit shops. It can get rid of goods that have failed to attract by offering them at bargain prices in the knowledge that many people who come to the store for these bargains will be caught by the more expensive and profitable goods that they see on their way to them. In fact, so outstanding are the advantages of such concentration of goods of all types in a central store that many people have argued that this should be the only shopping provision made in newly planned towns and that the unit shop is now an anachronism. Whether this is the right development or not depends on the qualities you rate most highly – efficiency of service and wide variety of choice with the bother of going some distance for them, or the comfort of knowing that you can run out for the odd box of matches or pound of sugar that you forgot to buy when you were out shopping.

The fourth method of retail distribution – the multiple shop, or, as the Americans say, the chain store – tries to combine the convenience offered by the unit shop with many of the advantages of large-scale distribution provided by the department store. They vary from the private shop which has done well enough to open a few branches in the neighbourhood to the giant concern with hundreds of branches all over the country. Where the number of shops is small, say half a dozen or so, and they are all near to one another, they do not differ to any appreciable degree from the unit shop; the owner probably specializes in buying the stock and in general supervision and can visit all his shops during the course of the day to keep an eye on the managers. He has the advantage over the unit shop that he can buy in large quantities and get the benefit of lower prices, quicker delivery, or easier credit terms, but, apart from this, there is little to distinguish this kind of firm from the single shop. But the chain store which has many branches dispersed in different towns has altogether different problems to cope with. Such chains have developed particularly in groceries, provisions, and meat – the things the housewife wants to be able to buy easily close by her home. In many cases they sell goods they have manufactured themselves, but all of them specialize in articles of standard consumption, many of which can be packed, labelled, and priced before coming into the shop. In this way, they get the advantage of centralized buying and processing and so can offer goods at attractive prices. As they depend on a quick turnover their goods are fresh and they can dovetail the likes and dislikes of different areas by removing stock from one branch to another as occasion demands. Most such chain stores have a standard design and decoration of their shops so that customers get familiar with them and treat them as old friends when they come across them in another town. The shop front thus acts as an advertisement and keeps the store in people's minds. They register its existence even when they don't want to buy anything at the moment.

The province of such stores is rather limited, for it is difficult to supervise a staff that is scattered in small groups all over the country; and they tend to confine themselves to the kind of goods that are suitable for bulk buying and whose sale can be done efficiently by routine methods. Where variety of choice is demanded or where personal knowledge or taste is required, they have neither the advantages of the department store nor those of the private unit shop.

Some chain stores have developed along the same lines as the supermarket; Woolworths and Marks and Spencers are the outstanding examples of this. Bulk buying, attractiveness of display, concentration on a restricted number of fast-selling lines, and ubiquitousness have combined to make both these stores into something of a national institution. Marks and Spencers have shown that the self-service principle can be introduced even into clothing, a branch of retail trading that one would have thought peculiarly unsuited to it. They have succeeded by concentrating on a comparatively small number of designs (which reduces the space needed for stocks as well as allowing bulk purchases from manufacturers) but most of all by the stroke of genius which permits any customer to return an article at will and get the money paid without question and without pressure to buy something in its place. This at once cuts out the need for fitting-rooms – an immense saving in space on expensive sites, and an equally big saving in the number of saleswomen needed.

There is still another branch of retail distribution which does not fall clearly into any of the categories mentioned so far, though it might perhaps be considered as a special kind of chain store – the Consumers' Co-operative Societies. These societies have a long history – the pioneer store was opened in Rochdale in 1844 – and they are by no means solely trading concerns. They are, in fact, an expression of a particular social philosophy and their development has been closely linked with that of other types of working-class association; but their principal work is that of shopkeeping and it is that side of their activities with which we are concerned in this chapter.

The Co-operative Society is an attempt to eliminate the profit-making middleman by organizing consumers into groups to supply themselves with the goods they want. Each Society is an independent self-governing body owned by its members, who constitute the purchasers of the goods stocked in its shops. It buys its goods in bulk at wholesale prices and resells to its individual members retail, and the profits that accrue are distributed amongst the purchasers every half year in proportion to the amount they have spent at the shop. One might ask, 'Why make profits at all? Why does the Society not sell to its members at cost price, at an amount that just covers the expenditure of breaking bulk, maintaining the shop premises, paying the wages of the sales assistants and so on?' There are two benefits to be gained by not doing so.

1. By charging the usual retail prices the society is fairly certain that its overhead costs will be fully met and that there will be no risk of cutting itself too close. It is not easy to estimate the exact share of the overheads that should be borne by each article of stock; if a generous estimate is made there will still be profits to distribute after some time and if the calculation is too cheese-paring there will be danger of losses to be covered.

2. The periodic division of the profits is very much liked by the members. A reduction in the price of weekly purchases by a penny or twopence would hardly be noticed, but the receipt of a few pounds at the end of the half year is a welcome event to the housewife of modest means. It is a form of saving which is done without effort and helps the household to meet special expenses at holiday time, or when some new equipment is needed, that would otherwise be a heavy burden on the weekly housekeeping money.

The size of the Co-operative Societies varies enormously, from the very small ones with one or two tiny shops to the huge concern which maintains department stores in the big towns and a large number of branches in smaller districts. There are close on thirteen million members of all societies together and as most of them buy for a household this means that probably about half of the whole population have some connection with the movement. This does not mean that these households buy all their goods from the society to which they belong. Indeed, that would be very exceptional. The societies deal mostly in the goods of general consumption, milk, bread, groceries, and the more or less standard kinds of furniture and clothing, rather than in those things which depend largely on the vagaries of individual taste. In fact, a recent estimate showed that 73 per cent of their total trade was in food, tobacco, and cigarettes. A great many of the goods they sell are manufactured solely for them by the Co-operative Wholesale Societies. There are two of these, one for Scotland, and one for England, from which the separate societies buy their stock. Not all of it, or even most of it, is manufactured by the C.W.S. themselves; they buy from makers in order to supply the stores and, as they also distribute their profits to the societies that buy from them, the individual customer eventually receives this also in his 'divi'.

The share of retail trade done by the Co-operative Societies has been dropping fairly steadily during the decade of the sixties; while the multiples increased their turnover by over 80 per cent the Co-operative increased by only 10 per cent and indeed, except in foods, the volume of their sales actually decreased. This is probably due at least in part to the fact that their clientele is drawn primarily from the wage-earning sections of the community whose purchases used to be heavily weighted on the basic essentials of life that the Co-ops were designed to provide at low cost. These groups now have much more to spend and enjoy a standard of living which – like the middle-class one – includes a variety of goods and a wealth of choice to which the Co-op stores have not yet adjusted themselves. To some extent the Co-ops find change difficult simply because they are not solely commercial organizations but have a social philosophy and political affiliations. Each store has a good deal of autonomy and committee members are often unwilling to close down a small shop – even if it is demonstrably inefficient – or allow it to be swallowed up by a larger branch.

Some societies have tried to stem the decrease by attempts to diversify but not always with success. The majority run flourishing wine and spirit departments, a few have their own travel agencies or act as agents for tour operators, some have been successful with garages and there is a growing awareness that the young consumer – the under 25s – now has a major part in buying power, and that he, or more likely she, demands a different kind of article from those which her mother bought. Nevertheless, up to the present most Co-operative shoppers are in the older age groups and predominantly working class and they continue to buy at the Co-op only the kinds of goods they bought in the very much less affluent thirties, so the Societies do not get a share of the much more profitable types of consumer goods on which ordinary stores rely for their profits.

The variety of goods stocked by a retailer is so large that the shopkeeper cannot keep in touch with the many manufacturers who make them and relies on a wholesale dealer for his supplies. It is the job of the wholesaler to act as a link between the shops that sell to the individual customer small quantities of many different goods and the manufacturers who produce a few types of article in immense quantities. He holds the stocks from which the retailers can replenish their stores to meet customers' requirements. But in recent years there has been a big growth in 'own brand marketing'; that is, manufacturers provide their own retail outlets stocked mainly by goods they have produced for themselves or which have been made to their specifications by other manufacturers. The most obvious example of this is Marks and Spencers with their St Michael brand but there are other firms, such as British Home Stores, Sainsburys, and Boots which sell other manufacturers' products as well as their own brands. In certain kinds of food 'own brand marketing' is responsible for as much as 30 per cent of the total sales but this is not general and if we take retail sales as a whole it is closer to about 10 per cent.

In branches of distribution – whether wholesale or retail – the size of the market depends to a large extent on the degree to which the goods for sale can be standardized. A housewife is quite content to order coal or groceries by letter or telephone because these things can be classified or described by name or number and she is confident that she will get exactly what she has ordered. She would hesitate to do the same when buying meat and salads and cheese (the careful French housewife would throw up her hands in horror at the mere idea!) but she would not even dream of buying a hat in this way. Some products, such as wheat and cotton, have classifications and labels which are recognized all over the world and immense quantities can be bought and sold by wire and wireless without any necessity for either side to see the goods that are the basis of their contracts. There are not, of course, many goods which have such a wide demand and that are suitable for standardized grading, but there are a very large number that can be bought by sample because, as they are mass-produced, the units of a particular type are identical. Many wholesalers depend on their travelling salesmen to develop their markets by visiting the retailers with a collection of samples of the different kinds of commodity available; and the same sort of 'sale by sample' is done by stores which distribute by post their illustrated catalogues showing their most attractive goods. Many households in the country or smaller towns buy a considerable proportion of their equipment and clothing in this way, and if manufacturers were able to evolve a more efficient system of standardization of clothing-sizes there is no doubt that this would develop much more than it has done. At present the sizes vary from manufacturer to manufacturer and purchasers realize that they run a serious risk in buying from the catalogue the sort of clothes that depend for their attractiveness on their fit; but already there is a wide market for the types of goods in which fit is unimportant.

Such developments of marketing as sale by grade and by sample are possible only in a community which has reached a high standard of commercial honesty. The purchaser must have confidence that the goods delivered to him will not only look like the sample he saw but that they are actually identical in every respect. Where the 'sample' is merely an illustration in a printed catalogue the buyer is pinning his faith mainly to the reputation of the firm, and many firms have spoiled their markets by over-glamorized illustrations and descriptions of the goods for sale.

There has been a remarkable increase in mail-order buying and some of the biggest firms have a turnover of well over £100 million a year. Such firms have the advantage of very low storage costs, for goods need not be kept in shops on expensive main-street frontages, but they have heavy outgoings in packing and postage and in high percentage commission to agents. Their success is probably due to two factors – first that they are strictly honest; the goods are exactly as described (or if they seem not to be so will be promptly exchanged). The second is that a certain period of credit is allowed. A recent estimate is that they account for well over 4 per cent of all retail sales.

IS ADVERTISEMENT A WASTE?

In an earlier section of this chapter, mention was made of the duty of the shopkeeper to inform the public of the goods he has available, and it was suggested that it was difficult to draw the dividing line between the expenditure in which he is involved for this purpose and the amount he spends on advertisement. Much of the lavish window dressing gives no information at all of the contents of the store but is intended solely to catch the eye and arouse the interest of the potential purchaser, and most of the amenities offered by stores are to be regarded more as decoys than anything else. The question that has now to be considered, therefore, is 'What part does advertisement play in our economic world? Is it an advantage or not?' It will be seen at once that the second of these questions is ambiguous, for it can be taken in two very different senses: (1) Is it advantageous to the advertiser? and (2) Is it advantageous to the community as a whole?

Here I am concerned principally with the second meaning. It is unlikely that firms would continue to spend so much on advertisement and to rack their brains to find new ways of attracting the customer unless they had come to the conclusion that it paid them to do so. The experience of most firms is that if they don't advertise they are sure to lose a considerable proportion of their trade to those who do. But suppose nobody advertised. Would there not be a net gain to the community, for all the labour and materials used in advertisement would be released for more productive uses? Before the war it was calculated that over £80 million was spent annually on advertisement, of which Press advertising accounted for £35 million, posters and direct mail advertising for £27½ million, window display for £10 million, and the remainder went on miscellaneous media such as films, radio, etc. In 1968 the Advertising Association estimated that the total was £494 million (1·4 per cent of Gross National Product) – of which nearly 64 per cent was on Press advertising, which included national and regional newspapers, magazines and periodicals, and trade and technical journals, 26½ per cent on television advertising, and the remainder on posters, outdoor signs, cinema and radio, window displays, samples, gift schemes, etc. This is a colossal total and it is worth while to consider whether the money was well spent. Let us try to make a profit and loss account.

IN FAVOUR OF ADVERTISING

1. Everybody agrees that the provision of adequate information is a necessary part of the work of the distributor. Hundreds of thousands of different kinds of goods are produced and we should waste an immense amount of time hunting them down unless the firms that are prepared to sell them tell us what they can provide. How is it possible to draw a line of demarcation between the means used by a firm to keep us informed of its wares and the efforts it makes to persuade us to spend our money on one thing rather than

another, or to buy from one shop and not from a competitor? The information will not 'register' with us unless it is attractively given and frequently repeated, particularly with regard to the things we buy at regular intervals. How is it possible to distinguish what proportion of the expenditure is necessary to bring goods to the notice of the potential customer without overstepping the line of offering unnecessary persuasion? For example, we should be ignorant of the new books that are published – and consequently miss all the pleasure they will bring us – if the publishers did not announce their names and authors through advertisements in the Press. They could, of course, give a closely printed list of titles in an obscure corner of the paper; but might we not justly complain that we had overlooked it and had missed the chance of getting a book that we should have enjoyed? As it is, books by which the publisher hopes to attract the buyer are announced in the spacious manner that is likely to catch the eye of the reader. How big must the type be before it ceases to be information and becomes advertisement?

2. Advertisement is necessary to introduce new commodities into the market and to explain their uses. Most of the things we now prize were not produced in response to the demand of the consumer; on the contrary, they seemed so strange that most of us would have been unwilling even to try them without a great deal of persuasion. We are creatures of habit even when the habit is irksome and inconvenient. Before the war, the vacuum-cleaner salesman-demonstrator was a familiar figure in every suburb. He brought his wares to the door and demonstrated their use on the drawing-room carpet, and this convinced many more people of the help they would get from possessing such a contraption than any amount of detached, impersonal statements giving lists of facts about its composition and purpose. Sewing machines, radio and television sets, bicycles, washing machines, typewriters – in fact, practically all the mechanical equipment of modern life – must be

included in this category of goods whose uses would be largely unknown without the persuasiveness of the advertiser who first got us to try them, and which have added greatly to the convenience or efficiency or amusement or pleasure of life.

3. Although advertisement costs must be covered by the selling price of the commodity, the result of advertisement may often be that the consumers get it at a lower price than they would have had to pay if it had not been advertised. The increase in the demand for the advertised article may be so great that production on a large scale becomes possible and opens the door to all the economies of scale mentioned in an earlier chapter.

4. Advertisement stimulates a continuous demand for an article, and this, by creating a stable market, reduces the waste, both economic and social, that is associated with instability in production. (See chapters 4 and 10.)

5. Advertisement is a guarantee of quality. A firm that spends a lot of money in making itself known will not risk the loss of its reputation by offering shoddy goods or anything inferior to the standards it boasts of. The buyer can have confidence that the advertised article will be standard quality wherever he meets it.

6. The confidence felt by the purchaser in the 'sameness' of the advertised article simplifies distribution. Instead of spending a lot of time examining various qualities and consulting the expert salesman, the buyer can ask for what he wants by name.

As most firms supply a wide range of goods the confidence we have in one article predisposes us to try others from the same maker or distributor, and this again simplifies the buying and selling process. The variety of goods offered us is bewildering in its complexity; we can't pretend to know enough about them to choose intelligently, so when we see a familiar label or trade mark we are inclined to give the article a trial. This is very useful when we move from one place to another. We should have to spend a lot of time examining and comparing different products and qualities offered us by shopkeepers in the new place before we could find the thing to suit; as it is we can buy the advertised branded article wherever we go.

7. Advertisement stimulates the total demand for goods and thus encourages investment, production, and employment. Many simpler societies remain poor because wants are so few that they see no reason to work hard enough to make use of the natural resources at their door. The greater and more varied our wants, the greater the incentive to experiment and to work and in this way to raise the standard of living.

8. Advertisement often provides a lot of enjoyment to the public. Thousands of women get great pleasure from 'window shopping' or from the use of the amenities offered by the big department stores. The bright lights and flashing signs may often be garish and vulgar in design, but how much they add to the liveliness and gaiety of the streets was realized when they disappeared during wartime.

AGAINST ADVERTISING

1. Although the provision of information is essential, this function of advertisement accounts for but a small proportion of the expenditure on it, and, in fact, a very large proportion of advertisements do not even pretend to give any details of the composition or quality of the goods they advertise. The pretty girl with the toothy smile who figures so frequently on posters and labels has nothing whatever to do with the goods she advertises, and there is not even a pretence that a good complexion or slender legs have any relation to the cigarettes or chocolates or holiday resorts or the hundred and one other things to which they try to draw our attention. The main purpose is to catch the eye of the potential buyer and to make a particular name so familiar that the person automatically thinks of it whenever he has a need for the article to which it is attached.

2. The chief objective of advertisement is to arouse and stimulate new wants or to induce buyers to change from old wants to new. Its main appeal is to emotion rather than to judgement. The girl who is afraid of falling behind in the 'attractiveness' race is persuaded that this lipstick or shampoo will turn her into the glamorous queen of hearts she longs to be; the man who succumbs to the 'snob' car advertisement prides himself on the fastidiousness of his taste. Neither has the slightest knowledge of the things he purchases but obediently swallows the statements of the advertiser.

3. As the customer is not a good judge the advertisement is not, in fact, the guarantee of quality it claims to be. Whilst it is true that goods of markedly inferior quality will have a short-lived market, those that are not noticeably poor quality will continue to sell, because the purchaser remains ignorant that he is paying for more value than he gets. And even those that are found out mostly last long enough to provide their producers with a handsome profit before the public learn to distrust the advertisement. None of us can judge the quality of more than a tiny proportion of the goods we buy as part of our everyday life, and even though we may pride ourselves on being unaffected by advertisements and are unable to remember the names of the advertised articles we do, in fact, find ourselves buying goods of whose construction we knew nothing, simply because the names seem familiar to us.

4. The object of the advertiser is to convince us that his product is so superior to others that no other can be substituted for it. If he succeeds, he creates a monopoly which is based on the reputation he has gained, and has all the advantages in price control that accompany freedom from competition. It is quite possible that similar products offered by other firms do not differ to any appreciable extent, except in packaging and name, but if the potential customers have been persuaded by lavish advertisement of the excellence of those bearing a particular label they will not buy others even

if they are priced lower. In fact, most of us have so little knowledge of the majority of the things we use, that there is even a possibility that we may favour the more highly priced article, if its advertisements are particularly appealing, because we are inclined to associate high prices and high quality.

5. The creation of 'reputation monopolies' increases costs of production because it leads to redundancy of design. The advertised article must look different from its rivals even if it is fundamentally the same, and that means that some obvious difference in design must be introduced. Each competing type must, therefore, be produced on a smaller scale than would be possible if the superficial differences were eliminated, and stores must tie up their capital in keeping stocks of both designs, to suit all purchasers, when a much smaller margin would be adequate if the two makes were accepted as substitutes for one another.

6. Advertisement leads to extravagance. As its aim is to stimulate changes in demand, consumers throw away articles half used, because an attractive advertisement convinces them that the new thing will be more enjoyable or satisfying.

Which set of arguments wins on balance?

Chapter 7

WHAT IS MONEY?

DURING the Second World War prices were continually rising and soon after the end of the war, in 1948, the Government published a White Paper called *Personal Incomes, Costs and Prices*, in which a warning was given of the dangers that would be inevitable if inflation were allowed to continue. The main argument was that the rise in prices of non-subsidized goods and services was due to an acute shortage of the things that people wanted to buy and that, therefore, it would only be accentuated by increases in wages and salaries. No advantage could accrue to workers – and a great deal of disadvantage to the country as a whole – if wages were pushed upwards before production had expanded enough to ensure that there would be goods available for the extra money to buy. You can raise wages and salaries as high as you like – £1,000 a week per person if you like that figure – but the standard of living would still be no better than the goods and services available make possible.

This distinction between money and wealth is one which has been forced on our attention throughout the post-war years but never more so than during the second half of the sixties and early seventies. In fact it would not be too much to say that the inflationary spiral has become one of the most serious of our domestic problems. Wages and salaries go up at an alarming rate and by percentage amounts that would not have been thought of in the wildest dreams of negotiating bodies a few years ago. Every group tries to get enough to compensate for the rise in prices that has already taken place and a bit more so as to cushion future rises that it is feared are going to happen. There is thus a never-ending race between our money incomes and the prices of all the things we want to buy.

Why has this happened? Who decides how much money is worth and why does it not remain the same all the time, as a yard does or a pound weight? This chapter tries to answer these and similar questions.

THE FUNCTIONS OF MONEY

First, what do we mean by money? It sounds a bit Irish to say that money is anything which behaves like money, but that is really true; so that we can most easily discover what money is by getting an idea of the work it does.

1. It acts as a medium of exchange. In the simplest form of exchange, money is not necessary. The brisk barter that goes on amongst schoolboys is a good example of this. John has more marbles than he wants, James would like more marbles and has stamps that he could spare; they do a deal. As there are not a great many articles that enter into this kind of trading most boys have a pretty shrewd idea of their relative value and no more higgling is needed than adds spice to the negotiations. In earlier times, when most households produced for themselves the greater part of what they consumed, this simple form of direct exchange of goods for goods was all that was required. Nowadays, however, the position is very different because we are all specialized in our work whilst there are literally thousands of different articles that make up our pattern of life. If we had to get all these by barter we should have to spend most of our lives tracking down the person who owned the things we wanted and who also happened to want in exchange the kinds of things we had to offer. Money gets over this difficulty. We sell for money knowing that we, in our turn, will be able to buy what we want by offering money in exchange for it.

2. It acts as a measure of value. In Chapter 2 I described the way in which we all continually measure our preferences against one another in choosing whether we want a little more of this or less of that. Think how difficult it would be

to do this if we had no common measure of our relative preferences. Or how could we express our indebtedness to people who had done a job for us? Suppose there was no money and we had to pay wages in kind – so much meat and bread and houseroom and so on. How could we cope with the differences of taste between those who liked beef and loathed mutton or those who didn't mind what clothes they wore but adored concerts? By reckoning values in terms of money each person is able to translate the value he receives into any specific form he likes and so gets a great deal more out of it.

3. It acts as a unit of account. How could we save for the future without money? If we want to put something by for our old age, there would not be much point in hoarding a few bottles of milk or half a pound of meat every week; but if we save the money value of these things it certainly is worth while to have it available to spend on the things we may want in the future.

Money, then, is anything that does these three things, and anything could be used for them as long as people had confidence in it. It doesn't matter very much what the thing is, provided that people believe that it is safe to accept it in return for their goods or their work, because everybody else will also accept it when they want to buy; so the one all-important characteristic of anything we use as money is that it should be widely acceptable. Many things have been used at different times in different countries – slaves, cattle, sheep, furs, tobacco, cowrie shells, gold dust, and so on. They were generally the things that played a very big part in the life of the community that adopted them, so that their value was pretty well understood. Gradually gold ousted other things from use in all developed countries, because it is easier to carry about than most of the others, and one bit of it is as good as any other bit of the same weight (which isn't true of slaves or sheep or furs) and it can easily be divided into recognizable units without losing its value – i.e. coins – (which again is not true of cattle or slaves!) but it still depended for its use as money on its general acceptability, just as did the other goods I have listed.

Until after the First World War it was thought that nothing could be used as money unless it was also wanted for itself and not simply as a medium of exchange (gold, for example, was used for medicine and in industry as well as for currency) but this belief has long ceased to have any foundation in fact. In the days when we used gold coins, before 1914, I doubt if anybody ever said to himself, 'Well it's really quite safe to accept this gold sovereign because if the worst comes to the worst and I can't find anybody who will take it as money, I can always use it to have a tooth stopped or take it to a goldsmith and have it made into a ring for the wife.' Long before we gave up the everyday use of gold coins they had become simply token money, i.e. they were accepted as money and not because they had intrinsic value. Nowadays this is recognized in most highly developed countries and we are quite prepared to use forms of money which are worthless in themselves – such as paper notes and nickel coins – but which we know that everybody in the country will accept as tokens of so much value. Sometimes this confidence may be lacking and then the money ceases to circulate because people will not accept it. This happened in the chaotic period which followed the First World War, when there were revolutionary changes in government in some countries; and for a time their trade came to a standstill because farmers refused to sell their produce for money in which they had ceased to have confidence. Much the same happened in Germany after V.E. day, and until the currency reform of 1948 cigarettes were more widely accepted as the medium of exchange than any more customary form of money.

THE VALUE OF MONEY AND ITS MEASUREMENT

A yard of ribbon measures today exactly the same as it did in 1939 or, indeed, in any other year since the yard measure was established. Why doesn't a £ measure the same amount of value as it did before the war? The yard is an arbitrarily determined length; we have said 'This length is a yard and we'll always mean exactly this length when we say "a yard"'; but the value of a £ cannot be fixed by law in this way because it is simply what it will buy and the things that can be bought don't stay put. They are continually changing in amounts and varieties, and anybody who has money to spend can buy any bit of the goods available for sale that he happens to fancy. Not only does the value of a £ change but it is very difficult to measure exactly how much it has changed. When we say that a £ is worth less than it was we don't mean that it will buy less of this one thing or that, but that it will buy less of 'things in general', and there is such an enormous number of 'things in general' that it is very difficult to compare them with what we could have bought at any other time. With £1 now I could choose between an almost endless list of goods for sale, beginning with a bit of the world itself and including anything from that to so many packets of pins. It would take me a lifetime to draw up the list for today and even if I could draw up a similar list for 1939 they would both contain such an immense quantity of items that it would be useless to attempt to compare them.

In order to get over this difficulty to some extent we use a Price Index which, if it is well composed, can at least give us some indication of changes in the value of money, and a good deal of ingenuity has gone into the making of indexes for different purposes. As ordinary individuals, the prices that affect us most nearly are those of the goods that we habitually buy. Few of us would care a great deal if the prices of Rolls-Royce cars and champagne went up, because we never dream of buying these things, but when fuel prices double or the prices of our usual foods, we immediately realize that the value of our incomes has gone down. For a long time the Government has compiled a price index which is intended to give some idea of changes in the value of money spent by an ordinary household. The trouble is to determine what is an ordinary household, for although there are few of us nowadays who are either very rich or very poor there are extraordinarily big differences between the patterns of expenditure of a dock labourer and a school-master, even though their present earnings are not widely different.

The problem first became acute at the beginning of the First World War, when it was quickly realized that prices would rise steeply and that it would be necessary to have some clear way of measuring changes in real wages. Through force of circumstances there was no time for any comprehensive investigation into the pattern of working-class expenditure, and a good deal of guesswork had to go into the making of the index. Some ten years earlier, in 1904, a couple of thousand of 'typical' working-class budgets had been collected and these gave some indication of the kinds of expenditure that bulked most largely in these households. For lack of anything better it was assumed that an index weighted in these proportions would provide the means for measuring changes in the real value of wages as prices altered. All that this Cost of Living Index attempted to do was to calculate the cost to a working-class family, month by month, of the purchase of the same goods and ser-vices, and in the same proportions, as had been bought for £100 before August 1914, assuming that the pattern of ex-penditure was the same as it had been in 1904.

Nothing more could have been done at the time. There was neither labour nor leisure to find out how people really did spend their money and whether a rise in the price of sugar would have more or less effect on the standard of liv-ing than a rise in, say, the price of fuel or clothes. More-over an inquiry undertaken then, even if there had been time to do it, would not have been of much value, for war-time shortages naturally caused involuntary changes in ex-penditure (just as they did in the Second World War) which would be reversed as soon as goods could be freely produced again. As time went on the index grew fantastically inappropriate; for there has probably been no former period in which the habits of the life of the mass of the population have undergone such profound alterations as during the present century. Particularly in the deflationary period of the twenties, when prices were falling rapidly, the combined effect of nation-wide collective agreements and unemployment insurance benefits introduced into wage rates a greater degree of rigidity than they had ever possessed before, so that for those who were in employment real wages rose considerably. At the same time the spread of mass production methods in the production of consumption goods has brought a wide variety of commodities within reach of the working-class family and established new conventions of living. One has only to compare the clothing of the working-class woman of today with that of pre-1914 to appreciate the revolutionary changes that have been brought about. Fifty years ago the working girl had one 'best' dress which had to last so many years that it could have no more than a nodding acquaintance with fashion; but the development of synthetic materials such as man-made fabrics and mass-produced clothing have reduced prices so greatly that the majority of working-class girls today can follow the mode just as do their richer sisters. What has happened in clothing has happened in many other things, and the wage-earner today has as varied a pattern of consumption as any other class. Furniture, kitchen equipment, curtains, radio, and TV play an important part in his household budget, and drink, tobacco, and entertainments in his personal one.

The 1914 Cost of Living Index assumed a very sparse way of life in which there was no margin for anything but the fundamental essentials. According to that index 60 per cent of the income of the working-class household went on food, 12 per cent on clothing, 16 per cent on rent and rates, 8 per cent on fuel and light, and only 4 per cent was left for everything else. No allowance was made for drink or tobacco, nothing for furniture or household equipment, and nothing for transport or other services.

A revision of the index would certainly have been undertaken earlier had it not been for the prolonged depression in many important industries; but it was believed that an examination of budgets at a time when nearly 3,000,000 households were living on unemployment insurance benefits or allowances would not be of positive value in indicating the normal pattern of consumption. The inquiry was not, therefore, undertaken until 1937–8 and its results were not available until shortly before the war; so that action had to wait on a more favourable moment. A representative committee was set up to advise the Ministry of Labour when the war was over and a new Interim Index of Retail Prices was based on its recommendations and introduced in June 1947.

The new index took account of the much wider variety of goods and services that figured in working-class expenditure; and, based as it was mainly on the results of the 1937–8 investigation, it is interesting evidence of the way in which the proportion of the income spent on food and clothing drops as a higher standard of living allows a larger margin for comforts and luxuries. The proportion of income spent on food had fallen from 60 per cent to 34·8 per cent and on clothing from 12 to 9 per cent, despite the fact that in both these categories the worker enjoyed a quality, quantity, and variety that were denied to his predecessor forty years earlier. That rent and rates had dropped from 16 to 8 per cent was due mainly to the fact that rents had been controlled throughout the greater part of the period, while fuel and light showed the least change, from 8 to 6·5 per cent. But the most striking alteration was to be found in the new categories of expenditure included for the first time and which showed that 21·7 per cent of the income was spent on drink and tobacco, 7·1 per cent on durable household goods, 7·9 per cent on services (transport, etc.), and 3·5 per cent on miscellaneous articles.

The new index was published for the first time in July
1947, with mid-June as the base date, which means that
from that date the index measured the amount of money
that would have been needed by an ordinary working-class
household to buy the same goods and services, and in the
same proportions, as it could have bought for £100 in June
1947. In 1953 the figure was 140, which shows that prices
had risen 40 per cent since June 1947.

As its name implies, this Interim Index was recognized,
from the start, to be something of a stopgap measure until a
more permanent index could be constructed; and, in De-
cember 1950, the Cost of Living Advisory Committee were
called together to consider whether conditions of spending
could yet be regarded as sufficiently stable to justify the holding of a new full-scale budget inquiry to provide the facts on
which a new index might be constructed. In a report dated
June 1951, the Committee recommended that a new large-
scale inquiry into household expenditure should be undertaken and that this time it should include a much wider
range of incomes than formerly, covering not only the mass
of manual wage-earners but also most people earning small
and medium salaries.

This recommendation was accepted by the Minister of
Labour and a large-scale inquiry into household expenditure
was made in 1953-4. The new Index showed changes that
had taken place in the pattern of consumption. Food took
about the same proportion as before, and rents were still
controlled; but clothing and footwear were no longer
rationed as they had been at the time of the earlier survey
so these items figured much more largely, and consequently,
though people were still spending a great deal on drink and
tobacco, these two items together had fallen from 21·7 per
cent of the income expenditure to under 10 per cent.

These variations showed how important it was to take
account of changing habits as quickly as possible if the Index
was really to be of use in measuring changes in the value of
money as these affect the budget of the ordinary house-

holder. There has probably never been any earlier period to compare with the last decade in really big alterations in the consumption habits of the population. The 'affluent society' is not just a slogan; it expresses an enormous change in the way people live. Better housing, furnished with all sorts of material equipment – washing machines, spin dryers, record players, TV, etc. – better and more frequent changes of clothing, cosmetics, motor cars and scooters, holidays and sport – all these are no longer confined to a privileged minority, but are part of the expenditure pattern of the majority of the population; and there seemed every reason to believe that, with increasing economic productivity, the changes would continue.

It was therefore decided that there should be an annual Family Expenditure Survey to provide a constantly up-to-date picture of the ways in which people spend their incomes and that, beginning in 1962, the weighting pattern of the Index of Retail Prices should be revised each January on the basis of the information obtained from this Family Expenditure Survey for the three years ending the previous June. The idea of a three-year average was to iron out temporary fluctuations that might be caused by some special circumstances, particularly in the purchase of durable household goods. One of the consequences of this annual revision of the weights to be given to each group of expenditure (food, household goods, fuel, etc.) is that it is no longer possible to get an accurate comparison of movements of prices as a whole between any one year and another year some time back : but it *is* possible to see how prices have changed in comparison with the previous year. During 1969 the average level of retail prices as measured by the General Index rose by 5 per cent compared with a rise of over 6 per cent in 1968 and about 2½ per cent in 1967. For 1970 the figure shows a big jump, nearly 10 per cent over the previous year.

But the danger of such an index, however carefully compiled, is that we may expect it to do more than it is really capable of. The pattern of expenditure on which the weights are based is by no means universal, and, though we know this, we often use the index as if we didn't. We are inclined to say 'Prices have risen so much per cent' without reminding ourselves that this is true only of the prices included in the compilation of the index. There are thousands of working men and women who neither smoke nor drink or who spend much less on these commodities than the 12 per cent of their incomes as shown in the Index weights. To them quite other prices would be of prime importance in measuring the value of their wages to them. And besides these personal variations there are great regional and occupational differences. There are even significant variations in the pattern of expenditure of the same family at different periods of life – when there are several young children, for example, to be kept out of the father's wage and when some or all of these have started in employment.

On the whole, middle-class and professional households spend more than average on what may be called 'general overheads' – house rent, education, insurance, etc. Such expenses are usually the subject of long-term contracts and do not change as prices of food, clothing, tobacco, etc., change : so that an index which does not give an appreciable place to those commitments does not provide even an approximately true indication of changes in the purchasing power of the incomes of these social groups.

As we have seen, the Index covers a much wider range of incomes than the earlier one in the attempt to get over this difficulty; but as these groups are a minority of the community, it can succeed only to a very slight extent. Yet the Retail Price Index is the only one we have and although we know that despite the refinements that have been introduced into its compilation, it can do no more than give merely an indication of the effects of changes in prices on the value of people's incomes, we get into the habit of appealing to it in all circumstances and, particularly, when new rates of wages and salaries are under discussion. Often, indeed, agreements are tied to it, rising and falling by an agreed amount for every so many points of change in the index.

During the mid-seventies inflation, i.e. the rapid rise in prices, has become the prime preoccupation. Between 1971 and 1975 the annual increase in prices reached double figures and led to much controversy in the attempts to deal with it. There have been unprecedented demands for wage increases, the setting-up of a Prices Commission to monitor the rise in prices, Government subsidies to keep down the cost to the consumer of basic foods, and so on.

WHAT DETERMINES THE VALUE OF MONEY?

A price index measures changes in the value of money but it does nothing to explain *why* the value changes, and this is the question to which we now turn our attention.

When we decide that we cannot afford to buy something we want we often say, 'I'd like it but I haven't enough money'. Suppose that by a wave of a magician's wand each of us suddenly found himself in possession of twice as much money as before, would our troubles be over? Should we each be able to buy twice as much? Definitely not, as we have ruefully learned during these last few years. Each of us could afford to offer double the prices for the things we liked but, as the amount of the goods in the shops and warehouses would not have altered, we could get only the same quantity of them, though we should pay more for them. Here is one thing, then, that determines the value of money – the quantity of money relative to the number of goods and services for sale. The more money there is available for making purchases, the less will its value be; the smaller the amount of money in relation to the things for sale, the more value each bit of money will have.

But there is another thing to consider. We don't possess a fixed amount of money from which we constantly ladle out bits; we are continually receiving sums and continually paying out. We get a certain amount on pay-day and we spend parts of it during the period before the next pay-day. But we don't always spend at the same rate; sometimes we keep our money quite a long time before spending it, sometimes we spend it as soon as we get it. If there is a depression in trade and we are afraid that the future does not look too bright, we postpone buying whatever we can do without, until we see what is going to happen. The effect is just the same as if there were less money, and prices begin to fall. On the other hand, if we feel confident that we shall continue to earn good wages, we spend our money immediately we earn it, and the effect is the same as if there were a larger quantity of money, and prices go up. Once prices have begun to change the tendency is for the change to be exaggerated for the same reason. If we have made up our minds to buy a certain article – for example, a new coat or a radio – and we find that general prices are rising we think we had better hurry and buy at once, before the thing we want becomes more expensive; so we spend our money as soon as we get it and give prices a further push upwards. On the other hand, when prices begin to fall, we delay our purchases and wait for them to get lower still, and as there is less money circulating the level of prices goes down more.

HOW IS THE TOTAL QUANTITY OF MONEY DETERMINED?

Since the amount of money has such an important effect we have to know who settles it, and we cannot understand this until we are clear on the different kinds of money we use.

1. *Coins and Notes*

A weekly wage-earner usually receives his pay in cash – coins and notes. Both of these are legal tender, i.e. you have a legal right to offer them in payment of debts, but they are not both produced by the same authority. Coins are issued by the State through the Royal Mint, which has a monopoly of coinage and produces the number that experience shows to be necessary for the general convenience of the public. We use these coins only for small day-to-day expenses, and they form a negligible proportion of the total amount of money. Notes, on the other hand, are issued principally by the Bank of England (the Scottish banks also have the right to issue notes, but their total is too small to be of much practical importance). But the Bank of England cannot issue whatever it likes; it is governed by the terms of an Act passed in 1928 which allows it to print notes to equal the value of any gold it has in its reserve plus a fixed 'fiduciary' issue the amount of which cannot be altered without the permission of Parliament.

2. Bank Deposits

Many people receive their salaries in the form of cheques instead of coins and notes, and most wealthier people meet their expenses by paying cheques. A cheque is not money in itself (it would not be generally acceptable if you did not know the person or firm who had signed it), but it gives the owner of it the right to receive the amount of money named on its face. It is, in effect, a letter to a banker telling him to pay out of the account of the person (or business) signing it the amount specified. It has the great advantage over notes that it can be made out for the exact amount of the debt (there are not notes, for example, of the value £3.71 and the payments we have to make are mostly these untidy amounts) and can be sent safely by post, because it can be drafted in such a way that it is of no value to anybody but the person for whom it is intended.

Although the recipient has the right to ask the banker for cash, he usually does not do so; instead he pays the cheque into his own account and his banker collects the amount due from the bank on which it is drawn. If both persons deal with the same bank, this is very simple; the sum standing to the credit of A is increased and that standing to the credit of B is decreased. If, however, A banks at Barclays and B at the National Westminster the sum would, in theory, have to be transferred from one bank to the other; but there are thousands of cheques drawn every day by the clients of each bank in favour of clients of all the others, so that, through the medium of the Bankers' Clearing House, the banks can balance their mutual indebtedness and leave only the excess due from one bank to another to be paid over. Even this is not paid in actual cash. All the banks hold accounts at the central bank, the Bank of England, and the amounts due from one to the other are paid by transferring the necessary fund from one account to the other. In this way an enormous amount of monetary exchange can be done without the transfer of any cash at all; it is done entirely by book-keeping, by the transfer of bank deposits from one account to another. So that although cheques are not themselves money, bank deposits are.

HOW BANK DEPOSITS ARE CREATED

How does a person get an account in a bank and so acquire the power to draw cheques? The most obvious way, of course, is by putting some of his money into the bank for that express purpose. But not all bank deposits come about in that way; sometimes they represent a loan from the banker. The banker is under an obligation to pay cash for any cheque drawn on an account he holds, but he knows by experience that a comparatively small proportion of those who could cash cheques will, in fact, do so – it is so very much more convenient to pay them into one's account in the way just described. He knows, therefore, that it is safe to lend his money to others who need it for business purposes. But he does not lend cash; instead he pretends that the borrower has put money into the bank and he agrees to honour his cheques up to a certain sum, i.e. he creates a deposit in his name.

By this method the banker creates money but he is not free to make as much as he likes. In this country there is no legal limitation to his power to lend; but he has to remember that anybody who has a deposit has the right to draw cheques for which cash may be demanded. In fact, a certain proportion of cheques must be cashed every day, for we all have day-to-day expenses to meet for which cheques are not suitable, and, moreover, weekly wages are almost always paid in cash, though it has recently become legal to pay them by cheque in order to counteract the wage-packet thief. The banker has learned by long experience what proportion of cheques will probably be cashed and he limits his loans accordingly. In general, he finds that he has nothing to fear if he takes care to have available enough cash to meet about one-twelfth of the possible claims that might be made, and he keeps his loans down to this proportion. If he finds he is getting near the danger line he raises the price of loans to would-be borrowers – i.e. he puts up the rate of interest – with the usual result of a rise in prices, a reduced demand.

Who, then, settles what quantity of money there shall be? That is a very difficult question to answer because, in fact, nobody does make the decision. The amount of legal tender that is produced, i.e. the number of bank notes issued by the Bank of England, is authorized by the Government, which gives permission for an increase when it thinks there is need for a further supply of cash. As wages and some salaries are paid weekly in legal tender, the banks have to be ready to cash bigger cheques when wage rates rise and earnings increase, and so during the last twenty years when there have been so many more people in employment at higher rates of pay than before, there has been a much bigger demand for cash for wage payments and the number of bank notes has risen.

But, as we have seen, most of the purchases that are made are paid for by cheques, which are not cashed but are placed immediately into another banking account; so that the quantity of this purchasing power seems to have very little relationship to the number of bank notes in existence. If business in general is prosperous men are eager to borrow from the banks in order to expand their production – i.e. to buy materials and equipment – and the banks, feeling confident that their loans will be repaid, are ready to lend. So, without any increase in the number of bank notes, there will be more purchasing power in circulation because people are buying goods and paying for them by cheques which the banks allow to be drawn on them. But if, on the other hand, trade is depressed and businessmen are afraid there will not be a market for their goods, they are not anxious to borrow from the banks and, even though the quantity of bank notes remains unchanged, there is less money as a whole in circulation because fewer cheques are being drawn. It is in this sense that we can say that nobody decides how much money there shall be as a whole, but this does not mean that it is impossible to *influence* the amount, and, in fact, this influence is now accepted as one of the chief responsibilities of the Government. The Chancellor of the Exchequer has several ways by which he can try to make us change the volume of our purchases. If he wants us to cut down he can increase the minimum lending rate and thus make it more expensive for those who want to buy on credit; or he can tax us more heavily so that we have a smaller proportion of our incomes to spend on goods of our own choice; or he can use his authority to try and prevent wages and salaries from rising (as he did in the 'pay pause' of 1962, or, in 1975, by restricting any increase in wage rates to £6 a week and decreeing that no rise in wages should be made more than once a year). The effect of these actions is much greater than the amount of the initial fall in demand for goods for if manufacturers fear that they will not be able to dispose readily of their products they are not eager to borrow from the banks to build extensions to their factories or to get new machinery. In this way the decrease in purchasing power is cumulative. If on the other hand he wants us to increase our spending because many people are unemployed and part of our pro-

ductive capacity is unused, he can do just the opposite : lower
the minimum lending rate and reduce taxation, as he did in
1971.

INFLATION AND DEFLATION

When the quantity of money in use increases more rapidly
than the goods and services for sale, prices go up; when the
opposite happens, prices go down. We call the first inflation, and the second deflation. Except in rather special circumstances (of which more will be said in Chapter 10) inflation is very much more often experienced and, indeed, the
effort to control it has proved one of the most difficult economic problems of the last twenty years.

Why should we try to control it? What harm does it do?

The problem stems from the fact that all our economic
arrangements are made in money terms and assume that this
money represents a stable amount of value. When this
assumption proves false the agreements into which we have
entered turn out to be very different from what we intended
when we made them. If every single price changed at the
same time and to the same extent, an alteration in the value
of money would not matter very much. We should always
say 20p where before we had said 10p, and £20 where before we had spoken of £10. But of course this is not so. First
of all, there is a time element in many contracts. Suppose,
for example, I have taken the lease of a house for five years
at a rental of £450 a year. It does not matter how
much prices rise – or the value of money goes down – I
continue to pay £450 until the lease comes to an end. Supposing that money loses a quarter of its value during my
lease, as happened during the post-war decade, I gain because I am paying less in value to my landlord than was
arranged when the lease was signed; and he, poor man,
loses. All the things he spends his income on will have gone
up but the money he gets from his house stays the same.

When the lease ends the landlord will be able to put up
the rent, so his loss is fairly temporary; but there are many

prices which are not the subject of a definite contract with a named period of duration, but which are difficult to change because people are so accustomed to them that they will not alter willingly. For example, the penalty for pulling the danger signal in a train was until recently still £5, just as it was a quarter of a century earlier, though £5 was worth less than a third of what it was then. Again, most people expect to be able to go to the theatre or a concert for very little more than they used to pay before the war though all the costs of producing concerts and plays – which are made up of fees to composers and writers, salaries of performers, wages of stage hands, prices of 'props', and so on – have risen with all other prices. And it is difficult to persuade trade union members that the weekly contributions they paid in the thirties are no longer enough to buy them the skilled help and other amenities they got for them then.

Almost all of us live on the payment we get for our work but these payments do not rise automatically as prices go up. It depends on how much pressure we can exert to get our wage agreements altered. Highly organized trade unions can push up the wages of their members even in advance of a rise in prices; but those who are not so highly organized or who, for some social reason, are less willing to strike – nurses, doctors, university teachers – are left behind, though this is no longer as true as it used to be. Recently even those groups which traditionally have never contemplated strikes have been readier to use industrial action to force their claims. Worst off of all are those who live on fixed incomes; retired people who have put all their savings into an annuity, or into fixed interest-bearing securities, or who are in receipt of pensions from their former employers. Those on State retirement pensions suffer in this way but these can, eventually, get their pensions increased by legislation, though there is generally a long period of deprivation before this is done.* However, those receiving private pensions sink lower and lower in the economic scale.

* It is now promised that these pensions will be reviewed annually.

The effect of inflation, then, is to bring about an entirely arbitrary redistribution of incomes and generally at the expense of the worst-off and weakest sections of the population. Everybody whose payment is fixed loses, and the longer the period that must elapse before it can be changed, the greater the loss. Everybody else gains at their expense.

But it has other bad effects also, for it upsets the basis on which reasonable calculations can be made. One of the most important characteristics of a highly developed economic society is our willingness to plan ahead; to put aside part of what we could enjoy now, to make provision for the future. And if we did not do so it would be impossible to produce the factories and machines and the different types of material equipment on which an expanding economy depends. If the value of money is unstable all the decisions people make are thrown out of balance; it is impossible to judge accurately whether it is worth while to save and how much; if the value of money drops quickly it soon becomes evident that it is not worth while to save at all, for whereas an article that is bought has *some* value in that it can be used or can be sold to somebody else, there is a chance that the money value of the savings may become worthless. Once the habit of thinking ahead for the future is lost it is not so easy to develop it again.

Then again, if prices are going up and are expected to continue doing so, businesses *must* try and budget for a wider margin of profit, for they know that everything they will need to buy for restocking – raw materials, machines, transport, labour – will be a higher price when they come to buy them. Thus inflation upsets the basis on which sensible economic calculations are made and in doing so also helps to undermine the stability of social institutions. Big windfall profits are made by some and crippling losses by others; it is as if our economic life were run as if it were a gigantic football pool.

Chapter 8

IMPORTS AND EXPORTS

BEFORE the Second World War the pattern of international trade was largely taken for granted. We had been brought up on the idea that Britain was 'the workshop of the world' and we were inclined to think that it was part of the natural order of things that we sold our manufactured goods all over the world and bought a large part of our food and raw materials from other countries. Nowadays, however, matters have changed so greatly that the volume of our exports and imports is a constant subject of report in B.B.C. news bulletins and we compare their relative values with as much concern as a nurse examines the temperature chart of a feverish patient. Since the formation of the European Economic Community (the Common Market) in 1958 and the long-drawn-out discussions with regard to Britain's entry into it, international trade has become one of the most important and controversial of all political issues. Why has international trade broken into the news in this way? Why is the situation now different from before the war? Why can't we cut out the whole trouble and produce what we want for ourselves? And, if we can't, what settles the kind of things we do buy and sell?

There is probably no part of our economic life about which there is so much confusion of thought. This is partly due, perhaps, to the fact that anything foreign is a bit more difficult to understand than domestic concerns, and partly because the whole subject has got itself so mixed up with politics that it has many sentimental and emotional associations which blur its economic outlines. For example, there are thousands of people who are indignant that we buy goods from some countries that do not import very much from us; they argue that we should trade only with those who trade with us. But they would never dream of choosing the butcher from whom they buy their meat on any such principle. There are thousands, again, who have an uneasy feeling that it is less laudable to buy foreign goods than home-produced ones. Such slogans as 'Buy British', 'Keep trade in the family', which were very common before the war, are examples of this belief, based on sentiment rather than reason, that it is unpatriotic to buy from foreign sources.

DOMESTIC TRADE AND FOREIGN TRADE

Yet, of course, fundamentally trade between people in different countries is no different from trade between people in the same country; it is merely one example of the specialization of production, which is so much more efficient than trying to do everything oneself. Note that I have said 'trade between people in different countries' and not 'international trade', for that, in fact, is what it usually is. During the Second World War and in the period of great scarcity immediately following it the Government was responsible for buying from other countries the quantities of goods which formed the essential elements in our consumption (such as meat, wheat, bacon, eggs, and so on) because it had undertaken to see that we all got certain rations at prices that everybody could afford to pay. But this was a very unusual procedure and is one feature of that central planning of our resources, spoken of in Chapter 2, which was a necessary concomitant of the rapid switch-over of production from its usual work to war purposes. Before the war it was very rare indeed to find Governments playing a big part as traders with one another, and that is true again today. So when we speak of *international* trade we mean simply trade between two individuals or firms situated in different countries, and not trade between two governments. Even this is ambiguous. England and Scotland are two different countries but any commercial activities between, say, a firm in Glasgow and one in Manchester are included in the domestic trade of the United Kingdom. But if Scotland became an independent political entity, exactly the same items of trade would be listed as exports and imports, and would thus figure as part of our international trade.

If then there is nothing very different between domestic and international trade, as is evident from this example, why do we make such a fuss about it? There are a number of good reasons.

1. Countries differ from one another in laws and customs, language, food, manners, political rights, and so on; and most of us are so conservative in our way of living that we should hesitate a much longer time before moving to another country than we should before moving to another place in our own country. But it is not only a question of moving ourselves; it is more difficult to get to know about the businesses in a foreign place; we realize that foreigners may have quite different tastes and wants from our own, so that, although we should invest capital or open a sales agency abroad much more readily than we should move there ourselves, there is nothing like the same ease of movement, even of capital and goods, as there is between two parts of the same country. As a consequence, specialization of production does not reach quite the same degree of development. When the cotton industry was first established in this country it was begun in several places, but gradually the outstanding advantages of Lancashire seemed so apparent that the whole industry was concentrated in that area. If the different counties had been separate countries it is unlikely that this would have happened, or, at least, certainly not so quickly.

2. Each country has its own monetary system, so that buying goods from somebody in another country entails getting hold of the right kind of currency to pay for them. In the years following the war, for example, we could not get hold of the dollars we needed to buy the many goods that America was producing and that we longed to have. We had to choose to buy from countries whose currencies we could ac-

quire more easily though their products did not appeal to us so much.

Moreover you cannot always be sure of being able to buy the other currency for exactly the same amount of your own. As was explained in the chapter on money, we accept currency for our goods only if we have confidence that we, in our turn, can exchange it for a definite amount of the goods or services we want. Sometimes this confidence is undermined because of international upheavals or because one suspects that the actions of the other country's government may lead to a fall in the purchasing power of its money.

3. There is always a danger that the country from which we buy important supplies may be cut off from us by war. It is not only that we may be at war with the country that supplies us, but that cargoes from a friendly country may be unable to reach us because of hostilities with another; as, for example, during the two world wars, the submarine danger destroyed, or delayed, essential material coming from America to Britain. Most countries, therefore, are unwilling to become completely dependent on others for certain things they consider particularly necessary to their economy, and they continue to produce, inside their own boundaries, things which they could buy more economically from abroad.

4. Sometimes we use our foreign trade as a weapon in political bargaining. We give special privileges to traders of certain countries in order to get concessions from them or to buy their political support.

5. In modern countries the government plays a big part in the control of economic activities, either in laying down minimum standards and conditions of employment or in the more positive control of the allocation of resources. But no government has authority over the activities of the producers and traders of a foreign country.

6. Quite a lot of difference between domestic and international trade is imaginary, though this does not reduce its importance in practice. We cannot get into our heads that buying and selling goods abroad is exactly the same in

essence as doing this at home. We do not think we are conferring a favour on one shop by buying an article from them instead of from another; we quite appreciate the fact that we do whatever we think suits our taste and our pocket. But if we buy from a foreign producer instead of a British one we feel we have to apologize for our choice.

Many people think that exports should consist only of the surplus of goods we don't want to use ourselves. Yet they do not think it wrong that the mechanic who makes the Rolls-Royce car cannot afford to possess such a car himself; they accept the fact that he specializes in making something he does well, and for which there is a demand by others, and that he must confine his own purchases to the amount of payment he gets for his work. Few of us believe that the greengrocer sells us merely the surplus of vegetables from his garden after he has taken what he needs for his family and none of us dreams of apologizing for buying our shoes from the manufacturer, instead of making them for ourselves at home. But we find it difficult to apply this to our external trade, and there are hundreds of thousands of people who believe that it is in some way 'better' or more praiseworthy conduct to buy from a home producer instead of from a foreign one. This belief leads many people to demand control of foreign trade in favour of the home producer, either by tariffs to prevent the easy entry of foreign goods, or by subsidies to the home firm to give him a competitive advantage.

WHAT KINDS OF THINGS DO WE BUY FROM ABROAD?

The things we buy from abroad fall into three categories. As far as two of these are concerned, we gain so obvious an advantage that it is not necessary to do more than mention them; but the third class takes a little more explanation.

1. Natural resources are not spread evenly all over the world, and people living in areas which lack the things

they want must buy them elsewhere. In this country there is very little gold or oil or uranium or bauxite; on the other hand we have a large supply of coal. We can acquire the things we don't happen to have only by trading for them.

2. Most things that are bought and sold, however, are not natural resources but goods that have been grown or manufactured. If expense were no consideration most things could be produced in most places, but the cost of production varies enormously from one place to another. For example, it would be possible to grow rice and oranges in England if we were prepared to create the necessary conditions. But this would cost a very great deal, and it is easier to buy them cheaply from areas where natural conditions are more suitable. On the other hand, in this country we can produce certain manufactures more cheaply than elsewhere, because of our big mineral resources, advantageous geographical position, and long tradition of good workmanship. So there is a general tendency to buy goods from other countries if they can be bought there at a lower cost than would be required to produce them at home.

3. But the third class of imports is more important and less easy to understand than these. It often pays us to buy from others goods which we could produce more cheaply ourselves, if we wished to make them. This is not such a paradox as it seems at first sight, for a moment's thought shows us that this is what we continually do as individuals. A clever businessman could probably do his own book-keeping more efficiently and more quickly than the man he employs for the job, but if he actually sacked the man and did the work himself he would be throwing away the substance for the shadow. It pays him to concentrate on the work he can do supremely well – the planning and organizing of the enterprise – and to buy or 'import' the services of a book-keeper. He can make much more in a day's work as an organizer than he can save by doing the book-keeping work himself. The same principle holds with the work of a whole community. It pays to specialize in those kinds of production

in which the comparative advantages are greatest and to buy from others goods in which our comparative superiority is less marked, even though we might be able to make them more cheaply than those from whom we buy.

The familiar phrase that Britain is the workshop of the world expresses pretty well the special emphasis of our share in international trading. On the whole, this country concentrates on the production of manufactured goods and imports chiefly foods and raw materials. Until this century, raw materials were a more important part of our imports than food, for many of the kinds of food we buy now were then either unobtainable or too expensive for the mass of the population. But the great increase in the size of the population during the second half of the nineteenth century swelled the demand for food so much that it was impossible to grow at home more than a small proportion of what was required. Fortunately the development of quick reliable steam transport and the invention of refrigeration allowed food to be carried great distances without spoiling and made available to us the immense resources of South America, Canada, U.S.A., Australia, and New Zealand. At the same time, the rapid rise in wealth showed its effect in increasing demands for delicacies and luxuries that had been almost unknown to the working man of earlier times, so that tea, coffee, sugar, fresh fruit, fish, and meat began to be consumed in much greater quantities. Before the Second World War, then, the amount of food produced at home represented a comparatively small proportion of the total consumed. Only in oats and potatoes could we consider ourselves self-sufficient (in each case home production was 96 per cent of the total) and of fish and vegetables we produced 85 per cent of our consumption, but for most other foodstuffs we depended primarily on foreign supplies. Only a quarter of our wheat was grown at home and about the same proportion of fresh fruit; only 43–5 per cent of butchers' meat and of pig products, 16 per cent of the sugar and 9 per cent of the butter.

One effect of this greater reliance on imports was to make our diet less seasonal. Our sources of supply were spread so widely over the world, comprising areas with different climates and seasons, that food was available from somewhere all the year round. In fact, when foreign supplies of all but bare essentials had to be cut down during the war, it came as a great shock to many people to realize for the first time that the agricultural cycle of seedtime and harvest is more than a picturesque figure of speech.

Yet despite the great increase in food imports, the value of imported raw materials was almost as great, and the majority of our most important industries, making both for the home and the export markets, depended for their existence on the materials bought abroad. Textile materials alone accounted for 27 per cent of the total of raw material imports, and timber for about half that amount. Even the quarter of our total imports that were classed as 'manufactured articles' contained many items that were bought as essential elements in our own manufactures rather than as finished products for consumption. Iron and steel, petrol and oils, paper (for newspapers) and chemicals and dyes are all listed as 'Articles wholly or mainly manufactured' because they are not sold until certain processes have been performed, and these between them represented close on 40 per cent of the value of imports in this category; yet all of them are bought primarily as raw materials for home industries.

When we come to look at our exports we find the emphasis entirely the other way. Four-fifths of all goods sold abroad appeared in the category 'Articles wholly or mainly manufactured' and, of these, textile materials alone accounted for more than 28 per cent; even more if we include the clothing made from these textiles as well as the fabrics themselves. The other main items were machinery, iron and steel manufactures, and vehicles (ships and cars) which, taken together, accounted for another 34 per cent. Even the food and raw materials which made up one-fifth of our exports of goods would not have bulked so large had it not been for the importance of one item – coal exports – which accounted for well over half the total value of our sales abroad of raw materials. Before the First World War, cotton and coal filled an even more important role than later. Until 1914 cotton exports alone were a quarter, in value, of all our sales of goods of all categories together, and 100 million tons of coal were sold abroad annually. By 1938 cotton's share of total exports had dropped to 10 per cent and coal sales to 46 million tons. Yet despite the drop in both these markets, these two were still amongst the most important items in our external trade. If we list our pre-war exports in order of importance, cotton goods easily took pride of place, machinery and iron and steel manufactures came second (though a good way behind), and coal, woollen textiles, and vehicles were close on each other's heels for third place.

The Second World War put us into great difficulties because we were concentrating the largest part of our productive resources on making the type of goods that were required for war purposes and thousands of working men and women were withdrawn from production to serve in the Forces, both military and civil. It is therefore not surprising that during that period our imports, which consisted so largely of food and essential raw materials, were much in excess of the amounts we sold abroad. Indeed had it not been for the generous credits provided by the Marshall Aid scheme we should not have been able to get through without a much greater lowering of living standards than we did.

INVISIBLE TRADE

One of the earliest lessons we learn is that we must do without the things we can't afford to buy, unless we want to land up in Queer Street. The same thing applies to trade between countries. We cannot continue permanently to buy more than we are able to pay for, and that means that imports and exports must balance one another – not, of course, each week or month, but over a reasonable period of time. In the immediate post-war years we bought much more than we sold for we were living on credit provided by the Marshall Aid scheme; but that was exceptional and temporary. Yet if we look at the records of international trade before the war – when no Marshall Aid or any other similar kind of generosity was available – we find that every year the value of our imports from abroad far exceeded that of our exports. In the last full year before the war – 1938 – records show exports to the value of £471 million and imports to the value of £858 million, and we should find a similar relationship in any other year we choose to look at. Were we then heading for the bankruptcy court? How did we manage to get more than we paid for?

The explanation lies in the fact that trade statistics cannot show all our imports and exports; they can show only those things that can be seen and recorded crossing political frontiers. But a great deal of trade is 'invisible' because it is in the form of services. When Americans came to England in the *Caronia* or the *Queen Elizabeth* they were importing our exported shipping services even though they seemed to be travelling in the wrong direction for it. British shipping does a large part of the carrying trade of the world, from one foreign country to another as well as from other countries to the U.K.; and whenever this service is done for a foreigner it is an 'export' just in the same way as a ton of coal sold abroad. Switzerland's most important export is an invisible one; it is the sale of hotel and guides' service to foreign tourists who come to enjoy the beauty of the mountains and lakes. Before the Second World War the amount spent by British travellers abroad was just about the same as the amount spent by foreigners here but in the last twenty years we have made a great effort to improve hotels, restaurants, and shows and now the tourist trade is one of our biggest exports. For as more people come to this country everything they buy – not only food and lodging, but theatre seats, transport facilities, souvenirs, clothes, and so on – is an addition to our exports even though all the sales are made in this country.

There are many such invisible items in trade – for example, banking and insurance services. As industrial development took place in England a long time before that of any other country, London became the financial centre of the world and British banks and insurance companies acquired such a worldwide reputation for honesty and stability that many firms and individuals in other countries used these services in preference to those of their own or any other country. Again, and largely for the same reason, many people in this country had capital that they were willing to lend when developments in other countries began to take place; this is an export of capital for which payment comes in the form of dividends, which allow British people to buy goods abroad for which no balancing export of merchandize need be made. In fact, imports and exports include everything, visible and invisible, for which payment has to be made by somebody living in one country to somebody living in another.

THE PROBLEM TODAY

One of the most difficult problems that faces us for the future is that our income from invisible exports is very much less than it used to be. This is by no means a new problem though it is much more serious than it used to be; but already during the inter-war period it was shrinking so much that there were occasions when we could pay for our imports only out of capital – for our total export of merchandise and services together was not enough to meet the cost of our purchases abroad. In 1913, the last year before the First World War, our invisible exports were so large that, after paying for all imports, we had £207 million left to invest abroad, but in the twenties they shrank so rapidly that by 1926 we were £14 million on the wrong side, and during the great depression of 1931 this deficit was as much as £103 million. If we take an average of the last years before the Second World War we were about £44 million down each year, i.e. in all these years we were living beyond our current means, and it was only because of the fact that our fathers and grandfathers had saved so much that we were able to live at the standard we did. Even had the war not taken place we could not have gone on in such a way much longer.

There were many reasons to account for this distressing situation. The goods which had formed the bulk of our exported merchandise before 1914, coal and cotton, were no longer in such great demand. They were still the most important items of our export trade but their value had shrunk seriously. Electricity, generated from water or lignite, was rapidly becoming the chief motor force in world industry, and steamers were built to burn oil instead of coal, so that other countries were much less dependent on our coal than they had been in the past; and the cheap textiles of India and Japan could be produced at a cost with which our cotton industry could not compete. These were not developments for which the war alone was to blame; they would have happened in any case. Britain could not have expected to retain for ever the great lead in export markets which she had gained as a result of her early industrialization. Other countries were gaining on her already by the end of the nineteenth century and competition would have been pretty fierce even had there been no war. But the war of 1914–18 accelerated trends that would probably otherwise have taken much longer to develop, and, at the same time, prevented the adaptation to changing circumstances which can be made so much more easily bit by bit. The break in world trade lasted much longer than the actual years of fighting, for the post-war chaos in the foreign exchanges was so serious that it was not until 1924 that international trade can really be said to have been resumed on normal lines. The break was long enough to allow countries which had depended on Britain for their imported goods to establish new industries of their own or to turn to other sources of supply. Neither group was willing to withdraw when this country was once again prepared to supply its old markets, and our industries had to face a permanently reduced market for their traditional products. Ten years is a long period when rapid changes are taking place and British industrialists had been cock of the walk for so long that they found it particularly difficult to cope with the situation. There had been periods of bad trade many times before, but the export industries had always weathered the storm and advanced to still greater prosperity when it was over. Looking back over the past we are now aware, of course, that the twenties posed a different problem from that of earlier depressions; but this was not clear at the time, and most of the managers of businesses in these industries simply waited for the tide to turn, as it had done in earlier depressions. Instead of the ruthless overhaul of techniques and organization that the situation demanded, most of those who were responsible for policy tried to save themselves from ruin by agreements not to undersell one another or to reduce their output so as to maintain their level of prices. How unsuccessful this policy was can be seen from the unemployment figures. If we take the decade 1927–36 (i.e. when the direct post-war effects had worn themselves out and before rearmament began), we find that the average rate of unemployment in coal-mining was 24·6 per cent, in shipbuilding 40·8 per cent, and 22·1 per cent in cotton, despite the fact that the numbers nominally attached to these industries had fallen very considerably – in coal-mining, for instance, from 1,260,000 to 868,000.

The gap between the value of imports and exports of merchandise would have been even greater than it was during the inter-war period had it not been for the fact that the prices of agricultural produce and raw materials (our principal imports) fell so heavily at this time. The years following the First World War witnessed a new Agrarian Revolution which improved agricultural techniques and a higher degree of mechanization brought about a greater increase in productivity than could be easily absorbed by world markets (remember that demand for most basic foods is very inelastic; see Chapter 2), so that it took a small amount of exports to buy the things we needed from abroad. Yet even so, the deficit to be made good by invisible exports continued to grow, so that by the period just prior to the Second World War it was as much as 44 per cent of imports.

Unfortunately the value of the invisible items in our balance of trade did not keep pace with the burden they had to bear. Of these shipping was the most important, and, as ups and downs in world prosperity are generally reflected in the demand for shipping services, it is no surprise to find a serious fall in the earnings of British shipping during the thirties, the time of the greatest depression the world has ever known. Though they rose when trade began to revive they did not again reach the figure they had maintained in earlier times. Overseas investments had also been appreciably reduced during the 1914–18 war, for we were concentrating on the manufacture of munitions, instead of goods for export, and it was a long time before this reduction was made up. During the economic blizzard of the thirties the income from these investments rapidly declined and, by the end of the thirties, we could pay for our imports only out of capital itself.

So even if there had been no war in 1939 our position in world trade would have been a matter of serious concern, for we could not have continued permanently to live beyond our means. Our income from all sources (merchandise and services) was not enough to pay for imports of food and raw materials; and buying out of capital involved a continuously falling income from overseas investments. Either we should have had to find a means of increasing the value of our exports or we should have been faced with the necessity of cutting down our purchases.

The Second World War exaggerated this maladjustment between our exports and imports so greatly as to create an entirely new problem and one of much greater urgency. For the first two years of the war – until the Lend-Lease system was introduced by President Roosevelt – Britain could get her essential war requirements from the U.S.A. only by paying for them on the nail; and for this purpose the Government drew on investments that British people owned abroad, to the tune of more than £1,000 millions, about a quarter of the total. It was luck for us that preceding generations had saved so much, for, had it not been for the large volume of these overseas assets that had been accumulated in the late nineteenth and early twentieth centuries, the course of world events might well have been very different, and the Nazi régime might have become the dominant authority in the world.

By the Lend-Lease arrangement the cash payment for American war material was no longer necessary and the goods sold us by America were to be repaid after the war, not in money, but in kind. Even this, however, was forgone, so that, through American generosity, the value of the material supplied to us by the States became a gift, only very partially offset by the similar remission of payment for British goods and services supplied to the U.S.A.

Yet, although so much was provided without payment, our dependence on American war material created a serious position for our industries. It was agreed between the Allies that America should undertake the responsibility of providing a great deal both of our equipment and of essential civilian requirements. As a direct result of this scheme, there was a much larger proportion of our population engaged on direct war service than of that of any other country, and the conversion from a war to a peace economy was consequently more difficult. Many important industries had been compelled to cut themselves down to token size, and workers in millions had been drafted from civilian to essential war jobs. This could not be immediately reversed as soon as the war was over; time was needed to allow people to get back to their usual work and for factories to have a chance to re-equip themselves. It was in order to provide this essential breathing space that the American Loan was negotiated, by means of which America agreed to supply us with quantities of imports, payment for which was to be made over a long series of years. Unfortunately, no sooner had this arrangement been made than American prices began to rise, and an amount of credit which had been calculated to be adequate for the three years which conversion might be expected to take was exhausted in half that time. This unfortunate occurrence brought the problem of our international trade sharply into the forefront of discussion and made the volume of our exports a matter of acute interest to the general public. Once more the extraordinary generosity of the American people came to the rescue and, by Marshall Aid, offered us the necessary respite. Together with fifteen other European countries we received a supply of dollars with which to buy American produce whilst we reorganized our economy. Britain's recovery was so remarkable that we were able to do without this aid earlier than was expected and Marshall Aid was suspended on 1 January 1951. From that date we were self-supporting.

There was one serious and unfortunate exception to the general recovery of British exports; that exception was coal. Although the prolonged depression of the inter-war years had cut down its market so drastically, it still remained one of our chief exports and 46 million tons were sold abroad in 1938. After the war, even with strict rationing of home consumption, the output of the mines was too low to allow for more than a token million or two million tons of coal for export; and during the winter of 1950–51 we actually had to import from abroad to meet our own needs. If we had still been able to export the pre-war amount we should have gone a good way to pay our way earlier, but coal production remained obstinately low. On the other hand, manufacturers of all kinds showed a happier record and the gap between imports and exports shrank a great deal.

Does this mean that our problem was purely temporary and that we need not worry about it in the future? Unhappily we cannot be so optimistic as the recurring 'balance of payments' crises since the early fifties have made clear.

THE FOREIGN EXCHANGE

It was mentioned earlier that one of the big differences between domestic and international trade is that in the former all the people concerned are using the same currency, whilst in the latter they are not. In the years following the war the 'dollar shortage' was one of the main topics of political conversation because of the difficulty experienced by most countries in getting enough dollars to pay for all the things they wanted to buy from the U.S.A. How do we get hold of any dollars at all? We have to do so in the same way that we get possession of anything else we want, i.e. buying them with our money, that is, sterling. There are many people in America in the opposite position from ours; they have bought goods from England for which they must pay in sterling, and the only way they can get hold of it is by giving us dollars for the sterling we let them have. If there are more people who have bought goods from America than there are people in America who have bought goods from us, there will be a bigger demand for dollars than for sterling, and we shall have to pay more sterling for each dollar. That is why our foreign exchanges were controlled for so many years and we were not allowed to buy foreign currency without Government permission. For example, we could not go abroad for holidays and spend as much as we thought we could afford out of our incomes but we had to cut down to the limit of currency we were permitted to buy – at one time as little as £25 per person in a year. This restriction remained in force in relation to dollars for a longer period than with other currencies, in fact until 1958, because of the enormous quantity of goods we needed to buy from America whilst our own economy was reorganizing itself. We could not export enough to create such a demand for sterling as would have equalled our desire to get hold of dollars and, if we had been allowed to buy as much as we wanted, the value of our money in relation to that of America would have gone down rapidly. Marshall Aid enabled us to buy the essentials by giving us the dollars to pay for them; but there are so many things other than essentials that we all like to have that if there had been no controls our demand for the dollars to pay for them would have raised the rate of exchange against us so seriously that our food and raw materials would have become much more expensive.

This, in fact, did happen despite the restrictions, for during 1949 the gap between exports to dollar countries and imports from them continued to grow rapidly, so that serious inroads into our gold reserves had to be made to pay for what we bought; and in September of that year Sir Stafford Cripps, the Chancellor of the Exchequer, announced that we had felt ourselves compelled to alter the value of the £ in terms of dollars. Instead of being able to buy 4·03 dollars for a £ we should, in future, get only 2·80. This had two effects:

1. By making everything we bought from a dollar country more expensive in terms of our money, it induced us to cut down our purchases.

2. By making everything we sold to a dollar country cheaper in terms of *its* money, it persuaded them to buy more from us. But this second result could continue only so long as we did not raise our prices. If we allowed our prices to go up, this would cancel out the advantages we should otherwise get.

This was the real difficulty. As we have seen, we buy a great deal of food and tobacco from America and the devaluation of the £ made these more expensive. If wages went up on account of this rise in the cost of living, so too must costs of production, and hence selling prices of our exports – unless, that is, both workers and management appreciably improved their efficiency at the same time.

Devaluation, therefore, is not itself a solution to the maladjustment between imports and exports; it is, rather, a recognition that such a maladjustment exists. By automatically raising the cost to us of imports, it forced us to cut down our purchases of those things which must be paid for in dollars, and thus lowered our standard of living. If we were content with this situation and prepared to resign ourselves permanently to this lower standard, we could bridge the gap between imports and exports in this way. But if we wanted to get back to our old standard, or raise it still higher, we had to find some way to increase, very materially, the value of what we sold to dollar countries; and we could do this only by offering them the kind of goods they wanted, at prices that compared favourably with those of our competitors.

This 'balance of trade' problem has been a constant post-war dilemma. The great rise in incomes we have enjoyed encourages us to buy all sorts of things – household equipment, motor cars, clothes, etc. – many of which are either imported from abroad or are made of imported materials. Unless our own productive methods are so efficient that we can undersell our competitors in world markets we do not export enough to pay for these imports and either the value of the pound goes down in relation to the currencies of other countries or we must send them our gold reserves to pay for the excess of our purchases.

In the immediate post-war period the problem was primarily that of the balance of trade with America; for Europe had suffered so greatly that most countries were trying to get American goods. But in the more usual circumstances trade is multilateral, i.e. there is no need for the amounts traded between two individual countries to balance one another in order to keep exchanges stable. For example, before the war the United Kingdom bought from the rest of Europe almost twice as much as she sold in that area, but, on the other hand, she exported much more to the tropics than she bought there; and the large proportion of her imports which were paid for (as shown above) by invisible exports did not necessarily come from the countries to which she sold shipping and banking and tourist services.

So far I have written as if the only demand for another country's currency was to pay for goods or services received;

but we often buy the currency of another country for a quite different reason. Suppose I believe there is going to be serious inflation in my own country – that is, that the price level is going to rise very high; I might try to export whatever capital I possess to another country where I thought it might have more chance of keeping its value. Or suppose I feared that there was going to be a revolution and that my capital would be confiscated; again I might try to export it to a country I judged to be safer. In such circumstances I should be buying another currency because I thought it a better storehouse for my wealth, and not to pay for the goods I had bought. Yet my demand would have exactly the same influence in increasing the relative value of the currency I bought and would make the rate of exchange of the currency I was selling less favourable. The trouble with such demands is that they fluctuate violently with every change in the state of political nerves and make the foreign exchanges jump about in a manner that is incalculable and unpredictable. Such fluctuations are a terrible nuisance to ordinary trade, because you never know from one day to the next how much the goods you buy are going to cost you. You contract to buy them at a certain price, which you have mentally converted into your own currency, but by the time you come to pay for them the rates of exchange may have altered so completely that the price represents something quite different from your calculation, and a transaction which would have brought you a reasonable profit is changed into a thumping loss. One of the most serious problems with which we are confronted in the modern world is the prevention of the jumping about of this 'hot money' which sends foreign exchanges haywire.

Until the First World War we had a gold standard, and one of the chief reasons for the attempt to recover and retain it was that it prevented more than a very slight change in foreign exchange rates. If you always had the choice of paying your foreign debts in gold (which you could always buy at a fixed price) as an alternative to bargaining for the other country's currency, it is fairly obvious that the rates of exchange between the two currencies could not vary by an amount which exceeded the cost of buying and transporting an appropriate amount of gold. But the gold standard had disadvantages which proved so great that it was decided they were not compensated sufficiently by the stability of the foreign exchanges, and the Exchange Equalization Accounts which were set up in the thirties, by this country and the U.S.A., were an attempt to achieve the same ends by other means. The aim was to separate the buying and selling of 'hot money' from the sale of currency to pay for goods and services. The money which jumped about for political and psychological reasons was not allowed to become part of the stock of circulating money; so that wads of it could come into the country or leave it, according to the state of people's nerves, without having any effect on ordinary trade.

Other attempts have been made to try and overcome this difficulty of fluctuating exchanges.

1. *The European Monetary Agreement*

This came into existence in 1958 to replace another organization – the European Payments Union – which had been in operation since 1950. The economic chaos into which the war had thrown most European countries led to heavy demands for goods of all kinds but, in particular, for raw materials and machinery; but so little other than war materials had been produced in the preceding years that the foreign exchanges could not operate in the normal way and direct barter of goods had to be substituted. This led to such delays and so much distortion of the trading pattern that the Organization for European Economic Cooperation (O.E.E.C.) was set up in 1949 to try and bring some order into the situation. In the following year it established the European Payments Union as a regional clearing house between its member countries – Austria, Belgium, Denmark, France, West Germany, Greece, Iceland, Ireland, Italy,

Luxemburg, the Netherlands, Norway, Portugal, Sweden, Switzerland, Turkey, and the U.K. This system allowed all payments between people in these countries to be made by a monthly net settlement with E.P.U. irrespective of the country of origin or the destination of the goods for which payment was due. As a result intra-European trade doubled in volume in the next six years.

It has been the hope of the O.E.E.C. that there should also be a liberalization of trade between member countries by the gradual abolition of quotas and tariffs amongst them but this did not happen. By 1958 it was felt that the economies of most countries were sufficiently re-established for international payments to be made through the normal foreign exchange channels and E.P.U. was given up but the European Monetary Agreement was put in its place as a stand-by in case the need should arise again in the future. Each country puts a certain amount of its currency in the charge of E.M.A. which enables it to ensure that the rates of exchange between these countries do not fluctuate by more than a narrow margin.

2. *The International Monetary Fund*

The I.M.F. was set up as a result of the Bretton Woods Conference in 1944 when the importance of stable exchange rates in the promotion of world recovery when the war should have ended was already recognized. Each country has a quota, which determines its subscription to the Fund (of which 25 per cent must be paid in gold and the remainder in its own currency) and the extent to which it can draw on the Fund. There are now about seventy member countries, which agree to maintain the value of their currency at a stable rate in relation to those of fellow members, and not to devalue without the consent of the Fund. The Fund will help a member that is temporarily in difficulties by selling it currency up to 25 per cent of its quota in any one year. The idea of this is to allow it a breathing space during which it can take whatever steps are required within its own boundaries to enable it to recover its position.

3. Eurodollars

One method of overcoming the difficulty of fluctuating exchanges has evolved more by accident than design. After the Second World War the dollar began to replace the pound as the chief trading currency, and it became customary to express values, of whatever country, in terms of their dollar equivalents. American industrialists and bankers were spending a great deal in Europe with the result that people in many countries had large supplies of dollars in their hands and it gradually began to be realized that these could form a pool of credit which could be exchanged for any other currency. London, with its very highly organized money market, was the first to recognize this opportunity and the business has largely become centred there. This is the Eurodollar, which has no physical existence and is not controlled by any Central Bank or Government but which does an enormous amount of work. A Eurodollar is a claim to a dollar in the hands of somebody outside America who does not want to transfer his claim to U.S.A. but to use it for other purchases. Eurodollars thus move round various countries in the form of credit transfers to meet the needs of borrowers and lenders.

4. The Sterling Area

As Britain was the first big trading country of modern times it established a network of trading relationships all over the world and sterling became the recognized medium of exchange in many areas whose own currency had only limited acceptability. Even now, despite the enormous development of the external trade of U.S.A., about half of all international transactions are settled in sterling. Those countries whose economies are particularly closely linked to that of the U.K. have formed a huge banking system for which

London keeps the central reserve of gold and dollars. This is the Sterling Area.

It is a voluntary association in the sense that no country is compelled to remain within it but no country can become a member without the consent of the others. Although all the member countries have their own currency each is linked to sterling at a fixed rate and international payments between them are made in sterling. The U.K. keeps a collective reserve of dollars and gold for payment to be made outside the Sterling Area and any country which earns more dollars than it needs to spend pays the amount into the pool and those which earn less can draw on this reserve. This means that provided each member tries to expand its exports to dollar-using countries so that there is not too great a drain on the fund there is a large area within which payments can be made easily without any exchange problems and within which even capital can move freely from one country to another.

But there are difficulties. Britain's commercial strength has declined and she has found increasing problems in maintaining sufficient reserves to meet the demands made; and any doubt that might be felt on this score is cumulative in this respect. Sterling was acceptable all over the world because the extent of Britain's trading was so large that it was universally believed that any debts incurred in sterling would invariably be met; but if there arises a doubt that they might not be, people immediately try to convert their sterling into another currency in which they have greater faith. Pounds are offered for sale and the takers are unwilling to buy at the usual rate and this means that in order to keep the exchange value stable the Government must intervene and the Bank of England must be prepared to pay out dollars. This is why the balance of payments comes to be so serious a matter of concern that it is constantly the subject of discussion on the radio and TV and a rise or fall in the reserves is mentioned in the news programmes. In 1966–7 the loss of confidence in the pound was so marked that the

Government reluctantly found itself compelled to devalue; that is, to lower the rate at which pounds would be converted into dollars by 14 per cent, so that instead of giving 2·8 dollars for a pound only 2·4 would be paid in future. This meant that anybody who owned sterling lost one seventh of its foreign exchange value at a stroke.

So many of Britain's economic problems are magnified by the fact that sterling is an international currency that there are those who argue that we should now recognize that we are no longer the dominant international trading country in the world and, however much it may hurt our pride, no longer try to maintain sterling as a reserve currency. Any failure to increase, or even maintain, the volume of our exports lands us in difficulties so that we are forced to introduce policies that we should not do if we were solely concerned with our own domestic economy. Hence the 'stop and go' see-saw that has been one of the main characteristics of our post-Second-World-War history.

Even dollars are sometimes mistrusted as happened during the latter half of the sixties, not because America was exporting too little but because American businessmen were so prosperous that they were buying industrial properties in Europe at such a rate that dollars became so plentiful that their value weakened. In such circumstances the only alternative is to pay in gold, the one substance that everybody is willing to accept. Why this should be so is a psychological mystery but as long as it is so it becomes the currency of final resort. After sterling was devalued the loss of confidence in the world's monetary arrangements was so marked that tons of gold were moved from centre to centre, partly from nervousness that both dollars and sterling might become less valuable and partly as a speculation that America might be compelled to raise the fixed price of gold in dollars. To prevent the second of these movements the central banks agreed among themselves to sell gold only to one another at an 'official' price leaving the speculators to sell to one another at whatever price the market brought about.

In the seventies the high price of oil – the fuel most in demand by all countries and particularly by the manufacturing ones – and the great increase in the trade of Germany and Japan, led to renewed chaos in the foreign exchanges. At the same time the recession in America made many people less willing to hold dollars; this had as its corollary a higher demand for European currencies and consequent constant fluctuations in their value in relation to one another and to the dollar.

TARIFFS AND FREE TRADE

There is probably no economic issue which has engendered more heat than the fierce controversy between those who wish our trade with other countries to be free from restriction and those who wish it to be controlled in order to protect the home producer. There have been times when the supporters and the opponents of tariffs have seemed like two armies locked in a religious battle in which each is convinced that he has God on his side.

First of all let us get clear what the argument is about. A tariff, in the sense used in this controversy, is a protective import duty, that is, it is a tax imposed on goods entering the country from abroad, when no such tax (or a much smaller one) is levied on similar goods produced within the country; and the effect, of course, is to make the foreign goods relatively more expensive and so induce us to buy more from the home producer.

Is this a good or bad thing to do? Well, it all depends what we are aiming at. A course of action may be advantageous from one point of view and disadvantageous from another, and what we think on balance depends which point of view we think the more important. This simple fact is generally forgotten when people get really excited about tariffs, and this accounts for a good deal of the bitterness of the dispute.

You might argue, for instance, that agriculture provides a

way of life which is of value in itself and that a community which allows itself to become entirely urban and industrialized is too unbalanced for social health. In this case, you might believe that it was worth while to encourage a large farming industry, because of its social or cultural effects, despite any economic disadvantages it might have. Or again, you might insist that security is more important than wealth and that it is wiser to make sure that certain essentials are produced at home, even if we have to pay more for them, so as to ensure supplies during war. But the essential thing is to face the fact that these objectives – whether the better way of life you want with a balanced community, or the greater security by making certain of essential goods – have to be paid for; and not to assume that because a thing is desirable for one reason it follows that it must inevitably be equally desirable for all others. The sensible course is to accept the fact that the tariff will make us poorer, and then to decide how much poorer we are prepared to be for the sake of the other things we want. How much more security, for example, for being such and such an amount poorer?

You will notice that in the foregoing paragraph I have written as though tariffs would certainly be condemned if economic issues alone were involved; and indeed, this is, on the whole, true. This is one of the very few questions on which economists are agreed. This does not mean that no economists are in favour of tariffs; many support them for social and political reasons, but they are agreed that they do not lead to greater wealth than free trade, that, in fact, they do the contrary. It is not difficult to see why they are so sure of this. A tariff interferes with the freedom of choice of the purchaser, and consequently reduces the value he gets from the spending of his income. As we saw in Chapter 2, the great advantage of the price economy is the opportunity it provides for the consumer to lay out his income in the way that will satisfy his wants most nearly. Though we have sometimes restricted his right to do exactly as he would like, we have generally done so on grounds of social justice or

administrative convenience. If a tariff is necessary in order
to induce us to buy from the home manufacturer rather than
the foreign, it follows that the home articles are offered at a
higher price for the same quality, and this means that, if we
wish to satisfy this want, we can do so only by laying out
a larger part of our income on it than we needed to do before, and so have less left to satisfy all our other wants.
Suppose, for example, that, quality for quality, imported
wheat is cheaper than home-grown and that, in order to
ensure that the British agricultural industry shall not decline
and shall be able to sell its dearer produce, we put a tariff on
wheat from abroad, the effect will be to raise the price of
bread to the whole community. The demand for bread is inelastic (see Chapter 2) and so we should not cut our consumption very appreciably, but should have to spend more
of our weekly income on bread than before. As our incomes
would not rise to allow for this, we should have to decide
what to cut down, and each of us would choose the thing he
cared least about; for some it would mean less on clothes;
for others fewer chocolates or fruit, or cheese, or a visit less
to the cinema or the dogs. It is true that the farmers and
their workers would be better off than before the tariff, for
the former would have a bigger and more profitable market
for their goods and be able to offer steadier employment to
their workers. But ours is an urban civilization; only about
3 per cent are engaged in agriculture. So 97 per cent of us
would find our incomes less valuable in comparison with the
3 per cent who would gain.

The difficulty in realizing this comes from the fact that
all the gain is concentrated at one point – the protected industry – and can easily be seen, whereas the price paid in
reduced consumption of other goods and services is widely
diffused and so is overlooked. It is not only the loss each of
us feels in having less satisfaction out of individual incomes,
but also the fall in profits and employment in all the different industries that must be cut down because we cannot
buy as much from them, the reduced need for shipping and

dock work and transport to carry the imported goods, the smaller demand from abroad for our exports because the foreign producer cannot buy when his own sales fall off, and so on.

There are circumstances, however, in which, even on purely economic grounds, a good case may be made out for the imposition of a tariff. We force people to spend money on education and public health measures that they would not have spent if left entirely free to make their own choices, and we justify this, partly, it is true, on social grounds, but also because we consider it a sound capital investment. A healthy well-educated community will make better use of its resources and, as the individual is not always sufficiently far-sighted to realize this, nor sufficiently reasonable in his behaviour to act on it if he does, we take the decision out of his hands and, as a community, invest part of our national wealth in this kind of collective provision. There are similar possibilities of developing valuable economic resources through tariffs.

The relative advantageousness of carrying on a particular industry changes from time to time, as knowledge grows, and as increased transport facilities bring sources of raw material supply and new markets within reach. For example, the growth of manufactures has become more possible in the New World since the development of electricity as the chief source of power; and the rise of the dyeing industry in this country has taken place only since the increase in knowledge of industrial chemistry. When an industry begins, it has many technical and marketing problems to solve, which may involve it in heavy expenses, and it may happen, therefore, that a comparative latecomer in a particular field may have great difficulty in getting a foot into the market because of the long established prestige of its competitors. If it could get a chance, it would eventually prove itself fully competent to take its place amongst all rivals – the difficulty lies in persuading possible consumers to give it a trial. If it were given a privileged position in the home market, this might give it the time to get over its teething troubles, and grow up to stand on its own feet, and so it is often argued that new industries, which look as though they would be able to become independent of artificial support within a reasonable time, should have a special claim to protection during their infancy.

It is significant that the majority of tariffs of the modern world came into being because of the force of this 'infant industry' argument, and this draws attention to the difficulty associated with it. It is much easier to put a tariff on than to take it off. It is almost impossible to persuade an industry that it has reached man's estate and must begin to fend for itself. Whenever such a suggestion is made all sorts of arguments are put forward by the producers in the industry to show why the moment chosen is peculiarly unsuitable, and all the organized pressure of those connected with it is brought into action to support their protest; so it is extremely rare for an industry that has once been granted the protection of a tariff ever to consent to come from its shelter and face the bleak winds of foreign competition.

TWENTIETH-CENTURY TARIFF POLICY

The period since the First World War has seen a remarkable break with tradition in our trade policy. During the nineteenth century restrictions on imports were removed bit by bit – the climax coming in 1846 with the repeal of the Corn Laws – until by 1860 they had completely gone, and foreign goods competed in British markets on equal terms with the home-produced article. This freedom lasted until 1914, when it was interrupted by the circumstances of war, and, a year later, by the deliberate imposition of import duties. Since then more and more restrictions have been introduced. The early tariffs afford a good illustration of the point made above that tariffs once imposed, for whatever reason, tend to stick; for the first duties – the McKenna Duties of 1915 – had the object primarily of cutting down bulky and inessential imports, such as motor-cars from the U.S.A., in order to save dollars and cargo space, and not that of giving a free field to the home producer. But they remained on after the war because, by that time, the motor-car industry had got too used to them to be willing to do without them, and they continued (with one short break) until they were merged in the general tariff in 1938.

Apart from the McKenna Duties, tariff history from 1918 to the outbreak of war in 1939 shows three separate trends.

1. The desire to protect certain industries whose products might be essential in time of war. The Safeguarding of Industries Acts 1921–6 were designed to encourage home production of those things which, while unimportant in themselves, might be regarded as key products to other more important types of manufacture. It is easy enough to define a category of this sort in general terms, but much more difficult to determine what goods fall within its boundaries. Almost everything is a key to something else and, in fact, many thousands of things that did not seem essential requisites of our civilization, such as dolls' eyes and fabric gloves, got themselves on to the list.

2. The desire to protect the gold standard by cutting down imports as a whole so as to prevent a drain on gold resources. The temporary legislation passed for this purpose gave way to a more permanent scheme, and by the Import Duties Act of 1932 a full system of protection was introduced. The Act imposed a general tariff of 10 per cent on all imports, but provided, on the one hand, for a Free List of certain types of goods and, on the other, allowed additional duties to be fixed on the recommendation of the Import Duties Advisory Committee, a body appointed by the Treasury to advise the Government. The general tendency of the thirties was for tariffs to rise; the rates on manufactured goods were approximately 20 per cent *ad valorem*, but 33 per cent or even higher on McKenna and key industry goods.

3. The desire to bind the Commonwealth together by

economic ties as well as those of affection and sentiment. As long as foreign goods were admitted freely into Great Britain no privilege could be granted to the Commonwealth, but as soon as tariffs were established it was possible to do this by remitting the tariff or reducing it in amount. This policy began as early as 1919, but its scope was limited until the introduction of the general tariff, and by the Ottawa Agreement Act it was agreed that all Commonwealth products should enjoy preferential treatment in British markets, varying in amount from 10 per cent reduction on the ordinary rate to as much as 33 per cent or, in a few industries, even more. The effect of this policy was to bring about a remarkable change in the direction of our external trade. In 1931 the U.K. bought less than a quarter (23·2 per cent) of her total imports from Empire countries; by 1938 this had grown to 40 per cent. And, similarly, during the same period, the percentage of British exports going to the Empire rose from 32·6 per cent to 50 per cent of the total exports.

Import duties are by no means the only way by which a Government can control the volume and direction of international trade, and, indeed, in the inter-war years they came to be one of the less important methods. Three other ways will be outlined here.

I. CONTROL OF FOREIGN EXCHANGE

During the thirties, Germany, for example, strictly controlled the market for foreign currencies, not only fixing the value of a foreign currency in relation to German marks as a whole, but selling the same currency at quite different prices according to the purpose for which it was wanted by the purchaser. This is probably the most complete and most effective way of restricting imports to what the Government wants them to be.

There was a similar control on British external trade during the years following the Second World War when, as has been explained earlier, the amount of currency that any person could purchase was limited. The British Government exercised its control, not by charging different prices – in sterling terms – for currency wanted for different purposes but by limiting the total amount of another currency you could buy according to the reason for which you wanted it. Before 1958, for example, you could get very few dollars if you wanted to go to the U.S.A. as a tourist; but if you went on business – particularly to develop our export trade – you were given permission to buy much more. During this period restrictions on the amount of different currencies that one was allowed to purchase were much more important than tariffs.

2. SUBSIDIES

It was argued that it is possible to justify the protection of an infant industry which shows signs of growing to independent maturity, but that a tariff, once put on, is likely to remain for ever. Another way of protecting a young industry which does not suffer so greatly from this disadvantage is by subsidizing it. In this case, foreign imports continue to come in freely and consumers can buy them if they wish, but the home producer receives a grant from the Government, out of national funds, to enable him to sell below his cost of production without loss to himself. The advantage of this system, it is argued, is that the cost of protection is clearly seen in the national accounts and, as none of us is eager to pay more in taxation than necessary, there is likely to be continuous examination of the value we get for our money.

The most important example of this kind of protection before the war was the sugar subsidy, which was given to encourage the development of a British sugar-beet industry. The object was primarily political, i.e. to ensure an adequate supply of an essential foodstuff in case of war (and, in fact, the greater part of the domestic sugar ration during the Second World War was drawn from home production), but it was also believed that the industry would soon be self-supporting and that a grant lasting for ten years would give it sufficient time to establish itself. This hope was never realized and, when the subsidy was due to end, new arrangements had to be made to keep the industry's nose above water. Though the amount of the subsidy was calculated on a new basis, it averaged pretty much the same as it had been in earlier years, and the general effect was that it cost the Government about 12s. 6d. per cwt to produce home-grown sugar, whereas imported sugar cost only 5s. per cwt.

The same method was employed to encourage a larger production of wheat and other kinds of agricultural produce, though no other pre-war subsidy was proportionately as heavy as that given to sugar. During and after the war, however, we went in for subsidies in a big way. The aim has been to guarantee to farmers prices which are high enough to induce them to increase home food supplies very greatly, whilst at the same time keeping down the cost of living to the consumer. They have certainly been very successful in achieving this dual aim, but at very great cost. Whilst rationing was still in force the cost was as much as £500 million a year (and remember in the late forties £500 million was worth a great deal more than it is now). Even in the early sixties direct subsidies amounted to between £250 and £300 million a year – a sum equal to £800 per full-time farmer and accounting for 1s. of the 7s. 9d. standard income tax.

3. THE ALLOCATION OF IMPORT DUTIES

The third method of controlling the volume of imports is by the allocation of quotas and this again has been used particularly in relation to agricultural produce. The Board of Trade fixes the amount of certain foodstuffs to be imported and a share of this is allocated to each country that trades with us in these products.

This question of the protection of agriculture is one of the most important and most controversial issues of the present time. What size of agricultural industry ought we to aim at? Should we return to our earlier policy of buying our food wherever we can get it most cheaply, a policy which has obvious advantages for an urban community, but which may put a strain on the supply of dollars and which leaves us in a vulnerable position in time of war? Or should we protect the industry by heavy import duties, or by guaranteed prices and subsidies, and so have a lower standard of living during peace-time, but a greater security in time of war? And if we decide on the latter course, how should we make sure that farmers use the land in the most efficient and economical way, so that the burden on the community of maintaining a large agricultural industry is not too heavy?

The problem is very closely related to that of the Common Market but before that can be discussed it is necessary to know something of the general development of tariff policy. It is not easy to give a short account of this because the attempts to evolve a greater degree of co-operation in international trading have been, and are, inextricably mingled with political issues. Very rarely have agreements been made purely for economic reasons; there has always been present the desire, more or less openly expressed, to achieve closer political affiliations between certain countries or to guard against the hostility (feared or actual) of others.

Very shortly after the end of the war an International Trade Organization was set up with the idea of guiding its members towards the elimination of political and exchange considerations from world trade so that exports and imports could follow the directions dictated solely by economic factors such as price and quality. It proposed that members should enter into arrangements for the reduction of tariffs and that no country should give preferential treatment to one source of its supplies to the detriment of others. But this organization was still-born and has never operated effectively. Rather more successful, though still on the narrow front, has been the General Agreement on Tariffs and Trade

(G.A.T.T.). This has held a number of conferences at which strenuous bargaining has been carried on and which has resulted in undertakings agreeing to reduce certain tariffs or to refrain from raising them further. In the early fifties these agreements were not as important in practice as they might have seemed because the shortage of many goods was so acute that people were prepared to buy the things they considered essential to their economic rehabilitation without giving much consideration to the prices they had to pay; and in any case, currency restrictions were a more positive control of international trade than tariffs. Since then G.A.T.T. has been overshadowed by the much more important developments of the European Economic Community and the European Free Trade Association.

Complete free trade such as existed in this country from 1860 to 1914 is no longer a practical political possibility. Mid-twentieth-century agreements are based on the belief that this – however economically desirable in theory – is irrelevant in the actual political situation of the modern world, for we have to recognize that all economic activities are carried on within political frontiers, with all that that implies. Governments nowadays have a very large direct control of industry and trade. In practically every country they are themselves big employers of labour and, even in the areas in which private enterprise operates, Government policy affects every facet of economic life; through employment policy, through taxation, through assistance to the industrial development of special localities, through social insurance and social legislation, and through education and industrial training. In such circumstances the complete removal of tariffs does not mean that each producer is put on his competitive mettle to do a better job than any rival, at home or abroad, but that trade takes place within a political framework which forces commerce along certain lines.

Suppose, for example, we retain our present methods of subsidizing agriculture but that other countries remove all their tariffs on agricultural products. Ostensibly there would be free trade; but all the farmers in countries where there were no agricultural subsidies would totter towards bankruptcy, not because they were less efficient than British farmers, but simply because the latter could afford to sell at prices that did not cover costs of production, and make up their losses out of the subsidies provided by the Government out of tax-payers' money. If we wanted perfect free trade, therefore, we should have to do much more than get rid of tariffs; we should have to have international agreements covering all those branches of State intervention which influence the costs of production of people carrying on the same trade in different countries. It is this wider concept which has been the background of the agreements leading to the Common Market.

The first example to come into existence was the Coal and Steel Community, founded in 1951, comprising France, West Germany, Belgium, the Netherlands, Italy, and Luxemburg. Its aim was not confined to the abolition of all customs duties and quantitative restrictions between its members for the goods within its scope – coal, coke, iron ore, steel, and scrap – but it tries also to deal with the techniques of production and with the social consequences of its controls. For example, it estimates the size of the market, gives credit facilities where needed, helps in the contraction of coal-fields which prove superfluous to world needs, and provides a fund from which countries can draw substantial sub-ventions to enable them to give generous allowances to miners made redundant by its policy, or to enable them to be retained for expanding industries.

A similar integrated institution is found in Euratom, which was set up to co-ordinate research programmes dealing with the use of nuclear power for non-military ends, because it was realized that the resources required, both for research and investment in this field, are beyond the capacity of all but the very wealthiest countries.

But it is the European Economic Community which is far and away the most important of these developments. This was brought into existence by the Rome Treaty, signed in 1958 by the six countries named above, with the following aim:

It shall be the aim of the Community, by establishing a Common Market and progressively approximating the economic policies of Member States, to promote throughout the Community a harmonious development of economic activities, a continuous and balanced expansion, an increased stability, an accelerated rise in standards of living, and closer relations between its Member States.

This includes:

(a) gradual elimination of all tariffs and quantitative restrictions between Members;

(b) establishment of a common customs tariff and common communal policy towards non-members;

(c) free movement of people, services, and capital between Members;

(d) a common agricultural and transport policy;

(e) common standard of industrial training;

(f) creation of a Social Fund to improve employment opportunities and to help raise standards of living;

(g) changes in respective legislation where necessary for the functioning of a Common Market.

From the beginning the U.K. was in difficulties over the Common Market. It is very likely that the true nature of the problem was not fully realized during the mid-fifties when the discussions were going on because most of the British politicians did not believe that the six countries would be successful in bringing the negotiations to a successful conclusion and so took the invitation to participate rather too lightheartedly. But whether Britain had taken these preliminary negotiations seriously enough or not, it remains true that there is a fundamental problem to be solved, for closer integration between European countries – whether on the political or the economic level – cuts across Britain's position

as the centre of a world-wide network of Commonwealth
relationships. Geographically Britain is a small off-shore
island of the European continent and if larger political and
economic units are demanded by the circumstances of mid-
twentieth-century life, it seems that her obvious place is
with other European countries. But she also has special ties
– political, economic, traditional, and emotional – with all
the countries that are included in the Commonwealth. If the
E.E.C. had been a purely free trade area this difficulty
might have been more easily overcome, but it is important
to realize the difference between a free trade area and a customs union. The Common Market is a customs union; that
is, the Member States agree to reduce or abolish trade restrictions between themselves but they also agree to establish
a common tariff barrier between all of themselves and the
rest of the world. Ever since the Ottawa Agreements in the
thirties the U.K. had given special preferences to imports
coming from the Commonwealth, and the economies of
many of these countries were geared to these preferences. If
the U.K. joined the Community the preferential tariffs on
goods coming from Commonwealth sources would have to
be given up and exporters from Commonwealth countries
to the Common Market would have been in exactly the same
position as any others.

Great Britain therefore did not take steps to enter the
Community at the outset but she soon began to feel the
effects of her non-participation. The trade of the six Members was expanding rapidly, capital was flowing into their
industries, and firms with headquarters in other countries
were hastening to set up branch factories and subsidiary
companies there so as to share in the prosperity. Some
people in this country urged the Government at once to
recognize that it had made a mistake in remaining outside;
others – and these prevailed – proposed an alternative association comprising countries which were not members of the
E.E.C. At the end of 1959, therefore, the European Free
Trade Association (E.F.T.A.) came into being. It included

Austria, Denmark, Norway, Portugal, Sweden, Switzerland, and the U.K. This agreement provided for the abolition of tariffs in four instalments to be completed by 1970, with the exception of tariffs on certain agricultural products, and import quotas were to be increased by 20 per cent each year, except where special difficulties arose.

E.F.T.A. did not, in fact, make a great deal of difference to British export trade, for the populations (and therefore the potential demand for goods) of her fellow members were comparatively small. Moreover, the tariffs of the Scandinavian countries were already so low that there was not much room for reduction. It was for this reason that Government policy changed so radically and that the U.K. applied for membership of the European Economic Community. It is, however, very different to ask to be admitted to a club which has already proved itself a roaring success, from entering as a founder member when its future is insecure, and there were long and often bitter arguments over the terms of entry. The main problem centred, as before, on the position of the Commonwealth and, in particular, those countries whose economy is based on large exports of agricultural produce to the British market.

What were the arguments for and against Britain joining the Common Market? Let us first consider those in favour.

1. In a growing number of manufacturing industries the very large organization has an enormous advantage. As was seen earlier, in Chapter 4, the economic advantages of mass production depend upon the use of machinery instead of hand labour for each process in the course of production. This is worth while only if a very large quantity of identical articles is required, for the machine, unlike a human being, does the same thing over and over again until it is reset or redesigned. The rise in the standards of living of people in most Western countries provides a big potential demand for goods, and the larger the market the greater the possibility of having both mass-production methods and

variety of design because there are enough consumers wanting each design to make production *en masse* practicable. The size of the British population is 55 million; that of the countries in the Common Market is 185 million. The advantages offered by this large number are obvious.

2. The new and developing industries are those in which the economies of scale are particularly important. If, for example, you are a manufacturer of pins, access to a market of 55 million is certainly large enough to allow ample facility to make possible the introduction of the most efficient techniques. But this would not be equally true if you were making aircraft, or electronic computers, or even such household equipment as refrigerators. Moreover, technical developments in the production of these things are taking place so rapidly that only very large firms can afford the capital for research and experiment on which an increasing share of the market depends.

3. Western Europe is one of the richest areas in the world and its standards of living have risen greatly and are likely to continue to do so. Such a market is vastly more profitable than that of an equal number of people who are only just rising above the subsistence level.

4. The fact that the six countries lowered their tariffs on their common boundaries whilst maintaining them towards other countries resulted in members buying more from each other instead of from outside sources. It is true that the exports from the U.K. to the Six went up because their great prosperity made them very big buyers; but it is certain that these exports would have shown an even larger increase had there been no tariff barrier to surmount.

5. Trade between Britain and the Commonwealth is no longer as important a share of the total as it used to be. At one time Commonwealth countries depended very largely on this country for their manufactured goods but this trading pattern has been changing since the First World War. Countries that were then cut off from their traditional source of supply, partly because the U.K. was too busy

making munitions to have labour and capital free to make its customary exports and partly because of the hazards of transport, had an opportunity to establish and develop their own industries. In the half-century that followed many became highly industrialized and, instead of buying from us, were competing with us for world markets. On the other hand, our trade with Europe went up greatly.

In 1954 39·4 per cent of our total imports came from the Commonwealth and 43·5 of our exports went to those countries. In 1961 the figures were 27·4 of our imports and 32·5 of our exports. (Canada is excluded from all these figures as her trade is, for obvious reasons, more closely geared to the U.S.A.) By contrast with this fall, our imports from the European Economic Community accounted for 11·6 per cent of the total in 1954 but had risen to 15·4 per cent in 1961, and our exports to the E.E.C. which represented 14·2 per cent in 1954 had gone up to 17·3 per cent in 1961.

Britain's rate of growth had fallen far below that of the other members of the Common Market. In the decade following the signing of the Rome Treaty the national income of the Common Market as a whole rose by 9 per cent per annum whilst the British one increased by only 5·9 per cent, their industrial production rose by 6·4 per cent per annum in comparison with the British rise of 3·5 per cent and their domestic production per head of the population increased by 4·1 per cent in comparison with the British rise of 2·6 per cent.

This does not mean that all British manufacturers are too conservative and slow to introduce more efficient methods. Some sections of our economy can bear comparison with the best in the world; but there are a large number that are content to go on in the same old way to which they have become accustomed, because they feel fairly sure of the domestic market. If they were forced to compete with the manufacturers in the Common Market they would be compelled to pull their socks up if they wanted to survive. There were many supporters of Britain's entry into the Common

Market who rated this as the most valuable of all the advantages that might accrue.

Now let us consider the case against joining.

1. Everybody, both supporters and opponents, recognized that entry into the Common Market would eventually bring big alterations in the pattern of trading and this would involve changes in the relative sizes of industries. Some of our firms would find themselves unable to compete with those from abroad and would decline; others would expand under the stimulus of such a large market. This is inevitable : in fact, it is part of the object – to ensure that goods are produced by those who can do so most efficiently and economically, to the benefit of the consumer. Such changes bring in their train many personal and social problems. It is no easy matter for people who have earned their living over a long period in one industry or occupation to have to change to another, particularly when, as so often happens, this also requires moving to another locality to live. But this kind of change is not confined to the effects of the Common Market; it is a constant element in a dynamic society. Industrial development now is very different from what it was ten, fifteen, twenty, or any other number of years ago; it is part of the price paid for a higher standard of living. The essential corollary to this continuous need for change is a social policy which ensures that those thrown out of their old jobs receive adequate maintenance whilst they are being retrained for other work. Experience has shown that when an economy is expanding quickly these adjustments are much easier to accomplish.

2. The Commonwealth is one of the most valuable and remarkable institutions that has ever existed. Any action which might lead to its disruption or even to a weakening of the ties which bind its members would be a serious disadvantage not only to Britain and her fellow countries in the Commonwealth but to the world as a whole. Most of the countries in the Commonwealth were already self-governing and more would become so; but they were bound together by

ties of sentiment and affection, by common associations, historical development, and similarity of institutions which enable millions of people of different colour, race, and religion to act together in a greater degree of harmonious co-operation than has been achieved by any other grouping of populations. It would be a great loss if the other members of the Commonwealth felt that Britain had let them down in any way and had taken action for her own interest without taking into full consideration the possible repercussions on them.

If Britain's entry into the E.E.C. allowed those members of the Commonwealth to join or to be associated on equal trading terms no harm would be done to their economies; but if not, some of them would be faced with major readjustments of the whole of their productive organization. This was particularly true of New Zealand, which depended for her wealth mainly on her agricultural industries whose chief market was in this country. In fact, in 1961 51 per cent of her exports came to Britain, though by 1969 this proportion had dropped to 38 per cent.

If Britain became a member of E.E.C. and no special concessions were given to New Zealand the latter would find herself faced with a new tariff wall to surmount before being able to reach the market on which she depended for so much of her trade. If, on the other hand, special concessions were given to soften the blow, or if the period of time fixed to delay the full operation of the tariff were lengthened, New Zealand would have an opportunity to reorganize her industry and to search for new markets. In any case, however, it would be a matter of serious dislocation to her and would, undoubtedly, involve her in great strain.

Although the situation would not be without its difficulties for Canada and Australia, it would be nothing like so grave for them; 71 per cent of Canada's exports went to the U.S.A. and 73 per cent of her imports came from that source. Australia was rather more dependent on her trade with this country, from whom she drew 22 per cent of her imports and to whom she sold 14 per cent of her exports.

3. The chief argument against joining was the effect that could be expected on agriculture and the probable consequences on food prices. If you look back to pages 180–81 you will see that the agricultural industry in this country is in a special position. Certain branches are protected by tariffs or by import quotas which restrict the amounts to be bought from other countries, and this has allowed them to grow to a size that would not have been possible if they had been in full competition with outside suppliers. But much more important in protecting agriculture is the rather complex system of subsidies, guaranteed prices, and deficiency payments. The general aim of these payments is to keep down the prices of the main foodstuffs to consumers whilst at the same time guaranteeing to the farmer prices which will completely recompense him for any losses he might incur in producing the quantities that the Government encourages him to set as an output target. Though the total cost of agricultural support has been reduced during the last decade it still costs the taxpayer just under £300 million a year. If Britain entered the Common Market this support would have to be given up eventually (although not necessarily all at one stroke).

What would be the result to the agricultural industry?

There is little doubt that the deficiency payments allow a number of marginal farmers to keep their heads above water and that they would not be able to do so without them unless food prices rose far above the present guaranteed prices. This may be due to the fact that they are cultivating land which is not very fertile or which is disadvantageously situated in relation to transport and markets. But it may also be due to the farmer's lack of knowledge of modern farming techniques, inadequate capital to buy the best machinery, or poor organizing ability. Such farmers would have to give up. But we must remember that this has been happening since the end of the eighteenth century when we began to import food in large amounts and turned our energies towards becoming an industrial nation. The ques-

tion we have to try to answer is, 'Do we want to maintain a
larger agricultural industry by taxing ourselves in order to
provide subsidies for farmers who otherwise would not be
able to produce at prices that consumers are prepared to
pay; or do we prefer to concentrate on a smaller industry
which through knowledge, efficiency, good land, and so on,
is economically viable without any buttressing?' This is a
political – not an economic – question and therefore is not
discussed here.

4. The removal of subsidies is of importance, of course,
to the consumer as well as to the farmer. We buy so much
of our food cheaply because part of its cost of production is
borne by the taxpayer. If this were no longer possible,
prices would have to rise to cover the full cost of production.
By how much would prices rise? We don't know; because
we don't know the answers to the questions raised in the
preceding paragraph. But those who had special knowledge
of agriculture and its markets believed that the increase
might be about 7 per cent.

Is this a serious matter? It must be considered in its context. Two considerations must be taken into account. First,
that the Retail Price Index rose by 5 per cent in 1970 though
we were not in the Common Market, so that the contemplated increase was nothing much out of the ordinary.
Second, that the average household spends about a quarter
of its weekly budget on food so that, if the prices of manufactured goods came down (because of the economies of scale
referred to above, or because of cheaper imports from other
countries) there might be a gain on balance even if food
prices were higher.

However, we must remember that the average covers a
multitude of variations. The lower-paid worker and even
more those living on pensions or social insurance benefits
certainly spend a great deal more than a quarter of their
incomes on food and even a slight rise in these prices would
bring hardship and misery. It would therefore be essential
to take this into account in our social policy.

In 1971 Britain made a third attempt to join the Common Market. She had tried to do so in 1961 and again in 1967 but in both cases was unsuccessful primarily because of the hostility of President de Gaulle of France. With his retirement and subsequent death the position eased and most members of the Community were anxious for Britain to join provided the terms of entry could be jointly agreed. But as the prospect became probable the opposition in this country organized itself to try to prevent a further application to enter. As a result there was a strong demand for a referendum to be held so that everybody could have an opportunity to express an opinion. This was an unprecedented step for no referendum had been held in Britain before (though this was not infrequent in other countries), and there were many people who opposed it on the grounds that there was no provision for it in our unwritten constitution. Despite this controversy a referendum was, in fact, held in 1975; there was a large vote and more than two to one voted in favour. Two other countries, Eire and Denmark, followed the British lead so that now the European Economic Community consists of nine members instead of the original six.

Since it was first established in 1958 the Common Market has not stood still and the aims it then set itself, whilst not different in character from the original ones, have now developed a somewhat different order of priorities. As far as political union is concerned there has been little advance, though in 1967 the Common Market for the first time negotiated as a single unit in the general discussions of G.A.T.T. on the question of reductions of tariffs in international trade as a whole. And now again – in 1975 – the E.E.C. is preparing to take part as a unit in the discussions to be held on the use of the world's energy resources.

And the question of developing a common monetary system has become something more than merely a pipe dream. This does not mean that such a system is likely to eventuate in the near future; when it comes to the crunch each country still acts in its own interest, as was shown by the devaluation of the franc in 1969 and the revaluation of the Deutschmark, but it does mean that deliberate steps could be taken to make a common monetary system a practical possibility. It would not be essential for every country to have the same units of exchange; the U.K. could still express its prices in pounds, France in francs, Germany in marks, and so on. But it does mean that within the Community the exchange value of these units would be fixed in terms of one another and this would involve a common policy of their Central Banks to keep these exchange values constant.

Far and away the most important, and most intractable, issue remains that of agriculture. In all industrial countries the proportion of the population engaged in farming has been shrinking but the rate of decrease varies from one country to another as a result of its history, culture, and political structure. In the U.K. less than 3 per cent of the working population earns its living in agriculture; in France it is 15 per cent and in West Germany 10 per cent, and in these two Continental countries there is a much larger proportion of very small family farms than here. As has already been shown Britain spends a lot of money every year in support of its agricultural industry, in direct subsidies and guaranteed prices, and in the effort to make agricultural techniques more productive; but in France and Germany the size of the industry is so much larger a proportion of the electorate that it has a much greater political influence. In both these countries the very small family farm attracts a great deal of financial support even though it is recognized that in modern times, with rapidly changing demands and methods, it is practically impossible for such farms to pay their way, despite the incessant work of the farmer and even more incessant and back-breaking work of his wife. The contrast between the lives they lead and the high standards of living of industrial workers, with the many holidays and free weekends enjoyed by the latter gives rise to constant friction and to ever-increasing demands by the farmers for still further help. It is estimated that 80 per cent of the existing farms are too small to keep one busy man efficiently occupied full-time, but the farming community is traditionally conservative in its living habits and though people may complain that their lives are poorer than those of their industrial neighbours they resent any attempt to get them to change, either by giving up farming altogether or by enlarging their holdings to enable more efficient methods to be introduced. Nevertheless more and more of the younger men leave the land each year, partly to earn the better wages in the towns and partly because their wives, more aware now than they used to be of how other women live, refuse to submit to such low standards of life. Already more than half of all farmers in the original Common Market are over 57 years of age; and in one way, this results in those who remain on the land being even more stubborn and conservative than would be likely with a wider age range.

The respective Governments have several ways of trying to cope with the situation : (1) Paying older men – those over 65 – compensation to induce them to give up their farms so that holdings can be consolidated to form more viable units. (2) Providing subsidies to enable farmers to buy equipment, though unfortunately not all these schemes are sensible. For example, one country makes grants to enable stalls for 15 cows to be built though it is known that no farm can make a profit on less than 40; at present two-thirds of Common Market farms have less than 5 cows though one man can tend a herd of 40 to 60. Other countries give grants to enable farmers to buy tractors though most of the tractors already existing in these countries are used to barely half their capacity. (3) The most important way of supporting is by guaranteed prices and purchases, of which butter has become, in a way, the symbol. Dairies churn out mountains of butter irrespective of market demands because they get a guaranteed price for it whether it is bought or not and even though it simply goes to build up ever greater and greater stores which nobody is prepared to buy.

Everybody but the farmers themselves agrees that the cost of maintaining these high guaranteed prices, already reaching astronomical proportions, will soon become unbearable and that the only way to establish stability in prices is to accompany such a policy by great structural alterations in the industry so as to make it more efficient. But whilst the maintenance of prices is one of the ways in which the Common Market works in concert the structural changes are a matter for each country to settle for itself according to its own political ideology and pressures. The chief countries in the Common Market hope that the problem will solve itself as more and more young men and women move into industry and that, consequently, the enormous cost of supporting thousands of farmers whom nobody wants and in producing tons of agricultural produce for which there is no economic demand will be reduced to reasonable proportions.

But this is the problem that Britain has had to face since becoming a member for she has had to follow the agreed agricultural policy; and as so small a proportion of this country's working population is involved in agriculture, this has meant large contributions to the funds of the E.E.C. in order to maintain numbers of unnecessary farmers whose products compete with our own. Three important questions must be answered: (1) How rapidly are the structural changes in Continental agriculture likely to be made to reduce the numbers of less than economically viable farming holdings and allow more efficient methods to become common? (2) Is it likely that Britain's membership will change current policies with regard to the level of guaranteed prices? and (3) To what extent will the industrial benefits to be reaped from access to the wider markets of 185 million potential buyers instead of 55 million compensate for higher food prices should these be unavoidable?

Closely allied to the agricultural problem is that of the fishing industry. Every country which has a sea coast sets restrictions on the right of nationals of other countries to fish close to their own shores. The members of the Community have, of course, given up such restrictions so far as fellow members are concerned and it was assumed that if the U.K. became a member her inshore fishing would be open to all the others. This is a more serious matter for the U.K. than for the original members of E.E.C. because her inshore fishing has been very carefully regulated – more so than that of most other countries – so that the seas near to her shores are extremely prolific fishing grounds. Inshore fishermen therefore complain that they would be giving up a great deal more than they could possibly gain by being free to fish near other coasts.

As a matter of fact, the more serious problem as regards fishing grounds concerns Iceland, which is not a member of the community. British taste in fish concentrates mainly on cod and British trawlers have been accustomed to get most of their cod from the prolific waters which surround Iceland. But fish is Iceland's only big natural resource and Iceland has tried to reserve this for its own nationals by denying access to foreign fishermen, first within fifty miles of its shores and now within two hundred miles.

Chapter 9

INCOMES AND HOW WE GET THEM

A CASUAL glance around is enough to show us that we don't all enjoy an equal share of what is produced – that there are rich and poor. It is certainly true that the difference is nothing like as great as it was a generation ago, but it still exists. Some people live in large well-furnished houses with plenty of good things to eat and to wear, whilst others have a poverty-stricken existence, counting every penny, in small, inconvenient rooms or crowded, insanitary cottages; and between these extremes there are countless grades of more or less. What settles the amount of income we get? How far is it true there is now a smaller gulf between rich and poor than there used to be? Is this likely to continue until we all have the same amount?

First let us get a picture of the different ranges of income and see how many people fall within each of them. Nowadays we can get a fairly good idea of this because, since early in the Second World War, the Chancellor of the Exchequer has adopted the excellent practice of publishing an annual estimate of the national income before announcing his budget proposals. The most comprehensive figures available are those published in Report No. 1 of the Royal Commission on the Distribution of Income and Wealth (Chairman, Lord Diamond) which was published in July 1975 and compares the numbers of incomes in different ranges in 1964–5 and 1971–2.

It is first of all necessary to explain why there seems to be so large a number of people with very small incomes in an 'affluent society' when we know, by common experience, that there are few earning such low wages as would be represented by the first categories listed. The explanation is that the figures include *all* separate incomes. For example,

an adolescent although living at home and partially dependent on the family is counted separately and, of course, the
majority do not earn big incomes in the first or second year
of employment. This is particularly true of girls. Then at the
other end of the scale there are the millions whose incomes
derive from retirement pensions and, as the number of
people over retiring age has been going up steadily this
comprises a very large group. Again there are those living
on social insurance benefits – widows with young children,
sick and unemployed persons. Lastly there are the people
who have worked for only part of the year, or widows or
divorced women and school-leavers who have come into the
employment field only a few months before the count.

The information given in the table opposite cannot be considered absolutely accurate for it is necessary for complicated
calculations to be made before the figures can be estimated.
As most of us get our living from our employment, P.A.Y.E.
is the principal source of information, but this gives only
the amount of earned income and many persons have other
sources; for example, dividends on shares, the rental value
of house property, interest on land, etc. Those whose incomes were large enough to fall within the range of surtax
had to make complete returns of all their income, whatever
the source, and for this minority the information is available; but there is no regular source of information about the
remainder who are the majority of income receivers. In
order to get an estimate of the totals of these incomes the
Commissioners of Inland Revenue periodically take a special
Incomes Census. To include the whole population in such a
census would be too formidable a task, so a sample survey is
made. Whilst the resultant figures, therefore, cannot be
guaranteed to give a wholly accurate picture of the distribution of personal incomes they can be accepted as providing a very fair outline of the general pattern of distribution.

But this is not the whole story. A good deal of what we
consume – and it is an ever-growing share of the total –

Distribution of personal income before tax by range of income, 1964–5 and 1971–2
United Kingdom   *Income unit: tax unit*[1]

1964–5		1971–2	
Range of income (lower limit)	Numbers of incomes	Range of income (lower limit)	Number of incomes
£ p.a.	Thousands	£ p.a.	Thousands
275	408		
300	1,814		
400	1,878	420	699
500	1,795	500	891
600	1,825	600	1,041
700	1,836	700	1,019
800	1,832	800	1,105
900	1,749	900	1,078
1,000	3,489	1,000	2,488
1,250	2,028	1,250	2,473
1,500	1,411	1,500	2,343
		1,750	2,149
2,000	592	2,000	1,564
		2,250	1,208
		2,500	776
		2,750	558
3,000	263	3,000	896
		4,000	291
5,000	121	5,000	136
		6,000	85
		7,000	49
		8,000	53
10,000	28	10,000	26
		12,000	20
		15,000	9
		18,000	3
20,000	6	20,000	10
Total	21,075		20,970

1. Incomes relate to tax units, the incomes of husbands and wives being aggregated and counted as one income.

Note: The numbers in the lower income groups are affected by school-leavers whose recorded incomes relate to part of the financial year only and who might appear in a higher income range in a full year. A similar situation arises, at all points in the income scale, in for example the case of deaths. Such factors must be borne in mind when interpreting differences between the two distributions but this does not detract from their value in illustrating techniques of measurement.

Source: The Royal Commission on the Distribution of Income and Wealth, Report No. 1, H.M.S.O., Cmnd 6171.

comes to us by virtue of our citizenship and not because of the size of our personal incomes. In some cases this takes the form of a definite sum of money which is handed over by the State to members of certain defined categories of people, e.g. those in the pensionable age-groups, or below school-leaving age, or out of work, or whatever it may be; in others we receive certain amenities, e.g. a free education, or food at less than cost price, or free medical attention, or other benefits which we should have had to pay for out of our income if they had not been provided by the State. It is obvious that we cannot all benefit equally from these 'civic rights' because we cannot, for example, draw a retirement pension unless we happen to be of the suitable age, and so this 'social income' modifies to some extent the distribution of the national income as shown in the table on p. 201.

Then again, all these benefits, as well as all the rest of the work done by the State – national defence, roads, and so on – must be paid for, and part of our income is taken from us by taxation to meet the bill. In recent years the amount taken by the State for these and similar purposes has grown so greatly that it is now close on a quarter of the total national income. Here again, the burden is not distributed equally on all incomes, i.e. we don't all pay a quarter of our income to the tax collector; some pay much more, some very much less, and this too, therefore, alters the relative amounts we have left to spend on what we choose for ourselves. So that before we can get a true picture of the distribution of income among us we have to take account of all these different factors – (1) the money we receive for our work; (2) incomes from property; (3) the extras we get as our part of 'civic rights', and (4) the amount we pay in taxes – and only then can we really see how far some people are better off than others.

We get our personal incomes from three sources – payment for work done, payment for the use of property and income from 'civic rights' – and each of these must be looked at separately.

1. INCOMES FROM WORK

The vast majority of us work for our living and the size of our incomes depends on what we get paid for our work. If we examine the earnings of people in any one occupation we find that they vary considerably. Miners, for example, don't all take home the same amount each week; it depends on how quick they are (and so what output they produce), whether they are regular in attendance or take a shift or two off, whether they work overtime, their luck in being on an easy or difficult part of the coal face, and so on. There are similar variations in other occupations. All this is fairly obvious. But these differences in earnings between persons in the same occupation are slight in comparison with the divergence in earnings between different occupations. There was a great deal of public comment when Dr Beeching was appointed Chairman of the Transport Commission at a salary of £24,000 a year; but it was pointed out that many chairmen of companies in the private sector in industry received much larger amounts than that. The same is true of a popular barrister or a well-known actor or pop-singer.

We have seen in the first chapters that prices are supposed to show where goods are wanted, so that a high price usually calls forth an increased supply. Why then don't the agricultural labourers become popular barristers and, by increasing the supply of them, bring down their price to something nearer that of the labourers? The answer is, of course, that although we are legally free to enter any occupation we choose, in practice we are prevented by circumstances. A barrister requires a very long education and training before he can begin to practise, and few parents can afford either the expense of the education or the cost of maintaining their son for so long a time. Moreover, to be a successful barrister demands certain qualities; both of intellect and of personal temperament, which are not very widespread; so that it is not enough to be rich, you must be rich and also have these qualities. As a consequence, only a comparatively few people can offer themselves for the higher ranks of legal work, and therefore the price is high. The same thing applies throughout. Whenever entry to an occupation demands either special types of capacity or long periods of preparation there is, relatively speaking, a scarcity of entrants, with the usual result of scarcity – a higher price. The skilled manual worker gets more than the unskilled because the time needed for learning his job keeps down the numbers who could possibly go into it. If the demand for that kind of skill declines (perhaps because of changes in industrial methods or because of changes in the buying habits of the public) then he is no longer relatively so scarce and his wages begin to go down. If, on the other hand, there is a sudden increase in demand, wages go up until a sufficiently large number of new recruits can be attracted into the industry. In the immediate post-war decade the earnings of coal-miners trebled whilst average adult male earnings only doubled, because there was an acute coal shortage and it was necessary to attract into the mines thousands of men who were employed at good wages in other occupations. This has changed completely during the sixties and seventies.

In some cases the skill required may be of the sort that is acquired 'painlessly' by many people in their ordinary lives, so that anybody who has lived that sort of life can easily do the work and offer himself for that occupation. This has been one of the factors that in the past kept down the earnings of both agricultural labourers and domestic servants – both skilled workers but neither it was thought demanding specific training. During the war the submarine danger and after the war the shortage of dollars combined to force us to concentrate more on home-produced food, with a corollary of a very big sudden increase in the demand for agricultural labourers and a rapid rise in wage rates to induce more people to enter the industry. The same thing was true of domestic service, as a result of the rapid expansion in the number of well-paid alternative employments for women.

Sometimes the difficulty of entering a particular occupation is due to social factors rather than the need for special training. There is still a good deal of snobbishness about our society, and in many jobs there is a tendency to choose from amongst those who have a certain manner of speech or who dress in a way that is considered desirable by those who make the appointments. If such persons are limited in number, the pay is proportionately high.

When we compare the earnings of different occupations we have to be careful to take everything into account. A businessman may make a good bargain which brings him in £1,000 profit; but we cannot therefore conclude that his income is £365,000 a year, because such a deal is not a daily event; and similarly the hourly earnings of a manual wage-earner are not a good guide to his income until we know how many times a year he is likely to earn that amount. Even this is not enough. Some jobs are regular, others are not. A civil servant is very unlikely to be involuntarily unemployed, whereas shipbuilding has had enormous changes in its volume of employment. If both kinds of work carried the same rates of pay the former would really be better paid, because the shipyard worker must reckon on some periods without earning and must make what he does earn spread out to cover the slack times. In some jobs again there is more wear and tear, and the workers cannot expect to continue earning at the full rate all their working lives; for example, the footballer knows that his professional life is a good deal shorter than that of a cricketer, and a man on heavy work in an iron foundry will have to give up his job at an age when the skilled carpenter feels that he is reaching his prime. Even if the wear and tear on the worker are not severe, there may be a risk that the occupation itself will decline and so cut short the working life of those who belong to it. Nowadays when the tempo of technical change has been so speeded up, this is a serious offset to all manual earnings, for, on the whole, the rate of obsolescence is greater among manual workers than among clerical ones. This is now changing with the introduction of such things as the dictaphone, the tape recorder and the computer, all of which alter the demand for clerical workers of the old type and similarly create demands for those with special skills and for technical and administrative workers.

In most occupations holidays are paid for; but in some they are not. Under the National Health Service the specialist has the right to a certain amount of remuneration when he is on holiday, but the general practitioner has to pay another doctor to look after his patients when he is sick or on holiday. There are similar expenses and perquisites attached to other jobs. The railway porter, the waiter, and the taxi driver can expect a very considerable addition to their recognized earnings through the tips they receive; the shop assistant, who gives a similar form of personal service, cannot, and this is only slightly compensated by the fact that he usually has the privilege of buying goods from the store at less than the ordinary marked prices. The miner and the agricultural labourer often get a cottage at a low rent and the miner usually also receives an allocation of coal at no cost or a very slight one; resident domestic servants and hotel employees generally receive free board and lodging in addition to their money wages. In some trades the worker provides some of his own tools, e.g. the plumber. The bank clerk and the schoolmaster must dress in the way that is considered suitable to the profession; they cannot save their 'good' clothes for the weekend as can the docker or the engineer. The salaries of civil servants are very much higher than they appear to be because they are the only big group of employees who do not pay a yearly contribution to their very generous pensions and in addition they receive a comparatively large capital sum, free of income tax, at the moment of retirement. There is no need to elaborate this further to make clear the point that a great deal more than the hourly or weekly wage has to be taken into consideration when comparing the remuneration of different occupations.

One of the most important changes that has taken place

in the post-war decades is the alteration in relative rates of pay. This is shown both in the changes in differentials in one industry and in the differences that have developed in the relative remuneration of different occupations.

For centuries the unskilled labourer in most industries received a rate of pay which was about two-thirds that of the skilled man; nowadays, in most, it would be closer to 90 per cent (though, of course, it varies a little from one trade to another). There are a number of factors which have helped to bring this about, the most important of which was the rapid rise in the cost of living in the ten years immediately following the Second World War. It was widely recognized that our economic rehabilitation, depending as it did on expansion of exports, would be seriously endangered if wages shot upwards and made our costs of production too high to allow us to compete effectively for world markets. Much effort was put into the attempt to control this movement (and Sir Stafford Cripps's 'wage freeze' was the predecessor of recent attempts to keep rises to a 'norm'). But at the same time it was realized that, as prices rose, the lower-paid workers were certain to be in real difficulties. The practice became usual therefore for wage rates to be increased by a flat sum which applied equally to all grades and an increase of, say 10s. (50p) a week, was a much larger proportionate rise for a wage of £5 than for one of £10. Repeated increases of this type gradually narrowed the differentials between higher- and lower-paid workers and by the time the practice was given up, and percentage increases became more common, the new relationships were established in people's minds and difficult to alter, however much resented by the more skilled workers.

Two other circumstances have worked in the same direction. First is the conscious egalitarianism which has been so marked a characteristic of popular belief during the last couple of decades – the conviction that marked differences in standards of living amongst members of the same community are hard to justify. In fact, most people find themselves in a cleft stick on this matter. On moral and social grounds they would like a world in which most people had roughly equal opportunities to enjoy the good things of life; but at the same time they are equally convinced that those who work harder or with greater ability or who have spent years training themselves or who have rare qualities, should have the reward for their industry and ability by being paid more. These irreconcilable beliefs form one of the great dilemmas of the present time.

The second circumstance is bound up with the changes in the structure of trade unions. As will be seen in the next section the recent tendency is for there to be fewer unions but larger ones. This means that the big unions now comprise all grades of worker – skilled, semi-skilled, and unskilled – and it is very difficult, if not impossible, for a union official to negotiate higher wages for skilled men, in order to provide an incentive to more people to train, without at the same time including the less skilled in the final agreement.

The biggest changes, however, are those that have come about in the relative earnings of different occupations. The obstacles to be overcome in entering those occupations which require higher ability and prolonged education, mentioned on pages 203–4 are very much less than they used to be. Since the passing of the Education Act 1944, those who have the ability to learn need no longer be prevented from doing so because of the poverty of their parents. Secondary school education is free – whether grammar, secondary modern, comprehensive or technical–and provided a student can get a place in a university on the score of his intellectual capacity, his local authority will provide him with the funds to pay his fees and to maintain himself.

Notice that I have said 'need no longer be prevented'; for although the opportunity is provided there are still able boys and girls who do not take advantage of it, either because they themselves do not wish to break away from the pattern of life of their family and friends or because their parents are unwilling to forgo the wages they might be getting in employment. There has, however, been a very marked increase in university entrants from sections of society who were largely excluded in the past; and as this kind of education generally leads to different types of job from those into which school-leavers go at sixteen, there has been, and will continue to be, an important change in relative scarcities.

The growth of joint stock companies and public corporations (the nationalized industries) as the typical units in our economy has been another factor in this situation. Both of these offer a large number of openings to people with ability, knowledge, and managerial skill who have no capital of their own. Before this development it was rare for those without capital, however much organizing ability they might possess, to get into managerial positions; but the joint stock company, by separating the ownership of capital from the management of the firm, opens up a career to talent so that those who, through the greater educational facilities provided by the State, can develop their potentialities, can enter occupations from which before they would have been shut out.

METHODS OF SETTLING RATES OF PAY

Trade Union Negotiation

If a shopkeeper makes a bigger income than a competitor we can assume that is is because he is more skilled in stocking the things the customers like, that he serves them more efficiently, or makes his shop more attractive and convenient, and so on. On the other hand, if he fails to keep his customers, his profits will begin to decline until finally he may have to decide to give up and look for some other way of earning a living. The point is that we should not expect to find all shopkeepers making the same amount each year nor be surprised at very great differences between them. But such a situation is unusual amongst employed people nowadays; and the vast majority of us earn our living at work for which a definite rate of pay has been contracted. In fact, 95 per cent of all occupied persons work for wages or salaries. (Is there any difference between these two? No. The difference is mainly one of custom or, perhaps, just snobbishness. Salaries used to be reckoned on a yearly basis and wages on an hourly or weekly or piece rate; but even this distinction was not universal, for example, the wages of domestic servants used to be fixed at so much a year, in addition to board and lodging. No. It must be admitted that the line of demarcation is more social than anything else.) Most, though not all, of this 95 per cent receive an amount which is based on an agreed rate and, even where it is not formally agreed, there is usually a standard method of calculation which is customary in the occupation. Most of these agreed rates are the result of collective bargaining carried on between representatives of the people who are to receive the pay, on the one hand, and those who employ them on the other.

Before this method of settling rates of remuneration grew up, the worker was often in an extremely disadvantageous position, for not only could the employer afford to wait longer to get what he wanted, but it was generally much less important to him to come to terms with an additional employee than it was to the man who must get a job or starve. A business which usually employs 500 or 1,000 men does not come to a standstill if one man is unwilling to work on the terms offered, but the worker loses his whole income if he does not manage to get employment. Except in the rare circumstances of an acute labour shortage, the employer could easily play on a man's fears of being undercut by somebody else who, because he had been out of work longer, was more desperate to land any sort of job, whatever the pay. But there was also a more subtle psychological disadvantage under which the worker laboured – that of recognized and accepted social distinctions. The employer is used to giving orders to, and having them obeyed by, just such a type of man as the one seeking a job, and he is accustomed to certain forms of respect in the manner in which work-men address him; it is difficult both for the employer and worker to differentiate between their reciprocal attitudes when one is the master of the other and their relation-ship before the bargain is struck when they are merely two citizens discussing the terms of their contract. The employer has a 'These are my terms, my man, take them or leave them' attitude, and the worker is inclined to assume that this is natural.

Trade unionism gets over these inequalities by eliminat-ing (or at least reducing) the competition between man and man for a job. Whilst no one individual is of supreme im-portance to the firm, the whole body of labour certainly is, and the employer, aware of his mounting overhead expenses, is as anxious to come to terms as the worker when the whole of his staff is involved. Moreover, as the size of the unions has grown and the paid official, representing often hundreds of thousands of workmen, has taken charge of the negotia-tions, the psychological disadvantage has become less serious.

A trade union is a voluntary association, and its power to protect its members depends to a large extent on its ability to get a monopoly of the possible recruits for the job. This is not an easy task, and the incidence of trade unionism is, therefore, extremely patchy; in some occupations the organ-ization is almost complete, in others it exists more as a hope than a fact. There are now (1975) between 10 and 11 million organized workers of whom two-thirds are to be found in only 17 of the 356 unions, for there has been a marked ten-dency during the last quarter-century for the number of unions to fall but for the individual union to grow larger. Coal mining, railways, textiles, building, transport, and the engineering and metal industries are the most highly or-ganized occupations, together with public employment, while agriculture, retail distribution, and many of the new consumption industries are to be found at the other end of the scale.

This is not a matter of chance. The building of a strong

trade union is a difficult and arduous business, and it is unlikely to be successful unless the circumstances are favourable. It takes vision and self-sacrifice on the part of the
founders and early supporters to develop a strong organization, because it is rare that anything positive can be achieved
for a considerable time. The majority of workers who would
be quite ready to support a going concern which can offer
obvious protection in their working lives, are not so ready to
give time and money to establish an organization which
cannot hope to make much difference to pay and conditions
for some years. It was not until permanent wage-earning
began to be accepted by large numbers of work-people as
the customary way of making a livelihood that trade unionism really got a chance to develop at all, and it has still not
grown to any extent amongst those sections of the population who can expect that their present occupation is likely
to be temporary. The largest group of such workers, is, of
course, composed of women, whose paid employment was
usually an interlude between leaving school and starting on
their life-work of looking after a husband and children –
and although it is now customary for them to return in
middle life a large proportion are part-time workers and
unwilling to add to their burdens by the effort needed to
organize – and wherever there is an outstanding proportion
of women working in an industry, trade union organization is
inclined to be weak. This is not true of those industries from
which women were excluded until recently and where unionism is a well-established tradition; in such circumstances
women generally do what is expected of them, that is, they
loyally join the union when they enter the trade, pay their
due, and keep the rules. But it is unusual for them to take
the initiative and start an organization if one is not already
in being.

But the presence of large numbers of women workers
does not explain the weakness of organization in such an
industry as agriculture, in which men are by far more
numerous; and here the cause must be sought rather in the

dispersed character of the work. Men work in twos and threes on farms which are often miles from each other. There is no meeting place ready to hand, and to add a long walk to a tiring day's work is more than most ordinary people can bring themselves to. It is doubtful if trade unionism would ever have grown so strong had it not been that most work is done in factories where hundreds of men with similar interests are inevitably thrown together, over periods of time which are long enough for them to become a coherent group conscious of their common interests. Wherever this factor is missing, organization is weak, if it exists at all – this is true of retail distribution, of clerical work, of domestic service, and of many branches of road haulage as well as of agriculture.

Until recently the largest unions developed from those that were founded by highly skilled workers, and it is still much more difficult to organize those whose work needs neither specific training nor accumulated experience, because in such occupations there is no well-defined constituency from which the membership can be recruited. In many industries the amount of skilled work has declined and only a nucleus of skilled workers is employed with a much larger number of operatives; but where the change-over from skilled to less skilled work has gone on continuously over a century, the tradition of organization has become strongly entrenched and most workers join the union as a matter of course. In the newer industries – particularly the consumption industries – which began on mass production lines and in areas which had not previously been industrialized, the majority of workers were semi-skilled from the start and trade unionism was consequently weak.

But there are two outstanding features of contemporary trade unionism; one is the growth of the general unions which between them now account for over two million members and comprise some of the largest individual unions in existence. Although the name generally applied to them – general labour unions – seems to imply that they are com-

posed of unskilled labourers, this is by no means the case.
They do, indeed, include an exceptionally large proportion
of this category but they also act as a sort of umbrella
organization for many miscellaneous occupations – some
highly skilled – which would find it too difficult or too expensive to run a union for themselves.

The other remarkable change in the character of present-
day unions is the growth of the non-manual organization.
The National Association of Local Government Officers
(N.A.L.G.O.), the National Union of Teachers (N.U.T.),
the Civil Service Clerical Officers Association, the National
Union of Public Employees, the British Medical Association
(B.M.A.), are now amongst the giants, and though they do
not usually think of themselves as trade unions their work is,
in fact, primarily concerned with negotiating the pay and
conditions of their members. But non-manual unionism is
heavily concentrated in public employment, particularly
amongst the less professionally qualified, such as clerks.
Four-fifths of organized clerks are in some form of public
employment and only about one sixth of the million and a
half in industry and commerce belong to a union.

More disputes take place between workers and employers
on the subject of wage rates than on all other matters together, and this is not surprising, because the two sides look
at wages from quite different points of view. The worker
sees his wage as the main determinant of his standard of
living. He knows that his whole life, and that of his family,
is conditioned by the size of his pay packet, and he is naturally concerned to see that he gets enough to provide for the
needs of those dependent on him. But to the employer the
wage bill is one of the costs of producing his goods, and unless he can keep these costs as a whole below the price that
the public are willing to pay for his products, he will soon
be out of business. The worker, therefore, relates the wage
to what it will buy for him and his family, and the employer
relates it to what the worker produces in return for it. Unfortunately there is no reason why these two relationships

should be the same. A man's family doesn't require any less food for healthy existence even if he does not produce so large an output or if its value in the market decreases; yet an employer who based his workers' wages on their needs, rather than on the economic value of their work, would soon find himself in Queer Street. No trade union, however powerfully organized, can force employers to go on paying higher wages than their workers are worth to them; the employer always has the choice of refusing to employ, either by going out of business completely or by cutting down the scale of his work and employing a smaller number of men, or by finding new methods of producing the goods that require fewer workers. In fact, the power of the trade union to maintain the selling price of its members depends, like that of any other monopoly, on the elasticity of the demand for the product, and as we have seen in Chapter 2 this, in its turn, depends primarily on the extent to which it is possible for the purchaser to find substitutes that he is willing to accept. If a higher wage means that workers work harder or better than they did before, the increase, of course, pays for itself by the larger output it has brought into being. Or if the employer is induced to reorganize his methods and eliminate waste, in order to meet the extra cost, again there is no difficulty. And both these consequences may be expected to result, wherever the wages have been kept unduly low and have led to either malnutrition of the worker or slackness on the part of the management. But there is a limit to these developments; a point is reached at which higher wages, valuable as they may be to the improved standard of living of the worker, cease to have any marked effect on his efficiency as a worker, and at which all the slack of poor management has been taken up. In such circumstances an increase in wages leads to a reduced demand for that kind of worker, so that those that retain their employment get the higher rate of pay, but a smaller number of workers keep their jobs.

But this is not the only effect. Industrial techniques are continually changing as new ideas are tried out, and the higher the cost of producing by one method, the greater the inducement the employer has to experiment with alternatives. Let us take a very simple illustration. Suppose that the errand boys of a certain district agree to organize to push up their wages, so that delivery of the groceries by a boy on a bicycle becomes a more expensive item in a shop's outgoings; it may then become worth while for the shopkeeper to give up his three errand boys and bicycles and employ instead one man with a small motor van. This substitution of methods is continually taking place, and, in fact, the constant effort on the part of the workers to improve their rates of pay has been one of the most potent forces making for technical progress. Most people are as lazy in mind as they dare to be and go on in the same old rut if nothing happens to force them out of it. A good deal of inventive genius has been given its chance because of the need to economize on more expensive types of labour, and, often enough, the improvements are sufficient to compensate for the higher cost of labour and enable the employer to employ as many as before at a higher rate. But this is not always so; and the trade union negotiator is faced with the need to make up his mind whether it is better to push the rates up further and risk some of its members being forced out of work, or to agree to a lower wage and have a larger percentage in employment.

The introduction of unemployment insurance has had a marked influence in this respect. When unemployment meant starvation or the workhouse, the trade union secretary realized that it was impolitic to pursue a course of action which would face his unemployed members with the alternatives of remaining out of work or accepting jobs at blackleg rates of pay. And a prolonged depression in a trade inevitably showed itself in agreement to lower wages. But the trade union has a very strong hold on the loyalty of its members and there are few who would dream of undercutting, so long as the unemployment insurance benefit provides, at least, sufficient to let one get along. The effect of this was seen during the chronic depression of the inter-war years when although there were at times as many as 23 per cent of the insured population out of work, wage rates fell hardly at all and when, indeed, if we take into account the fall in the price of foods during this period, the contrary was the case – real wages rose quite considerably. Here we have an entirely new phenomenon, and one that has, as we shall see shortly, a very important influence on the occupational distribution of the population. As a consequence, on the one hand, of wage rates fixed by collective bargaining, and, on the other, of the provision of a 'cushion' of social security payments to break the fall in the standard of living of those who are not earning a livelihood by their own work, there has come to be a very great element of rigidity in wages. Once rates have risen, it is extraordinarily difficult to bring them down, however low the level of prosperity in the industry and whatever the state of employment.

During the late sixties and the seventies a new feature has developed in the bargaining situation. Certain key unions have become so powerful that they have been able to compel employers to raise rates of pay without either altering the type of employment or the size of the labour force. Hence we have had important technical developments which remain unused because of the threat – or fact – of crippling strikes. Even if an agreement is reached that the new methods should be admitted there is a refusal to allow any of the unnecessary workers to be declared redundant. This was true of the dispute in the docks over the introduction of 'containers' which allow great masses of cargo to be moved from warehouse to ship – or the other way round – instead of being manhandled by dock labourers in the traditional way.

To some extent the increased power of the unions derives from the close contact between them and the Labour Party, a contact which is strong enough to allow the unions to dictate policy on many matters that would not, in the past, have been considered a part of their normal function. Examples are the controversy over the details of the reorganization of the machinery for settling industrial disputes, or the entry of this country into the Common Market.

Another factor which has played a big part is the general ignorance of the public of what actually happens in wage negotiations in various occupations. This ignorance is not confined to the less educated members of the community but equally affects the thinking of the many thousands whose work does not bring them into close contact with the types of work in which unions generally operate. For example, when a dispute is threatened or actually takes place the figures of the wage rates being paid or offered are publicized by radio and T.V.; but the commentators rarely have more than a nodding acquaintance with the facts. One of the most important ways in which wrong information is given is by quoting the basic rate paid in the occupation : nowadays hardly anybody gets this basic rate – it is simply the amount from which the actual rates are calculated, whether the actual rate is bargained for at plant level or whether there are other factors to be taken into account. It is extremely rare, for instance, to find any occupation which does not receive a very considerable amount extra because of working during times of day which have come to be considered outside 'normal' working hours. This does not mean that the worker is doing overtime but that the normal number of working hours happens to include some portion which takes place either earlier or later than the 8 a.m. to 5 p.m. which is widely regarded as the working day. This must happen whenever there is any degree of shift work.

Another misconception arises from the fact that workers' pay is always given as 'take home' pay, i.e. the amount left after the statutory deduction for insurance contributions and income tax. This is always compared with the salaries of managers which, by contrast, are stated as the full amount contracted for, though the higher the salary the smaller the proportion that is actually received because of the progressive nature of income tax.

The enormous rate of inflation during the seventies, due in large part to the rapid increase in the price of oil, has brought still another factor into wages bargaining. The most powerful unions have not been content to demand very large increases to compensate for the higher cost of living but have asked for even more in anticipation of future rises in prices.

The effects of an increased cost of labour differ, naturally, in different industries; it depends partly on the proportion of the total cost that is accounted for by wages and partly on the extent to which increased costs of production can be shoved off on to other shoulders. One would expect a different reaction to increased wages in coal-mining, for example, where, according to Colin Clark in 1930, the wage bill represented 62·4 per cent of the price of coal, from a similar movement in wages in the food, drink, and tobacco trades where wages represented only 7·9 per cent of the total cost. During recent years the greater part of the burden of the higher wages paid to agricultural workers has fallen on the shoulders of the taxpayer, for it is only because of the heavy subsidy paid to farmers by the Chancellor of the Exchequer that these wages have been economically possible while food prices have been kept so low to the consumer. Wherever wages represent a fairly small proportion of cost or wherever the effect of increased labour charges can be concealed by subsidies or other means, the degree of inflexibility of wage rates is enhanced, but it is now an important characteristic of all wage rates, even where these particular factors are not present.

A special problem arises in connection with the industries nationalized since 1945. The Acts of Parliament setting up the public corporations which run these industries contained a clause laying on the Boards of Governors the statutory obligation to maintain their enonomic solvency, i.e. they must take care that, taking one year with another, receipts cover costs. If the trade unions representing the workers in the industry demand higher rates of pay or shorter hours of work, the cost of running the industry goes up and the

Board of Governors must either put up prices to the consumer or fail to be solvent. If prices go up, sales may go
down seriously (this is the great problem of the railways,
bound as they are to meet the competition of aircraft, buses,
and private transport). If they refuse to raise wages they
may risk a strike with serious political repercussions. There
have been circumstances in which the Government has
intervened to force a Board to increase wages against its own
judgement in order to avoid such political repercussions.

During the mid-seventies earnings so far outpaced the rise
in the cost of living that the increased costs of production
which firms had to meet, together with the recession in world
trade (and hence a loss in exports) led to a fear of unemployment which began to dominate the whole situation. For
this reason the Government decided to intervene and to lay
down that for the time being no wage settlement could add
more than a maximum of £6 weekly. At the time of writing
it is too soon to know whether this will be maintained but
already a difficulty is to be seen. The Government's decree
was that the £6 should be a basis for consideration whereas
many of the unions regard it as an entitlement.

Statutory Wage-Fixing Machinery

Trade unions now cover over ten million workers, but a
good deal of this development is of fairly recent growth.
When the Second World War broke out there were only six
million organized workers, and even this showed a remarkable recovery from the four and a half million of the depth
of the depression in 1932. What about those who are not in
trade unions? Who fixes their rates of pay? Until fairly
recently it would have been true to say, 'In most cases, nobody'. The employer was the top dog and the worker had to
take what he could get. But this has changed, and there has
grown up a system of Wages Councils set up by the State to
provide a similar machinery for settling wages to that which

highly organized workers and employers have evolved un-aided.

Wages Councils, though not under that name, have now a long history. They were first established as early as 1909, when four Trade Boards were set up in four of the worst-paid and most unorganized industries, as an experiment in coping with the problem of low-paid labour. At that time, when Government control of economic activities was in its infancy, the mere idea of regulating wage rates was looked upon as almost revolutionary, and it was only the impossi-bility of discovering any other way of dealing with the scan-dal of the 'sweated industries' that forced the State to decide, very reluctantly, to try this method. But the form of control then devised proved so workable that it has remained the pattern ever since. The scope and, to some extent the powers, of Wages Councils have changed, but the *form* has hardly altered throughout the whole history of wage regula-tion. The principle on which it is based is that of reproducing as nearly as possible the voluntary arrangement spon-taneously developed by organized industries. The differences are those which derive from the more formal definition and procedure which are inevitable in something which is estab-lished by law instead of by voluntary agreement.

Each Wages Council is composed of three groups of people all nominated by the Secretary for Employment – two groups, equal in number, chosen to represent em-ployers and workers of every section of the industry, and three independent persons, one of whom acts as Chairman. In this way every interested group can have its say in de-termining the rates of pay and, although the independent members have the casting vote should the need arise, it is much more usual for the rates to be reached by agreement, without any necessity for them to throw their weight on one side or the other. They are there to help guide those who, by definition, are inexperienced in joint negotiation and to prevent a complete deadlock, but the fewer occasions on which they make use of the casting vote, the more successful their work.

There is another and very important difference between the work of the Wages Councils and that of trade unions. The agreements made by trade unions and employers' associations have no legal force, though, as a matter of practice, it is rare for such an agreement to be broken; but those made by a Wages Council are enforceable by law and persons may be prosecuted for not complying with them. The reason for this difference is easy to understand. In industries with a long tradition of negotiation, everybody realizes the futility of making agreements unless both sides can rely upon them, and, at the same time, the members of the organization on both sides can act as their own inspectorate, reporting breaches of observance to their officials. Where this experience of negotiation is lacking, and few employers or workers are members of representative associations, some substitute for this informal method of making and maintaining agreements has to be instituted. But though the bodies set up under the Wages Councils Act and the Catering Wages Act are nominated by authority and their agreements are given legal sanction, with an inspectorate to enforce them, the basic principles of the settlements are exactly the same as in industries that can do without this legal scaffolding. In fact, what seems at first sight to be machinery for fixing wages by law turns out, on closer inspection, to be the establishment of statutory provision for collective bargaining.

A NATIONAL WAGES POLICY

The success of these methods of establishing legally enforceable wage rates in the unorganized industries is a significant witness to the strength of the conviction that wages are, and must be, a matter of agreement between those primarily concerned, and not something to be imposed by an external authority. In recent years this belief has been challenged by the demand that the Government should formulate and carry out a National Wages Policy and not leave something which has such important indirect effects on the national welfare to be settled by the 'higgling of the market'. In the immediate post-war period the strength of this demand stemmed from the difficulties that confronted the community in the effort to persuade men and women to go into the industries that were of prime importance to our economic well-being when the whole trend of wage-movements attracted them to occupations which were much less essential. Expansion of exports was the overriding necessity and this could not be achieved unless we were able to sell at competitive prices. But to attract workers into these industries involved competing, in pay and conditions, with occupations that were producing for a very prosperous home market, and a wage high enough to induce workers to come back into the export industries in sufficient numbers raised their costs of production so much that they found it hard to sell their products.

Those who wish for a National Wages Policy at the present time still have this need in mind but other factors than occupational distribution have come to play a larger part.

Until the turn of the year 1962-3 we experienced full employment for over twenty years and even since then the unemployment which has developed has mostly been confined to a few areas – particularly Scotland, and the North-East. Over the country as a whole the incidence of unemployment was generally slight until the summer of 1971 and even in the badly affected areas the rate of unemployment was small in comparison with the situation between the wars. There has, in fact, been a chronic shortage of labour, especially amongst skilled trades, and this has enabled the unions to push up the wages of their members continuously in a sort of leap-frogging way. Each year – and sometimes at even shorter intervals – there is a round of wage demands. The success of those first in the queue alters what others consider to be the traditional comparative relationship and they, for this amongst more obvious reasons, demand similar rises. By this time the earlier increases have come to be thought insufficient by those who gained them and further demands are put forward. The effect has been seen in constantly rising costs of production and a constant tendency to inflation. The benefit of each increase is short-lived, for its extension to everybody else leads to a rise in the cost of everything on which incomes are spent and, instead of being better off, each group feels it has been 'done' in some way it cannot understand. At the same time the higher costs of production make exports more difficult to sell and the whole community suffers.

It is for this reason that many people have come to believe that the traditional way of settling wages by joint negotiation is out of date and that the Government should take a hand for two reasons: (1) to ensure that increases in wages as a whole bear some relationship to increases in national productivity and (2) to ensure that earnings in different occupations maintain such a relationship to one another that the essential industries are able to draw the share of the available manpower resources that they need in the national interest. It is true that this runs counter to a right that has been fought for, and jealously guarded, for a century and a half – the right to establish contracts by free negotiations between the representatives of the parties concerned; but this in itself is not conclusive for, after all, traditional rights must sometimes give way to national necessity.

Let us take the second aim first. By what means can we assess the 'right' relative earnings of different occupations? A wage, or salary, is a price and like all prices it has two functions. It rewards past effort and indicates where future effort is wanted. If we want more of anything we offer a price high enough to persuade people to produce the larger amount and vice versa. But how, in practice, could the Government or anyone else assess the relative payments for different types of work which would attract and retain all the various grades of workers where they are wanted? The truth is that we still know very little about the drawing power of wages. Wages are, of course, as has been said, a price, and changes in price always influence the readiness of both buyers to buy and sellers to sell. But if you recall what has already been said about the many factors to be taken into account in calculating earnings in different walks of life, it is easy to see that a comparison of prices paid for various jobs is not as straightforward as it seems. And there is another thing that is even more important than the difficulty of making fair comparisons between money earnings – one that we are only just beginning to realize – and that is that wages play a much less dominant role than they used to in determining the relative attractiveness of different jobs. Nowadays, a whole host of other factors have also to be taken into account. Thousands of workers have come to give a very high priority indeed to adequate leisure in their scales of values, and the kind of work that can be fitted into the ordinary fairly short working day and which leaves free the evenings and weekends undoubtedly has a strong pull, even though its earnings may not be quite so high as those of an occupation which demands longer hours, or shifts that go on all round the clock. This is a fairly obvious factor and one whose importance, one might argue, could be monetarily assessed. But what about social prestige? Here is something that is playing an increasingly important part, but one which is extremely difficult to measure by money. One of the strongest trends of the present century has been the effort on the part of the wage-earning family to get its sons and daughters into non-manual occupations. Earlier in the century, economic as well as social factors supported this ambition, for jobs in offices and shops usually offered a greater degree of security and more opportunities for promotion than the majority of manual occupations. Even at that time these advantages were often illusory; a clerk, it was true, was not turned off as easily as a manual worker, but if he *did* lose his job he was often longer unemployed. But with the spread of free education on the one hand, and the routinization of clerical work on the other, there are now so many people capable of doing these jobs that the pay is often lower than that of the manual wage-earner and the chances of promotion are only slightly greater. Yet this has not deterred the wage-earner, to whom the white collar and black coat of the office worker represent a step upwards in the social scale; and the right to be called *Mr* Smith or *Miss* Jones seems well worth some small drop in earnings.

The same consideration, in the reverse direction, has affected recruitment into domestic service, which, from being the most important of all the paid occupations of women, has sunk to a very low place. Social prestige is not the whole story here, of course. It would be interesting to speculate how much of the fall in numbers has been due to the wish of young girls to work in larger groups in the factories, where they have a chance of making friends and of meeting their future husbands, and how far other matters have played a part. It is impossible to generalize about conditions of this type of employment, for the majority of women work in households employing only one or two persons which differ greatly from one another, but, on the whole, the standard of board and lodging and the amount of free time compare very favourably with those available in industrial work, and the pay, taking into account the value of food, lodging, etc., is decidedly higher than the average of women's industrial earnings. But there is no doubt that factory girls look down on the domestic employee as in a lower social grade, and, despite the higher earnings, the scarcity of recruits persists. It is now extremely rare for any other than a very wealthy household to employ a resident domestic servant, whose place has been taken by the part-time married woman worker who is non-resident.

There are many other factors which play a similarly incalculable part in the choice of jobs. Some people dislike the loneliness of country life and would take less money, if need be, to get work in the town, with its lights and shops and cinemas; others are ready to do the opposite for the pleasure of living in the fresh air or of having a big garden. Part of the pre-war exodus from the land was said to be due to the unwillingness of young women to marry agricultural labourers, because of the lack of decent housing accommodation, with running water and adequate plumbing; and probably the speeding up of the housing programme in rural areas has done as much as, if not more than, the rise in wages to attract an increased number of workers. Sometimes it is not the *actual* conditions of an industry that act as a deterrent to recruitment, but the reputation that has lasted from the past, on the principle of 'give a dog a bad name'.

When we attempt to analyse the many things that play a part in the choice of jobs -- often enough while the 'chooser' is quite unconscious that he is influenced by them – it becomes clear that we should be in great difficulty in measuring their money value in order to establish relative wage rates that would attract the 'right' number of people into each kind of work.

When the Chancellor of the Exchequer imposed his 'guiding light' principle in the summer of 1962 he was trying to achieve the first of the two aims rather than the second; i.e. to keep increases in wages in general in direct relationship with the rise in national productivity. But in setting $2\frac{1}{2}$ per cent as the limit by which any increase in rates of pay should be governed he did, in fact, create a new, and quite arbitrary, relationship of different occupations to one another. Those who had had the good fortune to have achieved new contracts before the date were in a better position whilst those who were in process of negotiation were left behind. The result was anger, a sense of injustice, and a serious effect on the recruitment policy of those who happened to be caught at the unlucky end. Even so, the 'guiding light' had very little effect on the new rates of those who were not in public employment (the only sphere in which the Government could enforce its views) and who could insist – by means of strikes if necessary – on their right to settle pay as they had always done in the past without any control by the State.

Since that time the problems associated with wages have become the centre of the most heated discussions, which have, indeed, engendered rather more heat than light. The changes that have taken place in the economy have undoubtedly made wage rates rather more flexible than they were earlier (see pages 216–17). The largest manufacturing firms are mostly 'capital-intensive', that is, the amount invested in capital equipment has grown very greatly and the numbers employed have decreased so that, if there is a demand for higher payment for these workers, it generally pays the firm to concede (even if it believes that there is little economic justification for the rise) because any interruption to the running of the expensive machinery would involve them in such heavy losses. Such rises immediately set off a further train of demands from other workers who do not see why they should not enjoy similar benefits and so the race continues with each group making strenuous efforts to overtake the others. That there must be some reorganization of the methods of collective bargaining has gradually come to be accepted by the majority of people; the question is what form it should take.

Britain, unlike most other European countries, has long been wedded to the principle of voluntaryism in industrial relations. Elsewhere, though the form taken varies from one country to another, there is a certain amount of legal regulation of collective bargaining. In Germany and Austria, for example, agreements are legally extended to cover unfederated firms and unorganized workers so that their competition should not undermine agreements entered into by those representing the organized on both sides : and there are similar arrangements in other countries. In America and Canada, where in the early part of this century trade union organization had been not only weak but faced with extremely hostile opposition (sometimes reinforced by violence from the employers) steps were taken to compel employers to recognize the rights of unions to negotiate, and these were followed by further action to ensure that the unions, whose agreements were thus legally protected, should act in a democratic way.

In this country the first step in the overhaul of collective bargaining was taken by the setting up in 1965 of the Royal Commission on Trade Unions and Employers Associations under the chairmanship of Lord Donovan, and their report – the Donovan Report – was published in 1968. This report pointed out that there have developed two quite separate sets of industrial agreements during this last quarter of a century : the first is the formal national agreement embodied by the official institutions (the national executive of the appropriate unions and the similar bodies acting for the employers) and settling national rates of pay and conditions of employment;the other is the informal one which is the system created by the actual behaviour of managers, shop stewards, and workers in the individual plants; and unfortunately the two systems are often very far apart. As a result the actual earnings of groups of workers often bear only the most tenuous relationship to the rates collectively agreed and this is one of the most difficult problems when a dispute occurs. The figures cited as the basic pay, and on the inadequacy of which the disputants base their claims to higher rates, are generally widely divergent from the earnings actually received; but these earnings may, and mostly do, vary from one firm to another as a result of these shop floor negotiations and there is, consequently, a chaotic pay structure in any one industry and an even more chaotic one in comparison between different occupations. So the workers of one firm come out on strike – generally an unofficial strike, for 95 per cent of strikes are in this category (that is, not called by the union itself) – in order to gain parity with similar workers in other firms and these lead to further demands by workers who think themselves of equal economic worth in their industries.

With the aim of getting more order into industrial relations the Report made two important recommendations: the first was that companies should be obliged to register their agreements with the Department of Employment, the second, that there should be established an independent Industrial Relations Commission with a full-time chairman and other members (some of whom should also be full-time and others part-time) whose job it would be, on a reference from the Secretary of State for Employment, to investigate problems arising from the registration of agreements.

It is only the second recommendation on which action has so far been taken, and the Commission on Industrial Relations began its work in March 1969. Since that date the question of whether agreements should be registered, if so, how, and with what legal or other sanction, has been the subject of the most heated controversy. The Labour Government published a White Paper called *In Place of Strife* which set forth its policy on the changes that were required in methods of collective bargaining and the implementation of agreements. This met with such antagonism from the Trade Union Movement that many of its proposals were omitted from the Bill which was introduced; but before any action could be taken the Government fell and the Conservative Government which took its place introduced its own Bill – the Industrial Relations Bill – to embody what it believed to be its mandate from the electorate with regard to the reform of industrial bargaining. The Bill, which became law in 1971, was extremely large and it is not possible to give the full details here; but the most important clauses must be noted.

(1) There should be a code of industrial relations practice, approved by Parliament, which, though not directly enforceable, would be taken into account in any proceedings brought before the National Industrial Relations Commission or any industrial tribunal.

(2) Every worker has the right to belong to the union of his choice but equally not to belong if he so wishes, and mem-

bership of any union should not be made a condition of employment. Thus it would be an unfair practice for anybody to threaten a strike or take any similar action to compel an employer to make such membership a condition of employment.

(3) Every written collective agreement should be presumed to be legally binding unless there is an express condition to the contrary.

(4) Employers would be compelled to make available to any registered union any information necessary to it to conduct its negotiations and there should be power to compel any firm employing 500 workers or more to disclose certain types of information annually.

(5) The rights proposed in the Bill, such as in (4), would be allowed only to unions which had registered with the Chief Registrar of Trade Unions and Employers Associations (whose appointment is a further part of the Bill), whose main responsibilities would be to ensure that the rules of trade unions and employers associations conform to certain standards and are observed.

(6) It would be an unfair practice for anybody other than a union or employers association, or an agent acting on their behalf, to induce workers to break a contract in furtherance of a trade dispute. (The point of this is that unofficial stoppages do, in fact, generally cause workers to break their contracts and this would be considered an unfair practice.)

(7) There should be set up a new National Industrial Relations Court consisting of presiding judges nominated by the Lord Chancellor and lay members with special knowledge of industrial relations nominated jointly by the Lord Chancellor and the Secretary of State of the Department of Employment.

The Bill was greeted by organized antagonism from trade unions who insisted that if it became law it would undermine the whole system of trade unionism. As evidence of their opposition the Trades Union Congress urged its constituent unions not to register but there were disagreements among the unions as to whether to take this advice or not.

The whole question has now taken on a new dimension as a result of rapid and unusually steep inflation (for the last year, 1975, the rate in the U.K. has been 25 per cent). This has been caused primarily by the great increase in the price of oil – the chief fuel on which industry depends – coupled with a general world recession in industry and commerce. Unemployment has become a serious problem all over the world and it is generally agreed that this is largely the result of inflation, though in this country people differ in their conclusions about how much of the high total of workless (considerably more than that of our chief competitors) is due to very high wages and how much to the general world situation.

As a consequence of this a great deal of rethinking has had to be done. The Labour Party and the T.U.C. have consistently refused to countenance any statutory control of wage bargaining; but with the worsening of the position they have in practice changed their minds. Hence the insistence, supported rather grudgingly by the T.U.C., that until inflation has been brought down to a manageable rate, no wage bargain would be countenanced unless the increase in the weekly rate was kept below a maximum of £6 a week. Even here there is a big difference of opinion – the Government thinking of the £6 as a maximum and the unions thinking of it as an absolute entitlement. It is too soon to know what the effect will be, but the Government has thrown out dark hints that, if the maximum is not strictly observed, it might be necessary to impose some degree of statutory control.

EQUAL PAY FOR EQUAL WORK

Before leaving the discussion of incomes from work, something must be said about the relationship of men's and women's wages, a subject which has been a matter of controversy for a long time and which has once again been much in the limelight since the publication (in 1947) of the Report of the Royal Commission on Equal Pay. Put briefly, here is the problem. Over the greater part (though not the whole) of paid employment, women are paid less than men for comparable work. Why is this so? Should it be altered? and, if so, how?

Note that I have said 'for comparable work' and not 'for the same work', for, except in certain professions (medicine and education, for example), it is unusual to find men and women doing identical work. They may be employed by the same firm, and even in the same room, but they are usually doing different processes. In addition, there are many types of employment which are almost exclusively male (such as the Stock Exchange, the Church of England, and many industrial processes) and others which are exclusively female (such as children's nursing). But even in these, skill for skill, a man draws more pay than a woman.

Popular explanations of this situation do not stand up to examination. Most people, if asked to account for women's lower pay, would offer these explanations: (1) women are more bother and expense to the employer. More factory legislation applies to them than men, and most employers feel it necessary to offer them a rather higher standard of welfare amenities; (2) women don't produce as much as men; and (3) (the most popular explanation of all) women don't need as much because they have only themselves to keep, whereas men must provide for their families. How far is popular opinion right in finding the explanation in a combination of these? Let us look at them one by one.

1. It is true that much legal regulation applies only to women and young persons, but this does not mean that women's conditions are always better than men's; as a matter of fact, organized male workers have managed to get a considerably higher standard of protection by trade union negotiations than the law enforces for women. Moreover, the experience of the last half-century has proved conclusively that expenditure on good conditions is more of a

capital investment than an out-of-pocket expense, and most good employers provide as good 'amenities' for their male workers as for their female.

2. The second statement is frankly silly, as are most broad generalizations of this kind. The amount of work done depends partly on the type of work you are considering, and partly on the individual. In heavy physical work, which demands great muscular power or prolonged physical endurance, most men are capable of a much greater amount of work than most women (though there are, of course, some exceptionally strong women and some men below the average in strength); but in work which needs a quick deft touch it is usually the other way round; and in a great many jobs there is no sex differentiation at all. A woman teacher looks after just as large a class as a man teacher, and undertakes just as many, if not more, extra duties; a woman clerk can write as many letters as a man in a given time; a woman shop assistant can cope just as well with merchandise and customer. But even if it were possible to draw such a distinction when men and women are doing identical work, it would certainly not be possible to do so where, as is most usual, the processes are quite different from one another; here there is no basis of comparison. Even less could this account for the lower rates of pay in occupations where women are exclusively employed, as compared with men's rates where only men are employed.

3. But it is, of course, the third statement to which the majority pin their faith – that women *need* less than men. There are here two questions involved : (a) is this true? Do women, in fact, need less than men? and (b) if it is true, is it the explanation of their lower rates of pay?

Nobody with knowledge of the facts would claim that men, as individuals, need more than women, as individuals, for both have similar expenses for food, clothing, recreation, and the upkeep of their homes (whether by a wife in the case of a man, or by a mother, sister, aunt or landlady in the case of a woman). Most women, perhaps, spend less on food but more on clothes; as a total of expenditure the differences are negligible, and cigarettes, cinema seats, and such things are the same price for a woman as for a man. The big difference is in the cost of dependants, for man is normally the breadwinner of the family and woman is not. But to say that man is normally the breadwinner is not the same as to say that every man is actually supporting a family; and, in fact, the statistics show that this is not so. According to the evidence collected for the Royal Commission on Equal Pay, only just half of the married men under 65 who were covered by the contributory pension scheme (the most comprehensive of all the social insurance schemes) had any children at all under the age of 16. If we take the entire adult male population, without consideration of marital status, we find that the average number of children under 16 is 0·6, so that the total number of children dependent on the incomes of adult men is really very much smaller than we imagine it to be when we think of the 'average' family. The truth of the matter is that we generally ignore the time element in family responsibilities. Most men are responsible for children at some time in their lives, but they do not remain in this position permanently. If we take three children as the average family (a rather generous estimate) and assume, as is quite likely, that they are born within a period of 6 or 7 years, the complete period of dependency of the family is confined within a span of about 21 years. The heaviest burden falls on a man's income when all his children are growing up but still at school, and it begins to lessen as the children go out into the world, until finally his earnings have to bear the upkeep of only himself and his wife. For half of the forty-five years in which he can expect to earn his full adult wage he is likely to have no dependent children at all to support.

With regard to dependants other than children the position is not so clear, for the obligation to help with parents and invalid relatives is by no means confined to men. Unfortunately, we have not sufficient evidence to know accurately *where* the burden chiefly falls. On the whole, the women workers of the family are expected to shoulder a great deal of the cost of parents and younger brothers and sisters when their married brothers have young children of their own to care for, but later the older men, whose children have grown up, take their share of the responsibility. As far as the evidence goes, it seems to point to the fact that this burden falls slightly more heavily on women than on men, but it certainly doesn't compare with the cost of maintaining children. Children are not only completely dependent (with the exception of the help given by family allowances) but they remain so over a long period. This is not true of adult dependants, particularly now that so much social provision is available. Old parents often have a small income or pension, younger brothers and sisters grow up, invalids recover, and so on. There is no doubt that the big distinction in the needs that have to be met out of the incomes of men and women arises from the cost of bringing up children.

What about the second question? If we agree that, despite wide individual differences, men as a sex have heavier responsibilities than women as a sex, can we accept this as the explanation of the differences in rates of pay? If so, how do we account for the fact that a doctor gets more than a navvy, though the first may be childless and the other have half a dozen children? Or that the navvy himself gets much more than twice as much now as he did before the war? Or that employers make no inquiries about the number of children of their workers when calculating the contents of the pay packet? The answer is that needs play only a very small part in determining wages. As we have already seen, wages are fixed on an occupational basis. A wage is a price, and, like every other price, it mirrors the relative scarcity of the supply. Motor mechanics get more than they did between the wars, not because they now have large families (in fact, the reverse is true) but because there is now a keen demand for increased supplies of cars and more competition from other industries for the skilled men that make them; their increased wage is the result of the increased demand for their work.

Wages are not, of course, as starkly economic as this assumes. The parties to a wage agreement are not economic abstractions but ordinary men and women, who have grown up in a particular community, and whose minds have been shaped by the accepted ideas of 'right' and 'reasonable' which are current in their community. Most of us take for granted all the things we are used to and anything which is of long standing is likely to be looked upon as 'natural'. It is in this way that needs and recognized standards of living influence rates of pay and slow down wage movements that would result from purely economic influences.

As far as women's rates of pay are concerned, both the conventional and the economic factors have worked in the same direction and reinforced one another. On the whole, women's labour is relatively less scarce than men's, and this leads to lower pay, and, at the same time, the whole social pattern confirms the idea that women's needs are less than men's and that, therefore, women's pay *should* be lower.

Why are women generally less scarce than men? Chiefly because of the influence of the expectation of marriage on their paid employment *before* they marry. Almost all girls have to earn a living whilst they are single and until recently comparatively few used to after marriage (before the Second World War, only one in nine); and although the situation has changed, the attitudes of mind developed by the earlier long-standing tradition tend to remain. Nowadays the pattern of women's lives is very different from what it used to be : girls marry young – a third are wives before they reach their twenty-first birthday – and families are small so that most women have finished child-bearing and the care of very young children before they are forty. In consequence there are many more married women at work than there used to be; in fact, probably about a third of married women take some form of paid employment after an interval in the home looking after their babies. But despite the change, employment for women is not the same as for men. Few girls of 15 or 16 bother to look ahead to the time when they will be 35 or 40, so they do not find it worth while to train for any lengthy period. This keeps them out of all the skilled trades except those which are so closely related to the domestic arts that proficiency in them can be seen to have direct value in married life. How far this affects girls can be seen from the fact that, whilst 40 per cent of boys enter apprenticeship, only 5–6 per cent of girls do so and most of these are in hairdressing. Nowadays this does not exclude them from as large a field as it used to, for the proportion of highly skilled manual jobs is less than it was fifty years ago. But there is a large indeterminate area of minor managerial work which is the corollary of large-scale production with its thousands of semi-skilled operatives to be supervised and directed, and this has largely taken the place of the work requiring technical skill. There is rarely any prescribed preparation for such types of work, which demand certain developed personal qualities rather than any manipulative skill, and though women possess these qualities as well as men, they are not often employed in them. Employers don't want to promote workers who are likely to leave just as they are beginning to be really useful, and, to be fair, the majority of women have not shown themselves anxious to take on responsibilities in a field that they hope to be quitting for ever.

Women with high educational attainments find it difficult to get a foot on the managerial ladder in industry or commerce. It is not often that a male university graduate feels he must take a secretarial training if he wants to be considered for any appointment in industry other than those requiring specific technological qualifications, but most women graduates would have little chance of being admitted without some such additional bait to offer. Little blame attaches to employers for this situation. Every firm has its own individual characteristics and it is only after some years of experience that a person, however gifted, comes to understand them so intimately that he can undertake serious responsibility in management. The employer is always afraid – and with justice – that a woman will leave him because of her domestic responsibilities just at the moment when she has become so interwoven into the fabric of the firm that her loss causes a major upheaval. Though a large proportion of women return to paid employment when their children are of school age, they often wish to take part-time work so as to be able to continue with their home obligations, and this is much more difficult to provide in any other than routine work. Consequently, highly qualified married women are generally compelled to accept work far below their capacity when they return to employment after a break for child-bearing.

But even if we leave out of account the skilled and responsible jobs, the area of employment is still restricted for women. There are, of course, some kinds of work which need greater physical strength than most women possess, but mechanization is rapidly reducing the number of these. (For example, a woman cannot move heavy weights, but she can guide an electric trolley or work a lift as well as a man.) But when neither special strength nor special skill is involved, as is the case with the greater part of modern mass production methods, the line of demarcation between men's and women's jobs is much more difficult to explain. Here we have to admit that the greatest force is habit or convention. Many jobs which used to need skill no longer do so, but we go on thinking of them as 'men's' work because we are used to seeing men in them, and it is only when necessity forces us to try women in them (as during the two wars) that we are compelled to realize that there was no reason why we should not have employed women in them for years past. These conventional boundaries change very slowly as a rule. Sometimes the barriers keeping women out of a particular field have given way before a determined frontal attack, as was the case in the medical profession (this has still not been accomplished in the Church of England), but, more often, the change has been brought about by circumstances. The acute shortage of manpower during the two wars accelerated the process, and as the shortage has continued women have not been ousted from all the new jobs they undertook; but the strength of convention can be illustrated by the efforts made by the London Passenger Transport Board to get rid of women bus conductors soon after the Second World War, despite the general goodwill they had earned for efficiency, good temper, courage, and resourcefulness during the very difficult years of the blitz, and they were only compelled to reverse their policy because the acute shortage of all kinds of labour made it impossible to get sufficient recruits to man their buses without employing women.

It is, then, the restriction of the scope of employment which accounts more than anything else for the lower payment of women, and which, by continuing for so many generations, has fixed in people's minds the idea that women 'naturally' get, and should get, less than men. The great rise in the wages of domestic servants during the last thirty years or so is not due to a belated recognition of the dignity and importance of the domestic arts, but to the fact that the number of alternative employments open to young women has expanded so widely that the flood of potential servants has dwindled to a mere trickle; the same is true of the rise in the salaries of nurses and teachers, on account of the opening of other occupations for the middle-class girl.

It is significant in this respect to note the great difference in the salaries paid to secretaries and shop assistants in such towns as Bournemouth and Torquay compared with those paid for similar work in London or other big industrial and commercial centres. There are large numbers of middle-class families whose daughters wish to live in these pleasant residential areas but must still earn a living until they marry. The competition of a comparatively numerous group all seeking the same kind of job keeps their pay far below that ruling in the big cities.

The long period during which women workers could be

had for the asking has accustomed the world to look upon them as cheap labour. This is true not only of employers but of the women themselves, and of the men against whom they compete; and it is not surprising that it should be so, for it fits so completely into the social pattern of a world in which men occupy all the most important positions and enjoy the greater authority and prestige. The demand for equal pay is not, and never has been, voiced by women workers as a whole; it comes from the small class of middle-class women in higher and professional jobs, whose work is more often directly comparable with that of men, who are keenly aware of the individual capacity they bring into it, and who fiercely and justifiably resent the implications of women's general inferiority which is symbolized by sex differentiation in rates of pay.

Can this inequality be abolished? To answer this question we must distinguish between two fields of employment – the one in which the Government or a local authority is the employing body, and the one in which the ordinary business is the employer. In industry and commerce, wages, as we have seen, are determined by collective agreement between representatives of both sides, and equality cannot be imposed by an external authority, unless we are prepared to give up altogether this method of agreeing rates. As a matter of fact, most male trade unionists have now learned that, for their own protection against the competition of cheap labour, it is wise to insist that women employed on the same jobs as men should get the same rates; but this apparent equality is often illusory, for the area of overlap in men's and women's jobs is not very great in the industrial world, and women are usually given the work which carries the lower rates. It is hard to know how such an evasion of the spirit of an agreement to provide equality can be prevented until women are more organized and also until industrial women workers feel very much more concerned about equality of remuneration and of opportunity than the majority of them do at present.

Far and away the most effective means of raising women's pay would be to remove the conventional barriers to the scope of their employment. The trouble here is that, in the past, new openings have been established because of the eagerness of employers to use a supply of cheap labour, and, if there was general insistence that women should always receive the same pay as men, there is little doubt that fewer employers would be persuaded to overcome their traditional prejudices and engage women in jobs where they are un-familiar. This is a serious dilemma. On the one hand sex differentiation in pay almost certainly increases the number of occupations open to women and thus sends up the wages of women workers as a whole, but it is unjust to the individual woman who does the same work as a man for less pay; on the other hand, equal pay probably bolsters up employers' conventional reluctance to try women in new jobs and per-petuates the general restriction on the scope of their employment. The result is that those who *are* employed are more justly treated, but fewer are employed, and the probable effect may be to lower wages of women in exclu-sively women's jobs by increasing the number competing for employment in them.

In the other field of employment where the Government or other public body is the employer, equal rates of pay have now been established as an act of policy; for this is one of the occasions on which people have been more deeply con-cerned with the moral issues than with the economic factors concerned. The injustice of paying one person less than the other, when both are doing identical jobs, was so obvious that it was deeply resented. The demand for equal pay on the part of professional women, of which this change in policy was the outcome, was not primarily motivated by economic considerations; the fundamental reason for the claim was the resentment of the stigma of sex inferiority which the different rates implied. The insistence on equal pay was principally a demand for equal citizenship.

In 1970 an Act was passed to make it illegal to maintain

discrimination, as regards terms and conditions of employment, between men and women. This means that men and
women employed on the same work or, if not on identical
tasks, on work which can be regarded as being comparable
in demand, skill, decision, and effort, must receive the same
pay. It is obvious that the value of this Act depends on the
possibility of determining whether a particular job can, or
cannot, be shown to be of equal skill, effort, demand, etc.,
as that of a job done only by men and the Act provides for
an appeal to an industrial tribunal for this purpose. As it
does not come into force until 1978 it is too early for any
applications to the tribunal to have been made and we must
wait for some time to see how effective this Act is.

A further step has been taken by the passing of the Sex
Discrimination Act, which tries to open more occupations to
women and give them more opportunities for training. By
this Act it becomes illegal to specify the sex of applicants for
jobs except in a few defined areas, e.g. coalface workers in
mines. How far this will be effective is too soon to say but
several women's organizations are already urging women to
overcome their traditional diffidence in applying for jobs
that have long been considered primarily male preserves.
How soon are attitudes likely to change? Who can tell? For
example, there is no reason why a midwife should not be
male (despite the use of 'wife' in the term) but the majority
of women are accustomed to women in this capacity. Yet,
after all, many gynaecologists are men, and women are quite
used to their help.

I have mentioned the possibility of a man taking what has
been thought of as a woman's job to make it clear that the
Sex Discrimination Act works both ways. In fact, it happens
that one of the earliest cases brought up under the Act was
that of a man who complained that he had been unjustly
made redundant because he was the only man working with
a large number of women. He argued that he had been
selected for redundancy because he was paid considerably
more than the women and the firm feared that to retain him

would probably make them claim the same pay as he had been receiving under the Equal Pay Act. His claim was accepted and the firm was compelled to pay him adequate compensation.

One of the most difficult areas in which to change the relation of the sexes is the one which depends on promotion. It is rare to find those in control (who are mostly men) to be as ready to give a woman, however able she has shown herself to be, the chance to climb the ladder to higher posts, whether in a specialist field or in the more general one of management.

To help administer the Act the Government has set up an Equal Opportunities Commission to which anybody who feels she has been unfairly treated can apply; but it is still too soon to know how this will affect the situation.

2. INCOMES FROM PROPERTY

The second source of income is from the use of property – land, houses, capital, or anything else – and as it is obvious that the amount of income we get in this way depends upon the amount of property we possess we must see who are the principal owners. Most of us have some property (perhaps through buying Savings Certificates or by putting something into the bank) and with the higher wages that have been enjoyed since the war, there has been a great increase in ownership. Thousands of people have been able to buy their houses or are in the process of doing so and millions own a wide variety of valuable house equipment. And the practice of investing in industry by the purchase of joint stock securities has spread to sections of the community to whom it was quite unknown twenty years ago. But whilst ownership is very widely distributed it is also very unequally distributed. Our knowledge of the distribution of wealth is less detailed than that of income because wealth, as such, is not taxed at present and so the administration of the tax system does not give us the same amount of information as we get from taxes on income. The income derived from property is taxed, of course, and wealth itself is subject to tax when it is transferred from one owner to another, as in the case of estate duty and of capital gains. If a 'wealth tax' comes into force we shall similarly acquire information from this source.

The latest estimate has been calculated by the Inland Revenue and relates to 1973 :

Value of property	Number of persons (in thousands)
Up to £1,000	3,599
£1,000–£5,000	7,083
£5,000–£10,000	4,082
£10,000–£15,000	2,229
£15,000–£50,000	2,037
£50,000–£100,000	211
£100,000–£200,000 and over	110

As can be seen from this table the 81 per cent of the total owning any property have each too small an amount to make any appreciable difference to their annual incomes. The main difference consists in living rent-free, for by far the largest part is made up of houses and household goods. The remainder is in Building Society deposits, National Savings and life policies for which people are prepared to save, not because they hope to get an annual income from them but to have the comfortable feeling that they have a little nest-egg to draw on in case of emergency. It is only when we get to the higher ranges that addition to income becomes really important : less than 6 per cent of owners are in this category although between them they own the greatest amount of securities, whether in Government or company shares.

If we examine the ways in which people acquire property we find that this inequality accentuates rather than modifies the inequalities in incomes obtained from work. For the two principal ways of getting property are (1) by saving and (2) by gift, mainly, of course, by inheritance. The richer we are, the bigger the margin from which we can save and the more likely we are to build up our capital investments; so that, on the whole, it is the people who earn big incomes who also own property and, in turn, it is those with property who can afford the long education and have the social advantages which allow their children to enter well-paid occupations. Similarly, the effect of inheritance is to add wealth to wealth. People do sometimes divide their property at death amongst a number of poor relatives or servants, but this is sufficiently unusual for a legacy of a couple of hundred a year to an employee to be given quite a prominent place in the newspapers as 'news'. Most leave their property to their own kin, who are likely to be already in the better-off groups.

3. INCOMES FROM 'CIVIC RIGHTS'

Fifty years ago the individual member of the community was in a very much more precarious position than he is now. He was expected to be able to provide for himself and his family in all the vicissitudes of life, and only the grudging hand of the Poor Law or of private charity was held out to him if he slipped from economic independence. But during the last half-century we have built up a remarkable system of social services, the aim of which is to guarantee to every person a basic standard of living sufficient to prevent actual want. By means of national insurance, supplementary benefits, family allowances, and retirement pensions, every individual is assured a definite money income from collective funds if he is unable to provide for himself by his own work. The method of collecting the funds for these purposes varies from one to another, and not all of the money that is paid out comes from the national revenue. In the case of health and unemployment insurance benefits, for example, the greater part of the money comes from the compulsory contribution made by the potential beneficiaries and their employers, but even here a considerable proportion of the total is contributed by the National Exchequer. In the case of supplementary benefits, family allowances and non-contributory old-age pensions, the whole of the expense is borne by the State.

A great deal of our social income is, however, concealed because we get it in kind, instead of as a direct money payment. This is the case with the publicly provided education system, the National Health Service, the provision for Public Health, the libraries and baths and wash-houses maintained by local authorities, all of which represent services or goods for which we should have to pay out of our individual incomes, if they were not provided for us in this way.

Then other benefits are those which we derive from the subsidies to agriculture (see pages 180–81) which enable us to buy many of the staple foods at prices below their costs of production.

In 1968–9 the total expenditure on all the social services (whether direct money payments or the provision of services in kind) came to £8,708 million in addition to the £386 million of agricultural subsidies. Of this huge total, retirement pensions accounted for £1,410 million, the National Health Service £1,879 million, and education for £2,182 million.

How do we all share in the 'civic rights'? It is difficult to give a precise answer. In some types of service we can be fairly certain because a means test is attached to the receipt of benefit. This is so with supplementary benefits of all kinds and with the extra benefits beyond the minima that are provided for those in need. Until the National Insurance Act came into force in 1948 and brought us all into one comprehensive scheme, a great many sections of society had no claim at all on these funds, because they were designed only for manual wage-earners and non-manual workers with comparable incomes; and although we are now all included in these schemes, it is still true that the incidence of, for example, unemployment is so slight amongst the professional classes or the high business executives that it is unlikely that many of them would ever be in the position to claim benefit under them. By and large, therefore, these 'civic rights' incomes accrue to those in the lower income groups rather than to those in higher and to this extent offset inequalities in incomes from work and property ownership.

As far as the agricultural subsidies are concerned we can be fairly sure that the benefits are widely spread, for the foods chosen are those in general consumption; but that is not equally true of other items. Who gets most benefit from housing subsidies? It depends on the luck you have in becoming a tenant of a local housing authority and the policy this authority follows. Some, for example, charge rents that are far below the economic value of the property and the fortunate tenants are, in fact, receiving an addition to their income at the expense of the taxpayer and the ratepayer, including those less well off than themselves. Other authorities have developed differential rent systems based on the income of the tenant and the number of his dependants. Most authorities give preference in the selection of their tenants to those who have a number of young children but they do not usually turn the tenant out of the house when the children are grown up and leave home, so the tenant continues to enjoy subsidized housing accommodation when his income would be adequate to pay the full rent. When we come to consider the beneficiaries of the publicly provided services, such as health and education, the calculation is even more complicated because the individual has a good deal of choice in the matter. There are some who prefer to pay for the greater convenience attached to being a private patient of a doctor or a hospital, though they could have medical attention free of charge. Probably the majority of people take advantage of the National Health Service at some times and for some needs, and the amount of benefit they derive from it varies from one time to another. It is likely to be greatest when the children are young, irrespective of income; but it is impossible to do more than guess at the amount of benefit received.

We are all allowed to send our children to the publicly provided schools but many of the middle and higher income classes do not avail themselves of the right. They prefer to pay to send their boys and girls to fee-paying schools either because they believe they will get a better education in this way or because they hope it will help their young people when they later seek employment. In this respect it is the lower income groups that receive most benefit from the expenditure on schools provided by State funds. But on the other hand, though grammar schools are free and those who are admitted to universities receive public funds to pay for fees and maintenance, the proportion of children from middle-class homes found in both these grades of educational institution far out weighs those coming from less well-off working-class families, and consequently, this particular addition to income from 'civic rights' increases the middle incomes rather than the smaller ones.

Despite this, however, there is a rapidly growing proportion of pupils drawn from lower income groups both in the grammar schools and the universities and this tends to decrease inequality both directly and indirectly. The direct effect is obvious. Indirectly it influences the amount an individual receives as payment for work. As we have seen the differences are due primarily to differences in the relative scarcity of persons doing work which requires special qualifications, and as long as parents had to meet the full cost of educating or training their children, it was impossible for the great mass of the population to offer themselves for the better paid jobs, however valuable their inherent capacities might have been. Every extension in the educational facilities (and also in the health services that enable children to grow strong and healthy enough to take advantage of them) widens the field from which recruitment to the more highly paid types of work can be drawn. In so doing it affects the relative scarcities from both ends; it increases the number able to offer themselves for the highly qualified jobs and it reduces the number of those who, without these facilities, would have been forced to try to squeeze into semi-skilled and unskilled occupations.

TAXES AND INCOMES

The money spent on the provision of these 'civic rights' is only part of the expenditure incurred by the Government. In addition there is the cost of defence (now a particularly heavy one), the maintenance of law and order, the building and upkeep of communications, such as roads and bridges, the upkeep of the Government itself, both at home and abroad, the interest on the national debt, and so on. As a result of the war, as well as on account of the developments in the social services, Government expenditure has increased enormously, from £920 million before the war to over £36,047 million in 1975–6, a sum which represents nearly 40 per cent of the total national income. This gigantic sum has to be collected by taxation, and we must now turn our attention to the methods employed for getting it out of our pockets and into the coffers of the Government, so that we may estimate the effects of these taxes on the relative amounts of income that we retain for our personal use.

The kind of taxes that a country decides to impose depends very greatly on what it is trying to achieve, in addition to the collection of a certain amount of revenue. Throughout the present century there has been developing in this country a very strong belief that a nearer approach to equality is a desirable objective of social policy, and, as one consequence of this, our taxation system has become steeply 'progressive', i.e. larger incomes are not merely taxed a larger amount, but at a higher rate of taxation than the smaller ones. Egalitarianism is not the only reason for this trend. The very large totals that modern Governments have spent could not have been collected in any other way than by progressive taxation, but the 'steepness' has increased because people dislike wide differences in citizens' incomes. This aim also had much influence over the *method* of taxation, because it is not possible in all types of tax to differentiate the rates according to the income possessed by the taxpayer. From this point of view we can draw a broad distinction between direct and indirect taxes. Direct taxes – income tax, surtax, death duties – are those in which there is, so to speak, no intermediary between the tax collector and the taxpayer; indirect taxes – such as tobacco duty, the tax on alcohol, and so on – are paid by the taxpayer as, and when, he buys certain goods or services.

Direct taxes can be graded carefully, not only according to the size of the income as a whole, but according to the use made of it, so as to encourage the kinds of expenditure which are thought socially desirable. In the British income tax system, for example, the proportion of the income which is 'taxable' (i.e. on which the tax is actually levied) takes account of the number of dependent children to be maintained (and whether they are receiving full-time education beyond the statutory school-leaving age), of adult relatives who are dependent on the taxpayer, of the amount spent on life insurance, etc. (The allowance given in respect of earned income, it might be as well to note in passing, is not on quite the same basis. It is not due to the belief that it is more moral or praiseworthy to earn than to live on the income derived from one's property, for, after all, a good deal of such property may have been accumulated by saving out of one's earnings, but to the belief that an earned income is more precarious. If the earner is ill or dies, it disappears, and he must, therefore, if he is to act prudently, put aside part of his earnings for future eventualities; whereas the property income continues irrespective of the life or death of the owner.)

This grading is not possible with indirect taxation. The barmaid in the local or the tobacconist in his shop cannot inquire into the client's income and the number of children he has to support before deciding how much of the tax to add to the price of the beer or the packet of cigarettes. A flat rate must be imposed on all buyers, rich and poor alike. The burden of such taxes on small incomes is increased because of the absolute necessity to choose, for indirect taxation, the types of goods and services for which the demand is highly inelastic and, as we have seen in Chapter 2, this means that they form so integral a part of the customary pattern of expenditure that they are considered to be necessities. If this were not so, the tax, which to the consumer is exactly the same as a rise in price, would have the effect of reducing the quantities bought so appreciably that the Chancellor of the Exchequer would not get his revenue; whilst the unfortunate trade would be ruined by its reduced markets. (Indeed, one of the dilemmas with regard to the alleged heavy incidence of lung cancer among cigarette smokers has been the difficulty of reconciling the national concern for the health of the community with the problem of ruining a large and prosperous industry and cutting down the enormous amount of revenue raised by the tobacco tax.) In the last thirty or forty years we have tried to get round the problems of the burden of indirect taxation on smaller incomes by putting the main burden of indirect taxes on what might be called 'conventional luxuries', i.e. the types of expenditure which most people stubbornly try to maintain, despite rising prices, but in which a reduction of consumption on the part of those who find they can no longer afford them would not have any serious effects on welfare. In 1969–70 for example, over £2,000 million were collected from taxes on drink and tobacco alone, £1,302 millions from taxes on oil and a further £1,110 million from purchase taxes. (The last named is a little different from most indirect taxes. It was originally imposed in the effort to discourage us from buying goods that were inevitably in short supply because of the importance of cutting down imports until we had increased our exports. It proved so valuable as a revenue collector that no Chancellor of the Exchequer has been willing to give it up and it is now used primarily as a method of encouraging and discouraging productive activity in different fields of employment.) But whatever form they take, it has to be faced that indirect taxes are regressive, i.e. they bear much more hardly on the smaller incomes than on the larger. Most rich people spend more on drink and tobacco, of course, than do those with lower incomes, but they spend a very much smaller *proportion* of their incomes on these taxed commodities.

Another criticism that one might bring against these taxes is on the score of injustice. The demand for beer and tobacco is very widespread and, where it exists, it is very inelastic; but it is by no means universal. There are hundreds of thousands of people in the community who never smoke, and never drink, and such people evade, quite legally, a great deal of the tax burden borne by their fellow citizens. It is very difficult, if not impossible, to justify this discrimination except on the grounds of expediency.

In this case, why don't we cut out indirect taxation altogether and get all we need by the direct method? There are many who have argued that this would be the right policy to pursue, but we have to admit there are many obstacles to be overcome. The principal one is, perhaps, psychological. A direct tax is a constant 'nagger', whilst an indirect one tends to be overlooked, once we have got used to it. Few of us could say offhand how much of the price of a packet of cigarettes is represented by the tobacco tax, but we can't help but be aware of the amount taken from the pay packet each week or month for P.A.Y.E. income tax. If we are keen drinkers or smokers and it costs more to indulge our taste, we are anxious to earn more to make this possible; but if we are acutely conscious of the amount of our earnings that is taken for income tax we begin to wonder if it is worth while to do the extra shift or improve our speed when so little of the extra earnings actually reaches our pockets. It is generally accepted that it is right that exceptional effort should have exceptional reward – overtime rates, for example, are higher than rates for the normal working day; and businessmen expect to make higher rates of profit to compensate them for work that is particularly venturesome, or that requires special qualities or initiative. The trouble with a heavy income tax, particularly when it is steeply progressive, is that the higher the rate of pay, the higher the *rate* of taxation, so that what remains as payment for the extra effort may be less instead of more. This is one of the occasions when the cussedness of human nature makes it specially hard to reconcile a course of action of which we approve on social grounds with the way we behave as ordinary, rather selfish human beings.

A word must be said about the death duties, which have, at one time and another, aroused so many and such conflicting emotions. There are still many people who insist that any tax on capital must be unsound because it is on a par with 'killing the goose that lays the golden eggs'. As far as the relevance of this to the death duties is concerned it is based on a complete misconception of the nature of the capital. There is not, of course, anything like the hard and fast line of demarcation between capital and income that this belief assumes. A high income tax might just as well be thought of as a tax on capital, for it reduces the margin out of which savings could be accumulated; a death duty simply waits until the capital has been formed out of the savings and then taxes it. It is a question of timing, that is all; though the timing may be an important factor in the assessment of its effect.

On the other hand, there are many who believe that all inheritance is unjust, since the beneficiary reaps where he has not sown; and it is a fact that inequality has been perpetuated more by freedom of bequest than by any other one factor. The problem here resolves itself into two questions. (1) Is the private accumulation of capital necessary and desirable in our kind of economy? (2) If it is, would a very stiff set of death duties make people unwilling to save the necessary amounts? The answer to the first question depends on the extent to which industry and trade continue to be financed by private investors. There is no question that capital is essential and that it cannot be produced without saving; but the real question to be answered is: 'Who, in fact, *does* the saving?' Fifty years ago – even less – the question would have been hardly worth asking, for there was so little alternative to the private accumulations of capital, but times have changed, and this is no longer so. Nowadays a large part of the capital needed for industrial development is provided by the joint stock companies which, as a matter of sound financial policy, customarily build up their capital reserves instead of distributing the whole of the profits that have been made to their shareholders. The same is true of the productive activities of the local authorities, and, with the extension of the area of production under public ownership, there is no doubt that a similar policy is likely to be pursued by the public corporations.

How far are 'collective' sources of capital likely to be adequate to provide the amounts required? In a survey made a few years before the war, Mr Colin Clark stated the opinion that large private incomes had ceased to count as a source of saving, though, as he hastened to add, opinions might differ as to whether this was due to the level of taxation, low investment rates, or lack of investment opportunities. For it must be remembered that this survey was made at a rather exceptional time, when there had been a prolonged depression and there was no great desire to experiment with new ventures. Once a business is established and making substantial profits it can, perhaps, rely on its own resources for its further expansion; but until that time it must, like any new development, depend on the willingness of private investors to save their capital and to venture it in these new fields.

This brings us to the second question. 'Would very stiff death duties so far reduce the willingness to save that the needed capital would not be forthcoming?' The answer to this question cannot be given categorically, for it depends on the reasons for saving at all. Do we save primarily for the sake of leaving property to our children, and would we, then, cease making this sacrifice if our children were to lose, by heavy taxation, a great part of what we had left them? Many people believe this to be the case, but human motives are so complex that we cannot give a straight 'yes' or 'no' to such questions. Of course, most parents are fond of their children and there is a strong convention in favour of providing for them by legacies, but it does not seem, as far as we have evidence, that this desire is invariably the reason for hard work and accumulation. In a detailed investigation made in the twenties, Mr Josiah Wedgwood found that 33 per cent of those leaving big fortunes (over £100,000) during the preceding decade had had no surviving children and that 23 per cent were not even married; it is clear that these could not have been moved by family affection. Many men save because they are more interested in making a fortune, and in the power and prestige it confers, than in the more ordinary enjoyment of consumable luxuries; or perhaps they are anxious to retire early and have more time for their hobbies. Of course, family affection plays its part, and a big part, too. There are few parents who are not anxious to give their children a good start in life and who are not ready to make real sacrifices by putting money aside for the purpose. But most children have started out on their adult life long before their parents die, so that if this was the principal motive for saving, there would be no need to worry about the effect of taxes that are not imposed until the parent's death.

Apart from this, the desire for security is probably the biggest factor in encouraging us to save part of our incomes. Most of us like the idea that we have something put by for eventualities; some of us can go even further and hope to collect enough to enable us to retire and live comfortably, or to buy the little cottage in the country on which we've kept an eye. But, although these 'security savings' as a total form one of the big sources of capital accumulation, the amount saved by each individual on the average is comparatively small, and consequently the amount of death duty payable on it by his heirs is very nearly negligible. That the desire for security on the part of the saver plays at least as important a part in his motives as the wish to provide for his children is shown by the significant fact that, although death duties can always be evaded by handing over one's property a sufficiently long time before death, not every wealthy person avails himself of this right but most prefer that their children should inherit less in the future than that they should divest themselves of the powers and the privileges of wealth during their own life. Perhaps this is due to the fact that we all study *King Lear* during our schooldays.

There are, however, an increasing number of rich people who do take advantage of this legal opportunity to evade death duties and in recent years a great many wealthy men have handed over at least part of their capital to their families long enough ahead to enable them to enjoy it free of tax.

We have to agree, therefore, that there are many reasons for accumulation of capital and that heavy death duties would reduce only that part of the savings that are the result of the wish to provide for one's family after one's death; and even then only the savings that are large enough to be seriously affected, for there is always an exemption limit for modest estates. But there is still another point to consider. A death duty cannot, any more than any other tax, rightly be judged by itself. If the Government has to raise a certain amount of revenue and a death duty is thought to be a disadvantageous method, it must find some other alternative, and, presumably, a higher income tax would be the only choice. So the question resolves itself into 'Which is likely to have the more serious effect on savings – on the one hand, a heavy death duty levied when the savings are bequeathed at death or, on the other, a reduction or complete abolition of death duty but a proportionately heavier income tax?' Who knows? It is largely a matter of temperament. Some people would rather meet liabilities year by year and leave unencumbered property to their children; others would prefer to put off the evil day, enjoy the fruits of their industry now and leave less to their families in the future. On the whole, human nature being what it is, it seems likely that taxes that have to be paid in the future are easier to bear, and have a less discouraging influence on effort and saving in the present, than taxes which are levied each year with nagging persistence.

STRIKING THE BALANCE

What does all this add up to? How far do taxes modify the distribution of income? If we take income tax and surtax alone we have very accurate knowledge from the tables published each year in the White Paper on National Income and Expenditure. From the tables published we get the following comparison of the incidence of these taxes in 1938–9 and in 1967–8.

Distribution of personal income:

Total of income before tax	No. of incomes 1938–9	No. of incomes 1967–8
£125–£149	2,483,000	—
£150–£249	4,600,000	—
£250–£499	1,890,000	3,100,000
£500–£999	539,000	7,800,000
£1,000–£1,999	182,700	9,316,000
£2,000–£4,999	79,400	1,395,000
£5,000–£9,999	18,700	152,000
£10,000 or over	7,700	40,000

The amount paid in direct taxation, particularly in middle and smaller incomes, varies very greatly according to domestic circumstances (see page 251). The following table gives an indication of the amount of tax paid in 1970–71, not only in relation to different ranges of income but also to the number of dependent children. This shows that a married man with three children of school age does not begin to pay income tax until his income is over £1,000 though the single person with the same income is paying 18·7 per cent when he reaches £1,000.

Income tax and surtax are only part of the story, for about half of the total revenue is raised by indirect taxes, and these, as we have seen, bear more heavily proportionately on the

Income	Effective rate of tax (percentage)		
£	Single person %	Married couple with no dependent children %	Married couple with three dependent children %
Under 400	—	—	—
500	5·3	—	—
600	9·7	0·1	—
700	12·9	4·7	—
800	15·3	8·1	—
1,000	18·7	12·9	—
2,000	25·4	22·5	14·9
7,000	35·7	34·5	31·4
15,000	54·8	54·0	51·9
100,000	85·7	85·5	85·2

smaller incomes; so we should need to assess the amount of indirect taxation paid in these various income ranges before we could know the true effect of taxation as a whole. Unfortunately we do not know this with the same precision as we know the amount of direct taxation. Everybody is legally bound to pay the appropriate income tax, but nobody is *bound* to pay tobacco, or alcohol, or purchase tax, and the amount one does actually pay depends on how much one spends on these things and not on the size of one's income.

As we have seen when discussing the compilation of the Retail Prices Index, there is no such thing as a 'typical' pattern of expenditure, though there certainly are fairly widespread habits of consumption. We know quite accurately the total amount spent by the community as a whole on each commodity that is taxed, because we know how much tax has been collected, but we don't know how much has been bought by each individual, nor how much each family in different income ranges spent on them. Knowing the total that has been bought and with some knowledge of habits, we have to *presume* a certain amount of expenditure by persons in the various income ranges. The last published estimate of the amounts paid in indirect taxes made in this way refers to 1941–2. The authors of it* took a household, consisting of man, wife, and two children, and calculated how much such a family would pay in taxes on commodities and services, assuming that they consumed a moderate amount of the taxed articles. This was the result :

Income £	Percentage of income spent on direct taxes	Percentage of income spent on indirect taxes	Total tax burden
1937–8:			
150	2·9	14·1	16·4
250	1·4	12·5	13·9
350	—	11·3	11·3
500	1·7	12·8	14·5
1,000	10·3	9·0	19·3
5,000	28·3	4·2	32·5
10,000	38·5	2·8	41·3
20,000	47·5	2·0	49·5
50,000	56·6	1·1	57·7
1941–2:			
150	2·8	21·3	24·2
250	1·8	17·8	19·6
350	8·2	16·0	24·2
500	15·2	15·2	30·4
1,000	30·1	9·7	39·8
5,000	55·1	3·9	59·0
10,000	67·8	2·3	70·1
20,000	80·5	1·2	81·7
50,000	90·7	0·6	91·3

It may be surprising to find that the smallest incomes pay any direct taxes at all. The reason is that these incomes fell within the scope of compulsory health and unemployment insurance schemes and the workers' contributions are here counted as direct taxation. Those with incomes of £350 before the war earned too much to be included in these schemes, but too little to pay income tax; hence they bore no direct taxation. By 1941–2 this group had moved a little further up the scale. These tables show the regressive nature

* Shirras and Rostas, *The Burden of British Taxation.*

of indirect taxation, but by 1941–2 the high rates of income tax were more than enough to compensate for this; and, as very few people by that time had as little as £150 a year income, the taxation system as a whole had become, for the first time, progressive over the whole of its range.

Since that time there has been no equally detailed calculation made, so it is not possible to give a similar table for comparison taking into account present indirect taxes. Recently, however, the Central Statistical Office* has made an estimate on rather different lines. It has attempted to discover how much households of different income ranges, and with varying numbers of dependants, pay in taxation of all types in comparison with the social benefits they receive. The calculation is based on the material collected for the Family Expenditure Survey (see page 137) whose main object is to enable a realistic Retail Price Index to be compiled. The households co-operating in this survey are asked also to supply information about expenditure from which it is possible to work out how much they have paid in taxes on the goods they purchased and how much they benefited from subsidies paid on any of their purchases.

For other benefits the calculation is not so simple. How much an individual household derives from participation in the facilities provided by the National Health Service or the educational system must be determined on fairly arbitrary assumptions.

The calculation shows that the smaller the income the larger the amount it receives of net benefits after its taxes have been paid, so that its 'civic rights' result in an addition to the original income. The larger the income, the more the result is the opposite. Again, the more children there are to be supported the higher the income will be before outlay on taxes exceeds benefits received. The table showing the estimated effects of both taxation and social benefits is given in the chapter on the Welfare State. But it must be remembered that these estimates take no account at all of the advantages

* *Economic Trends*, February 1970.

derived by the whole population from government expenditure on defence, the maintenance of law and order, roads, public buildings, libraries, parks, etc., all of which must be met out of taxation.

Much of the redistribution that is now brought about is not simply from richer to poorer, if we define these terms solely by the size of the income one has; but it is also a redistribution according to family circumstances. In all income ranges those who are unmarried, or widowed people without dependent children, pay more in taxation so that those with children to support can receive more in social benefits. The same family, with an unchanging income, pays more than it gets at one time, receives more than it pays at another, and may revert to the earlier position later on as the children grow up. But whilst there is a great deal of what we might call 'horizontal' redistribution, that is, from people in one income range to others in the same range with heavier family responsibilities, there is also an immense amount of 'vertical' redistribution, that is, the larger incomes pay so very much more in total taxation for all purposes than the smaller ones that the gap between them is much reduced.

Thus the total effect of taxation nowadays is to bring about a greater equality of income than there seems to be if we look only at the range of incomes as they are *received*. The amounts received are very unequal; the amounts *retained*, after taxes have been paid, are much less unequal. If, in addition to this, we take into account the effects of the income derived from 'civic rights', whether in the form of direct money grants or in the value of food subsidies and social services, the movement towards greater equality is further strengthened. The combined result of taxation and social services together is to effect such a considerable redistribution of income as to merit its being called 'a silent revolution'. But every change in direct taxes and every change in the amounts and conditions surrounding welfare benefits alters this equation. For example, it is argued now that the

increased rates for prescriptions and for school meals or
willingness of local authorities to give rebates on council
house rents may impose a burden so much heavier on small
income earners with heavy family responsibilities as to reverse
this trend. An attempt to assess effects of benefits and taxation is made in the chapter on the Welfare State.

Chapter 10

UPS AND DOWNS IN PRODUCTION
AND EMPLOYMENT

In the early months of 1963 there was great distress, and
much discussion in Parliament and elsewhere, about the rise
in the unemployment figures. The number of unemployed
had risen to over 800,000. It is true that a large part of this
was due to the worst weather conditions we had experienced
for over a century. For weeks on end it was impossible to do
any outside work such as building or road-making and repair, and consequently not only were those in these industries out of work but also there was a slowing down in
occupations which, though carried on indoors, are closely
related to these; fixtures for plumbing installations, furniture-
making, house decoration, light engineering goods, and so
on. If we took away the amount of unemployment probably caused in this way, the percentage of insured workers
unemployed would have been about 3 per cent and it is some
indication of the great changes that have occurred that this
figure roused widespread disquiet. Forty years ago – in the
early thirties – there were three million men and women
out of work – 23 per cent of the insured population – and the
percentage of unemployed had fluctuated between this high
figure and 10 per cent throughout the whole period between
the two world wars. If we had ever got within nodding distance of 3 per cent we should have rejoiced in the belief that
this dreadful problem was practically solved.

But times have changed. Since 1940, until the exceptional
circumstances of the mid-seventies, we have more often suffered from a severe shortage of labour than any appreciable
amount of unemployment. How did this remarkable change
come about and why does unemployment occur at all?

The easy answer is that there was a lot of war destruction

to repair and arrears of civilian demands to make up. But this does not bear examination. There were similar needs after the First World War yet the year 1920 ushered in the beginnings of the worst period of mass unemployment we have ever known. And even if this explanation were adequate to account for the brisk employment in the immediate post-war years of the late forties it would not explain the later situation. But, even if we take just the years following the war, is this explanation satisfactory? After all, we cannot pretend that we all had everything we wanted before the war and that there was not the same lack of all kinds of essential goods during the thirties. Everybody would have been only too glad to have had more if he had felt that he could afford it, but most of us were afraid to buy even if we *were* in jobs and those who weren't in work had not the means; so the industries making the goods we would have liked to buy were depressed and their workers unemployed.

This was not an unusual state of affairs. In fact, ever since the beginning of our modern type of industry these ups and downs have been a feature of our economy. The fluctuations of the inter-war years were, perhaps, more violent and the depression more prolonged than in earlier times, but the same alternation of years of stagnation and gloom had characterized industry for a century or so; not only in Great Britain but in all highly developed countries. Records of the earlier part of this period are not very comprehensive, but there are enough indications to show that the experience was pretty much the same as we know it to have been during the time – i.e. the last hundred years and more – when our records have been fairly accurate. These records show that the 'ups and downs' usually took place every eight or nine years; sometimes the span was a little more, sometimes a little less, but generally, without trying to be precise, one can say that there was a period of prosperity and one of depression in each decade, and it is this fluctuation to which the name the 'trade cycle' has been given. For some reason, to be explained later, people began to take heart after a bad patch; orders were given to factories, who took on more workers, more money was spent to restock warehouses and to buy the goods we denied ourselves when employment was precarious, and soon the whole economy was humming with activity. But the good times did not last; warehouses became overstocked, orders were cut down, workers were turned off and had less to spend, and those still in employment put off buying things they could do without, as a precaution in case they also should have bad luck, and there we were back in the depression. Why did this see-saw take place?

The question is of much more than academic interest. Of all the features of our modern industrial civilization there is none that is more dreaded than the loss of one's job, partly because, as we have seen in the last chapter, most of us get our incomes from our work, but also because our self-respect and our sense of being of use in the world are closely bound up with the ability to hold down a job. Unemployment means a loss in income and a fall in the standard of living, but it also induces the despairing feeling that we are not wanted and that we have no place in the community. It is probably true to say that the widespread unemployment which results from depression, and the fear of it during more prosperous times, have caused more unhappiness and done more to undermine confidence in our present economy than any other element in our life. And the almost obsessional desire for security which is its corollary has had, and still has, an incalculable influence on our industrial structure, on political programmes, on the policy of the trade unions, and on our scales of values.

As far as the trade unions are concerned the ca' canny policy, the hostility to piece rates, the dislike of labour-saving machinery, the antagonism to the introduction of women workers, the restriction of the number of apprentices, and similar policies, have derived their main inspiration from the passionate desire to make sure that there is a sufficient number of jobs to be done. (Not, be it understood, that these various policies proved, in fact, to be the best ways of maintaining regularity of employment for those who pinned their faith to them, but yet they *did* pin their faith to them because they believed they would have this effect.) In the same way, business firms have tried to gain control of their markets by Price Associations and similar forms of amalgamation, with the aim of regularizing the demands and prices of their products. And no political party that had any hope of being elected would dare to omit from the forefront of its programme support for the measures required to protect the community from serious fluctuations in employment. In fact, so great an impression did the disastrous chronic mass unemployment of the thirties make on the whole population that all political parties have now accepted the view that the Government has the responsibility to try to maintain a 'high and stable level of employment'. In the White Paper on Employment Policy published in 1944 the National Government announced its acceptance of this responsibility. What, then, is the root of this instability?

CONSUMPTION AND CAPITAL MARKETS

All production must be carried on in anticipation of the demand for the goods wanted. If I decide to buy a new table for the dining-room I don't begin by growing a tree to provide the suitable timber; I go to a furniture shop, or probably to several, where I can expect to find a variety of tables of different designs and prices from which to choose. Yet these tables could not have been there without a long and complicated series of processes – growing and cutting the timber, getting it to England, seasoning it, shaping it to particular designs and transporting it to a shop in a suitable district, where I can have the opportunity of inspecting the result of all this work at my leisure. Many people have had to look ahead and guess that I, and others like me, would want to buy tables of this or that type, and have set the whole chain of events in motion. None of them could be certain that there would be enough of us ready to buy to justify all the costs involved in producing the finished article. They have had to back their own judgement, and gamble on their estimates, by undertaking all the expenses of production without any guarantee of being reimbursed by their sales to buyers. This is not, of course, a blind speculation; they have all sorts of pointers by which to judge – the experience of the past, their knowledge of changes in the size of population, the general state of trade, changes in taste, and so on – but nobody can foretell the future accurately and, however careful they are in their estimates, they may prove to be wrong.

In an earlier chapter it was explained that the word 'demand' has a special meaning when it is used by an economist; it does not refer simply to our wish or desire to possess something, but to a desire which is allied to an ability and a willingness to offer a reasonable price in exchange for it. So the job of the producer is to try to find out not just how many goods people might like to buy, but how many they would be prepared to buy at a price which would be enough to make it worth while for him to produce them, i.e. he has to try and estimate the *effective demand*. If he thinks effective demands will be less he cuts down production and there is unemployment; if he thinks they will increase there is the opposite result. So, in order to understand why there are alternations of employment and unemployment, we have to explain why effective demand changes in its volume in this way.

The amount we buy of things as a whole depends partly on our tastes, temperament, and obligations and largely on the amount of income we have at our disposal. The incomes we get are our shares of the wealth that is being produced. When a thing is sold, the price paid for it is divided up into wages for the workers who have helped to make it, salaries for the technical and administrative staffs, interest on the capital, rent for the site, payment for machinery and materials, and profit for the risk-takers; and it is the way in which we spend the shares we get which determines the demands (and consequently the volume of employment) for all the things we consume. So all of us are both income receivers and income spenders; the amount we get as producers, or as owners of property which others are using, determines the amount we have available to spend as consumers; and the way in which we spend as consumers determines the volume of production and the amounts we shall receive in return for our work, or the use of our property.

Few of us spend the whole of our income as we get it. Practically all of us (unless we are extremely poor or extremely improvident) put something aside for the future. We save to provide for old age, or for periods of sickness or unemployment, or to leave our families with an income if we die, or to educate the children or start them in life, and some of us (never very many at any time and very few indeed at the present rates of taxation) save because our incomes are so big that it is less bother to save a part than to think of more things to buy. Whether much or little, almost all of us save something; and on the whole, the more we get, the larger the margin out of which such savings can be made.

As a rule, the amount we save is largely a matter of habit – habit which, of course, can change as other habits do, but which does not alter very much, nor very quickly. Now, when a man says that he is saving so much out of his income, he means that he is not spending it, but that does not mean that no use is being made of it. He does not usually bury his savings in the garden, or hoard them in a money box, but, through the agency of the banks, joint stock companies and other financial institutions, he lends them to people who need capital to finance their businesses. The man who saves refrains from buying the new clothes or washing-machine or what have you that he might have purchased and, instead, the business that borrows his money uses it to buy tools or machinery or to install a lift or build a new workshop. There are thus two kinds of demand in the market: one for consumption goods, that is, for all the things you and I buy to satisfy our individual wants, and the other for capital goods, that is, for all the various stores and equipment that are wanted in production. So that what the individual thinks of as saving is, from the point of view of society as a whole, simply another form of spending. Now this is where the snag comes in.

When we buy goods for our own use we do so because we believe that they will satisfy our wants. We may make a mistake, but we generally learn by experience to shop carefully, and, as we are very much aware of our own likes and dislikes, we can usually tell whether the article is likely to fill the bill or not. But when a businessman buys tools or equipment, he does so in order to produce more cheaply, or more efficiently, or in greater quantities, the goods that later he hopes to sell at a profit. He does not want the tools for their own sake as we individuals want the food or cigarettes we buy, but only for the part they will play in making other things. This means that his willingness to buy machinery depends on his prospects of selling the goods, and as he doesn't know for certain that he will be able to do so, he will hold back unless he feels fairly confident; he may decide to be cautious and buy only a small amount of equipment this year, until he has a chance to see how things go. So that there is no guarantee that all the money which people save out of their incomes and are prepared to lend to business is, in fact, invested in the purchase of capital goods; and in this case, some part of the income is not spent either on things for the individual or on things for production. In such a situation the demand for goods as a whole is less, and general unemployment is the consequence.

If we look back over the records we see that there is a strong tendency for this to happen fairly regularly, because the purchase of capital goods has the habit of going in spurts. When a new industry is establishing itself, or when an old industry extends its market, or when its techniques undergo a really appreciable change, there is a big demand for all the types of equipment it uses, and the constructional industries – building, engineering, transport, and so on – become very profitable and active. The effect of this soon spreads outwards and influences other trades which seem to have little direct connection with the constructional industries; for as the shareholders and managers, the technicians and workers in these industries find themselves with larger incomes to spend, the consumption trades, which make the food and clothes and radios and bicycles that people spend their money on, soon find that their markets are expanding too. Now most capital equipment has a fairly long life and, once a business is equipped to meet its likely market, its demand for further tools will be pretty slack until its old machinery wears out, or until new methods are introduced which are important enough to make it worth while to scrap the old machinery even before it is worn out. Once the new machinery has become established, therefore, it becomes more and more difficult to find profitable uses for further supplies of it. Some investments fail to bring in the profits that were expected, so people begin to be less confident about the future and judge they had better hold back for a time before committing themselves to the new factory buildings or machines they had planned, until they see how things are going. As they cut down their investment in these things, the field for employment in the constructional industries is reduced, and with fewer workers in jobs and smaller profits being earned, it is not long before the consumption trades also feel the cold blast.

After the war the position was much the same as when important new methods are introduced. There were such large arrears in demand for civilian goods all over the world, as well as in this country, that manufacturers had no fear of producing too much for a profitable sale. So few things had been available for purchasers that they did not bother too much whether they were exactly what they would have chosen; they took what they could get and were thankful for it. But later a change became apparent. As reconstructed industries got into their stride and more goods reached the market, purchasers became more choosy and there were signs that we might go back to the swing from good trade to bad and back again.

Can this be prevented? Can the Government maintain a 'high and stable level of employment', as it has accepted the responsibility for doing? The problem we are up against is to try to make demand keep pace with production. There is no lack of the things we want; there is no danger of our power of production outstripping our total needs. What we need to do is to plan our demands so that purchasers are always ready to buy the amount that we are capable of producing. The trouble is that we cannot compel ordinary consumers to buy articles when they believe they cannot afford them, or fear that they may soon be out of work and would have been better advised to save their money. But the spending done by public authorities *can* be controlled and we can take care that it is well-timed. Every year the central government and the local authorities spend hundreds of millions of pounds on all the things that are now under public control – schools and houses and their equipment, roads and bridges, transport, civic institutions, and so on. A great deal of this can be planned in such a way as to fit in with private purchasing so as to be able to keep the total amount of demand, both private and public together, more stable.

This is not a new idea; it has often been suggested in the past and has even been tried to a slight extent, but it has never been attempted as a deliberate, carefully organized policy. To be really effective three conditions are essential :

1. The policy must be carried out on a large enough scale to make an appreciable difference to the market. The spending of a few hundred pounds in a niggardly fashion will not do the trick.

2. Plans must be made beforehand, so that public projects can be put in hand with economy and efficiency as soon as the time is judged ripe. As most such projects fall within the

province of local authorities and public utility undertakings, this necessitates a close relationship between these bodies and the central government.

The White Paper in which the Government announced its policy suggested that local authorities should be required to make their plans for a period of five years ahead and that a central committee should coordinate their programmes and adjust them in the light of the prospective employment situation. By temporarily withholding grants the programme of a local authority can be slowed down, or conversely, by financial assistance, it can be accelerated as the situation demands.

3. The policy must be carefully financed. In the past it has been a recognized axiom of public finance that the State raises each year enough revenue to pay its bills for the year. But if the Government decided to increase its expenditure during a time of slack trade it would not do much good if it had to depend on getting the money by higher taxes at the same time. In such a case taxpayers would have to cut down their own buying in order to pay their higher taxes and the whole effect of the Government purchases would be lost. It would be necessary, therefore, for the Government to finance part, at least, of its public investment by loans. At the same time it must be remembered that the Government must eventually raise sufficient taxes to pay its way, even if it does not balance its Budget every year.

Let us admit, at once, that this is not an easy programme. There are many public undertakings which cannot be postponed, because the loss in social welfare in doing so would outweigh the loss and suffering of a certain amount of unemployment. Again, most projects are necessarily large in conception and many are so closely interconnected that it is not practicable to delay one part when the rest has been begun. A new housing estate, for example, requires much more than the houses for the new tenants. Streets and recreation spaces, schools, libraries, hospitals, shopping centres, and cinemas must all develop at the same time, whether the employment situation demands increased activity or not. You cannot leave the roads unmade and abandon the inhabitants in a welter of mud, far from all the amenities of urban life, because ordinary non-Governmental demands have increased sufficiently to keep productive resources in full employment.

How difficult this policy is to implement can be seen from the situation that developed in early 1963 to which reference has been made. As I have pointed out, the unemployment was not spread evenly over the country; the unemployment rate in London and the south-east counties, for example, was only 1½ per cent, and in the Midlands, 2 per cent; but the northern district had 5 per cent and Scotland just under that rate. Tyneside, Merseyside, and the Clyde Valley were the worst-hit areas and even during the long period of booming trade, these areas have always had more unemployment than the average. There is good reason for this. In the chapter on the location of industry, mention was made of the problems that arise when a region is very dependent on one particular industry. If, for one reason or another – a change in world markets, or a change in consumer demands – this industry declines in size, it is not only those who earned their living in that occupation who are affected, but also all those who provide the ancillary services for the industry as well as those who produce the goods and services on which the people in that industry spend their earnings. Most people don't buy new houses and furniture, or TV sets, or spend a great deal on beauty culture when they are out of work, or fear that they might be soon; so even those occupations that are prosperous in other neighbourhoods suffer from the general decline.

This is what has happened in these localities. They are particularly bound up with shipping and shipbuilding, which had been suffering a recession not only in England but all over the world, though it is also true that Britain's share of the world shipbuilding market also declined relatively to that of other countries such as Japan and Germany.

Great effort has been put into the attempt to introduce a

more diversified economy into these areas by the methods described on pages 93–99 and when the national productive system was very buoyant this had considerable success. But when there are traces of general slackness this becomes more difficult and the demand arises for new public works to be started at once to give the stimulus necessary to make industry as a whole brisk again. But such big projects as electrification or the building of major roads cannot be undertaken at a moment's notice; they require an immense amount of preliminary planning, and the delays experienced in tackling the problems of these areas are a good example of the difficulties of relying on the use of public works as a means of dealing with a sudden increase in the numbers out of work.

The problems faced by these localities are not, however, caused primarily by cyclical fluctuations; they are the result of structural changes and more will be said of these later.

The greatest power for countering these fluctuations lies with the Chancellor of the Exchequer and it is the use of this power which has been the principal way of keeping the economy working at as high a level as possible since the end of the Second World War.

He has two methods he can employ. First, he can raise or lower the minimum lending rate (with the consequential changes on all other rates of interest) and impose more or fewer restrictions on the ease with which one can borrow. Banks can be prevented from allowing overdrafts or from giving credit except for particular purposes and hire purchase can be made more or less difficult. All such actions increase, or decrease, as the case may be, our willingness or opportunity to borrow either for production or consumption purposes, and this, of course, affects the amount of production undertaken. This method has been much used by all Chancellors of the Exchequer during the last thirty years. The long period of full employment has resulted in a continuous struggle to prevent constantly rising prices from having their effect on the international balance of payments. As the pound was threatened, credit restrictions were imposed and production slackened off, with its consequent influence on the level of employment; at that point the opposite procedure came into operation until inflation was once again a menace. This see-saw has been the outstanding characteristic of our post-war economy.

When this method of controlling the ups and downs of production was first discussed it was believed that very slight variations would be sufficient to have the desired effect. The theory was that businessmen would get so used to the idea that action would be taken to keep production moving on an even keel that the slightest rise or fall would be an indication of what was needed and would be enforced if necessary, so that they would take the appropriate steps without anything more being required. Experience has shown, however, that this is not so. When demand is brisk producers continue to step up their output even if the lending rate goes up a little, and a rate of 8 per cent or more with other credit restrictions has been needed to curb a too ebullient desire to expand. Unfortunately such drastic action has other serious repercussions as well as compelling firms to think twice about the amount they are producing.

On the other hand removal of restrictions and a lower lending rate do not of themselves induce expansion if industrialists have reason to waver in their confidence about the future. For example, recently high inflation with a large number of industrial strikes created a lack of confidence, and firms held back from ordering new plant and new factories even though they could get cheap credit.

The second method the Chancellor may employ is that of taxation. A marked reduction in taxes releases purchasing power which people can spend on their immediate wants and this, in its turn, stimulates production. But this is not as simple as it sounds. Which taxes should be reduced and by how much? Should the Chancellor cut down income tax and surtax so as to give producers more incentive to risk expansion? Or should he give larger rebates to family men so that they can buy goods of the kind needed by such households and thus indirectly encourage firms to expand? The decision cannot depend on purely rational calculations for there are serious political considerations to be taken into account. Choose the first and the Chancellor is accused of favouring the rich at the expense of those whose incomes are too small to pay any significant amount of income tax. Choose the second and he is told that industrialists do not find it worth while to risk expansion when heavy taxation removes all incentives because they bear all the losses themselves but have to pay over to the tax collector so large a proportion of any profits that may accrue.

Moreover it must be remembered that this method has many limitations. The Government is now responsible for an enormous amount of activity, the costs of which must be met out of taxation. It can endure a deficit one year; but eventually the funds to meet its expenditure must be raised, and the only way to do this is by taxation.

Another proposal which has been put forward is one which was tentatively adopted by the Government in the White Paper mentioned above but which has never been tried – though perhaps some of the increases in national insurance benefits may have been partially motivated by it. This is that the contributions payable under the social security scheme should be made to vary with the employment situation, rising when trade is good and falling when trade is bad. The aim, of course, is to leave employed people with more purchasing power when consumer demands are showing signs of falling, so as to persuade them to spend more freely, and the reverse when resources are fully occupied. It is doubtful whether such a scheme is really practicable or socially desirable. Financial calculations and administration would get into a hopeless muddle if the value of weekly insurance stamps was suddenly and frequently changed and as the main purpose of the insurance scheme is to provide people with a sense of security in this complex and unstable world, a new element of instability, arbitrarily imposed on principles which the general public would find very difficult to understand, is hardly likely to help towards the desired objective. The increases in benefits which came into force in the early summer of 1963 were made partly, perhaps, in the hope that they might have some effect on unemployment; but they had been long demanded before the rise in the unemployment figures because the value of the benefits had fallen so far below average wages; and in any case, the rise in benefits was accompanied by an increase in weekly contributions to pay for them.

Supposing that we were successful in ironing out fluctuations in the trade cycle or were able to reduce them so considerably that they were no longer a serious cause of changes in the volume of employment, does this mean that unemployment would be a thing of the past? Unfortunately, no, for there are many other causes of unemployment.

(a) New things are invented which suit us better than the things we had earlier, e.g. we like motor-cars instead of hansom cabs, or nylon underclothing instead of cotton, or electric fires instead of coal-burning grates.

(b) Our wants may remain the same but new and better methods are devised for satisfying them, e.g. electricity is used instead of steam power, automatic machinery in the place of hand tools, or cranes instead of human porters, etc.

(c) We want certain things at one season of the year and other things at other seasons, e.g. coal and mackintoshes and plum puddings at Christmas and hiking shorts and ice-cream in the summer.

All these changes in our demands inevitably affect the amount of goods that can profitably be produced in these trades, and, therefore, affect the amount of employment available in them. If we were all interchangeable as producers it would not matter that we wanted a lot of this at one moment and a lot of the other at the next. But as we are all specialized, some of us are left high and dry in our occupations while the tide of demand recedes and floods another channel. In the third of the changes mentioned above the tide will return; it is a seasonal affair and moves more or less regularly from one group of industries to another. But in (a) and (b) the changes in demand for workers are due to permanent changes in the *structure* of industry, and this entails a relative shift in the occupational distribution of the population.

Let us take the seasonal changes first. It is fairly obvious, even to a nation of townsmen, that farmers have different jobs to do at different times of the year and that they need many more workers, say, to gather the harvest than they can employ regularly all the year round; but we often ignore the fact that there are seasonal changes which are just as marked in other industries. For example, building, which must ordinarily be done in the open air, is more likely to be interrupted by snow and fog and rain during the winter months. Even without these special handicaps, as the winter days are shorter, it is impossible to get as much done as in the longer summer days. So builders are more likely to tackle their work in the summer months. This does not mean, of course, that men will down tools in the middle of a big job and wait for better weather, but it does mean that where a choice is possible, as it is in all the kinds of building which take only a few months to complete, more projects are likely to be begun in the spring than in the autumn. So all building workers can usually anticipate some weeks of unemployment as a regular feature of their work. The rate of building affects a whole host of other occupations that, as far as their conditions of manufacture are concerned, could be done the whole year round. Cupboards and doors, baths and cooking-stoves, and drain pipes are all made in factories that are unaffected by the climate but, as they are parts of buildings, there is no demand for them unless buildings are going up, so they, too, are seasonal in activity. The same is true of furniture and decorating.

Clothing is another big industry which is affected by the

seasons. We generally buy our lightweight clothes in the early summer and our heavier in the autumn, so all the workers engaged in these industries are extremely busy in the few months preceding the chief buying times and slack – working short-time or completely unemployed – afterwards. It might seem, at first sight, that there is no reason why the manufacturers should not go on steadily all the year round, even though we don't buy regularly; but we must remember that fashion makes the manufacture of clothes a speculative and chancy business at the best of times, and the longer the interval between making and selling the greater the gamble. So everybody employed in anything to do with the production of clothes or millinery can expect a certain annual amount of unemployment or short-time.

Another group of industries which is much affected by the seasons is that connected with hotels and catering. There is frenzied activity in July and August with minor peaks at Whitsun and Easter and Christmas, and very little work at holiday centres at any other time. As far as present experience goes, it seems that no amount of propaganda, with dashing posters showing the pleasure and enjoyment to be derived from taking holidays at the quiet times, can wean the British holidaymaker from his determination to go away at the same moment as everybody else; and a great up and down in employment possibilities for the worker in these occupations is the result. The same thing is true, consequently, of all the trades that cater for the people who have time to fill in and money to spend – the bus excursions and seaside amusements and so on.

Toy-making is another big industry which blazes into activity at one period of the year, in preparation for the orgy of present-giving at Christmas time, and hardly ticks over at others. Publishing, too, shares in this because so many people buy books for presents who would never dream of buying a book at any other time; so printers and bookbinders are busier in the autumn months than at any other part of the year. In both these groups it is social custom rather than climatic changes which cause the ebb and flow of trade; but social habit is almost as difficult to change as the climate.

Fortunately these seasonal factors do not affect all industries in the same direction at the same time; some industries are busy in the spring or summer and others in the autumn or winter. In fact, there is no month of the year in which some occupation or other is not having its busy period and some its slack time. So that, although there are pockets of dispersed unemployment, there are not a large number out of work at the same moment from this cause. And, on the whole, such unemployment is not very serious in its effects. It is sufficiently regular for workers to know they must reckon on it. This does not mean that each individual knows just how much slack time he will have to cope with, but he does know that there will be *some* people out of work in his trade and that, if he happens to be the unlucky one, the unemployment is not likely to be prolonged.

The effects of the changes in demand I have listed as (a) and (b) are much more important and much less calculable.

During the inter-war period these structural changes added enormously to our problems, because the industries which were shrinking in size happened to be concentrated in certain areas and the new expanding industries established themselves in quite different localities. So that people thrown out of work in the former had to face the misery of moving their homes, as well as learning new jobs, if they were to get absorbed into the new industries. Many attempts were made to encourage new businesses to settle in the areas where there was labour already available and, since the war, 'taking work to the worker' has become an accepted part of the policy for preventing unemployment. (See Chapter 5.)

This problem of structural changes points to one of the greatest difficulties in the control of unemployment. No policy for maintaining employment at a high level is intended to guarantee to each worker permanent employment in the job he happens to be doing, and if we are to get rid of unemployment as a serious menace, the ordinary citizen must be prepared to do his share and be ready to change his job when necessary. We are now a lot better off than previous generations, because we have learned new and more efficient ways of producing what we want. Our great-grandfathers spent nearly all their time and energy in growing their food and raw materials for their clothing and other essentials; consequently, their manner of life was narrow and poor. Then expanding knowledge and quick communication enabled us to get these things more cheaply from parts of the world where they could be produced more easily and set us free to make that wealth of manufactured goods which has so vastly raised the standard of living.

Suppose that our forbears had obstinately refused to go into the new industries, on the plea that they were agricultural workers and had the right to remain so all their lives. There would then have been no possibility of the immense variety of things – clothes, furniture, radios, record players, cinemas, motor-cars, bicycles, and aircraft – which we now take for granted and accept as almost essential to a reasonably good standard of living. The control of investment, with the object of maintaining stable demand, will not try to prevent further technical developments from taking place; it would be fatal to welfare if it did. All it aims at doing is to prevent a *general* decline in markets, i.e. to ensure that new avenues of employment open as old ones shrink. But this is no use unless people are ready to recognize the need to change their old jobs for new ones. This is a real difficulty because it is a psychological one. Most of us are pretty conservative in our routine of life and especially so in the way we earn our living. It is a great jolt to realize that we are no longer wanted in the work we are used to, and it needs courage to face this fact and to be willing to learn something new.

When I referred in Chapter 2 to the controversy about the reduction in the railway service I was discussing how far a nationalized industry should be expected to pay its way or whether it should continue to operate uneconomic activities. But there is another side to this problem which is by no means confined to nationalized industries; in fact, it is common to all occupations : that is, the effects on the people engaged in an industry when there are big changes in the market for its goods or when the techniques of production undergo radical alterations. The problem of redundancy has become one of the most worrying of all characteristics of our modern economy. Most people are very specialized in their work. Even if no long period of training has been needed they feel themselves identified with the occupation in which they have been employed for some time, and the thought of moving to a different type of job holds all the terrors of the unknown. This is particularly true when the industry has been carried on in such a way that it is almost co-terminous with a whole community. This is the case, for example, in the docks and the mines and, to a great extent, on the railways. The workers in these occupations generally live close to one another in the same neighbourhood so that the ties that bind them are not simply those of common working associations; hence there is usually great opposition to anything which involves a change in the number employed for those affected are neighbours and relatives as well as workmates. The coal-miners oppose the use of oil as fuel, the dockers try to prevent the introduction of labour-saving machinery, the railways resent the closing of unused stations or the reduction in the size of railway workshops.

The problem is made more serious by the extraordinary difficulty of establishing whether a falling-off in demand for a particular type of article is due to a temporary recession from which it will make a good recovery or whether it is the beginning of a permanent decline in its market. After the end of the First World War it took a whole decade for us to realize that the shrinking in our coal and cotton industries was not the result of a temporary post-war dislocation, but that there had been a permanent shift in the world's relative demands. As we are all inclined to think that our own work is the most important job in the world and hate the idea of any fundamental change in our way of living, there is always a strong temptation to be over-optimistic in our estimate of the situation and to assume that the trouble is not likely to be due to any long-term factors.

The great danger here is that people who find themselves out of work will take it for granted that it is the Government's job to bolster up the demand for their products (as part of the 'maintenance of the high and stable level of employment' policy) when what is really needed is the courage to face the facts that the industry is too large and that redundant workers must be trained for new kinds of work. Unless ordinary men and women have this courage and are prepared to change their occupation when necessary, no amount of Government action can keep unemployment from becoming serious – unless, of course, we also consent to have a lower standard of living than we need, in order to keep on with the old methods.

This problem is now more important than ever before because of the rapidity of technological change coupled with the peculiar age structure of the population. In the last century most workers could expect to remain in the same occupation for most of their working lives. Change took place, of course, and in comparison with the preceding centuries, it was quick change. But adjustment to the changing manpower needs could be made with greater ease because of the age composition of the community. The big increase in the population during the nineteenth century was caused by the fall in the death-rate of young children, most of whom, for the first time in history, lived to maturity and so became parents in their turn. Thus the proportion of young to old constantly increased. As industries changed in relative size and new techniques were introduced, the young people attached themselves to the expanding occupations whilst death and old age (agents of natural wastage) gradually reduced the numbers of those in declining ones.

Nowadays things don't work this way, for two reasons.

First, the rate of change has very much speeded up and, second, the fall in the birth-rate which has characterized this century has resulted in a very different age structure. Improved public health, higher standards of living, and better medical facilities mean that more people live to a ripe old age than used to; but only half as many young people are born each year for every thousand of the population in comparison with the nineteenth century. Thus the adjustment of the number of workers to the demands of industry cannot take place as painlessly as it used to. The majority of people entering industry now must face the fact that it is fairly certain that they will have to change jobs, and probably more than once, before they reach retirement age.

But there is also a less obvious factor which makes changes in the numbers attached to an occupation more difficult to bring about. It has been emphasized several times in earlier chapters that wages are a price and as such show the relative demands and offers for certain types of work. At one time, before trade unions were as strong and effective as they are now, a lessened demand on the part of employers showed itself at once in a fall in the wages offered and this induced those who had been employed in that occupation to look for something more remunerative. Higher wages in a developing trade acted as a magnet to draw more workers into it and lower pay in the overcrowded one helped to push workers out, though it always took time for this to become effective. Nowadays with over ten million organized workers in strong unions it is extremely hard for employers to lower wages – the most they can hope for is that the increases will not be as much or as frequent as those in more profitable or expanding branches of production – and this greatly strengthens the natural reluctance of workers to change from one kind of job to another. On the other hand, if the wage rate stays up there is more inducement to employers to cut down the numbers they employ or to find other methods – by reorganization or greater use of machinery – to get their products on the market. But here again they are often prevented from doing what they wish, and what they would have been able to do without question at other times, because many of the unions are sufficiently powerful to prevent – or at least postpone for some considerable time –the dismissal of redundant employees. A very large union – and with the amalgamations which have taken place in the last two decades there are many which are very large indeed – includes within its ranks many different branches of work other than the one whose value is decreasing; and a threat to bring out the whole lot on strike can cause so much loss to the employers that they agree to continue to employ workers they do not need so as to retain those whose work is essential to them.

Even if they hold out and the strike takes place the loss to the firms is likely to be greater proportionately than to the members of the union. Most of the large unions can afford strike pay, the family continue to draw their family allowances, and get rebates on P.A.Y.E. that has been deducted from their pay packets when they were working at a rate that assumed that their wages would continue at that level, and the lower paid workers can draw supplementary benefits in respect of their wives and children though not of themselves. In addition, as there was such a general shortage of labour as a whole after the end of the Second World War, it was often not too difficult for the men on strike to pick up other work until their own jobs were open to them again. All these factors resulted in a great degree of inflexibility in the employment market and there is little doubt that many occupations are seriously overmanned – and thus compelled to face higher costs of production – whilst others are desperate for increased numbers of workers.

But if the economy demands more flexibility and a greater readiness on the part of workers to change jobs to adjust to rapid technological change it is equally necessary for the community to recognize its responsibilities to those who have to do the changing. Nothing can eliminate all the suffering that arises from the realization that the work one has done – and perhaps loved – is no longer required : but that does not mean that nothing can be done to make it easier. There are several kinds of assistance needed.

(1) The first and most immediate need is provision for the maintenance of the unemployed on a more generous scale than we have been willing to finance up to now. Insurance benefit is now so low in relation to average wages (and consequently the standard of expenditure to which the majority of workers are committed) that the loss of a job means a catastrophic fall in standards of living and the possibility of falling into serious debt because of the inability to meet hire purchase payments on washing-machines, TV sets, the purchase of the house, and so on. As long as this is so we must expect the most strenuous resistance to anything, however valuable from the point of view of the economy as a whole, which threatens a loss of work to a particular group of workers.

(2) To some extent steps have already been taken to cushion the blow by the Contracts of Employment Act 1963 and the Redundancy Pay Acts, 1965 and 1969. The first of these gives the employee (and incidentally also the employer) the right to minimum periods of notice to terminate employment; for the employee at least one week's notice if the employment has lasted continuously 26 weeks, two weeks if it has lasted for 2 years or more and four weeks if it has been for 5 years or more. (The obligation on the worker is to give at least one week's notice however long he has been employed. The period of notice does not increase for longer periods of employment.)

The second entitles a worker to payment provided he has been employed continuously for at least 104 weeks by the firm, if he is dismissed because the employer is cutting down on the particular type of work he has been doing, and unless he is offered (in writing) alternative work which can be considered 'suitable'. The scale of payment relates to the number of years of service the worker has had with the firm : half a week's pay for each year of employment between the ages of 18 and 21, one week's pay for each year between the ages 22 and 40, and for each year between 40 and 64 (59 for women) one and a half weeks' pay.

The money for these payments is collected through weekly contributions to the Redundancy Fund made by employers at the same time as the flat rate national insurance contributions.

(3) But neither lump sum 'cushions' nor better maintenance benefits are enough. A man who loses one kind of work must be helped to find another and this requires training. In recent years the Government has greatly increased its Government Training Centres and more of them have been sited in the areas in which the principal industries have been declining. It has also made generous funds available to those firms which agree to retrain a number of adult workers above their own needs so that these men can hope to get employment in expanding occupations. But in this respect unfortunately more than Government action is required. Experience in other countries has shown that a man with some industrial experience can be trained to do skilled work in another occupation in six to nine months' time, provided that the training is carefully thought out, is carried on full time and is done by trained instructors; and the results of the Government Training Centres confirm this experience. But the snag is that the trade unions in this country have a 'dog in the manger' attitude to adult trainees. They are prepared to accept a limited number of ex-service men and disabled persons who go through the training centres but it is extremely difficult to persuade them to accept ordinary adult trainees from other industries. When they do, it is customary for these men to be placed on a special register which ensures that, if there should be any reduction in the demand for labour, they would be the first to be dismissed, irrespective of how skilled and industrious they had proved themselves to be. And one of the most important weapons in the fight against structural unemployment (which is likely in the future to be the one most important factor in the incidence of unemployment) would be the abolition by

the trade unions of their restrictions on the admission of adult trainees to their ranks. This is particularly serious because the demand for skilled labour constantly increases. With more and more mechanization and automation it is the demand for unskilled workers which declines but that for the skilled man gets larger and larger.

During the mid-seventies the incidence of unemployment has again become very serious and there is little likelihood that it can be materially reduced immediately. This is due to a number of factors : (1) There is a general world recession triggered off by the rapid rise in the cost of oil – the most important of the fuels used by industrial countries; (2) The loss or reduction in our export markets as a consequence of British lack of competitiveness in relation to other countries; (3) The serious overmanning in the industries which have in the past played the biggest part in our world trade; (4) The frequency of strikes (the majority of which are unofficial, that is, called by shop stewards rather than by unions) which makes it impossible for firms to honour the delivery dates given to their customers.

When world trade recovers, the amount of unemployment will go down; but the very fact that it has increased so rapidly after such a prolonged period of low rates of incidence creates a situation which is likely to make recovery more difficult. Overmanning and refusal to accept redundancy or to accept the need to change one's occupation, even if generous opportunities for retraining are offered, are all caused by the dread of insecurity. If standards of living are to go up, the great need is for mobility and willingness to allow technological knowledge to be fully exploited. It had been hoped that as the memory of the misery caused by the depression of the twenties and thirties dimmed the attitude to change would be more flexible. This experience of the seventies is likely, on the contrary, to harden inflexibility.

Chapter 11

THE WELFARE STATE

IN Chapter 9 mention was made of the fact that some portion of our incomes depends on our 'civic rights' that is, the amount or the value in kind of goods and services provided by the State and paid for from taxes. This chapter deals with the way in which these rights have developed and some of the issues connected with them. At the present time there are many different opinions as to how extensive this provision should be and whether it should be freely available to all or only to certain sections of the population.

The term 'The Welfare State' seems to have slipped unobtrusively into general use; and there is still no universally accepted definition of it. Nobody knows for certain who coined the term though it began to be used fairly commonly during the Second World War and it is probable that most people would find themselves in difficulties in explaining exactly what is meant by it. On the whole it refers to the methods by which the State, through all kinds of different services, tries to raise the standard of living of the population and help people to meet the vicissitudes through which most of us have to pass at one time or another of our lives. As early as the reign of Elizabeth I – 1601 – there was a statutory duty on certain public authorities to make some provision for those who were entirely destitute but most of the present services either began or have been greatly developed during the present century. Before then the ordinary man was expected to provide for himself and his family in all circumstances and to make arrangements for any periods when he might be prevented from earning by sickness, unemployment, or old age. How he did it was a matter for him to decide for himself and if he could not meet his obligations he had only two alternatives open to him : first, he could appeal to charity, either the generosity of some person to whom he was known or to a charitable institution founded by compassionate people in the past; or second, if the worst came to the worst he could apply to the local Board of Guardians for enough to keep himself and his family from actual starvation.

The situation is now very different. There is still a legal obligation on every adult to provide for himself and those who are directly dependent on him and the work he undertakes to earn the amount he needs for these purposes is a matter of his own choice. But there is a Youth Employment Service maintained by the State to help the young recruit to make a choice between the many alternatives open to him and a network of agencies provided by the Department of Employment to help all who apply – young and old – to get a job or to train for a new one. If no suitable job is available or if a person cannot earn because he is too ill or too old he can draw an insurance benefit or a retirement pension and if these are not sufficient to enable him to reach an acceptable standard he can apply for a supplementary benefit. And even when a man is normally at work he receives a money addition to his income in the form of family allowance for those of his children who are of school age. But quite apart from direct money payments there is a great deal of state help given in other ways. Education is provided free of charge and for those able and willing to pursue their studies to a higher stage, not only fees but maintenance are given. School meals are provided free of charge to those whose parents cannot afford to pay for them or below cost price to others. Local authorities build large numbers of well-equipped houses and flats which are let at rents which do not nearly cover their economic cost. There are special homes and schools for the physically and mentally handicapped where they can be helped to overcome their disabilities as far as possible, and homes for the care of children whose own families are unable to look after them properly and for the care of old people or others who are in need and have no family to look after them. Everybody in the community has the right to free medical attention and to the services provided by the hospitals, and equipment such as spectacles and dentures are available at prices much less than would be necessary to cover their full costs.

This change has not come about of itself. It is the result of the work done by thousands of people who felt compassion for the sufferings of others and who felt that it was wrong or unjust for people to be left to bear ills that could be remedied. It did not take place all at once nor was it planned as a comprehensive scheme; big social changes never are. Every change has demanded an enormous amount of thought and argument and discussion, and people have had to learn, bit by bit, through experiment, how to bring about improvements they thought desirable. Even what is thought desirable changes from one time to another for we have to remember that our values and ideas are moulded by the society in which we live and change only slowly. We are born into families which are part of a particular society and we grow up with the attitudes of mind that are taken for granted in that society. It is no surprise to us that a child brought up in England speaks English and one brought up in France speaks French. It seems natural to us but, of course, it is natural only in the sense that it is expected because it is part of the way in which human beings develop and become adult. But what is not so much taken for granted, though it is equally true, is that just as he picks up the language of the locality in which he lives he also picks up all the other ways of behaving in regard to food, manners, religion, ideals, customs, beliefs about what is right and wrong, and so on. By the time he is grown up he has become used to looking at the world in a certain way and it is not easy for him to change his whole outlook. Every group of human beings has accepted ways of conduct which govern the behaviour of members to one another and to the outside world. Some of these are given legal sanction and deviation from them is punished; but there are even more which are not established by law but which have come to be accepted as right ways to behave, just as in a school there are not only the rules laid down by the headmaster but customs about what is 'done' or 'not done'. Many of these customs alter as rapidly as fashions of clothes but some of them continue so long that they become established traditions which are accepted as if they were natural laws which cannot be broken and this means that any suggestion of change meets with a great deal of opposition because it involves altering the ways and attitudes of mind with which people have grown up.

During the last half-century there have been radical changes in the ways we think about the relationship between individual and community with regard to the responsibility for maintaining and improving the standards of living of the population. In some instances the change has been due to the influence of men with the greatness of vision and the intellectual power to think out things afresh and to open men's minds to new ideas. But much more often it is due to the fact that we are continually faced with serious problems which we have to try and solve as best we may. In such cases our solutions are mostly 'opportunist'; that is, they are not the result of some carefully thought out theory of how such matters should be dealt with but they are the efforts of men with limited knowledge trying hard to improve some situation or alleviate suffering with which they have been brought into contact. Later, perhaps, experience shows that this improvised way of coping with a difficulty can be improved upon but on the other hand it may prove so successful that it can be used in a more general way so that what had earlier been regarded as a revolutionary break in our customary mode of behaviour comes to be taken for granted as part of the ordinary course of events and later as so out of date that it should be radically improved. In very many cases the first initiative is taken by voluntary effort; by people who give their own thought, time, and money to try to help others. Then if this is thought to be successful efforts are made to get these new ways of dealing with life's difficulties applied more universally by making them part of the social provision made by the whole community for its members.

This is a never-ending process; it is going on today for we are constantly faced with new situations and difficulties for which some solution must be found. But each generation begins from a new standpoint because it has grown up in different conditions from the one preceding it, with different assumptions of what is 'natural' and 'ordinary' and with different ideas of what to expect from life. And often enough we find that the methods that had been tried earlier had wider repercussions than had been foreseen and so must be reconsidered and reshaped or even given up completely in favour of some other scheme.

The body of social legislation that is comprised in what we call the Welfare State has brought about so many changes in our patterns of living and in our beliefs with regard to the line of demarcation between individual and communal responsibility that is worth asking why such profound changes have taken place in so comparatively short a period of time. The answer is to be found in the word 'industrialization' and all that is implied in it. Until the end of the eighteenth century the majority of the population lived in villages and very small towns and were mostly engaged in agriculture and the services allied to it; and communications were very much less than they are today. Roads were so few in number and so badly made that they became almost impassable in winter and this meant that each small area was much more dependent on itself than anything with which we are familiar today. Most households provided most of their everyday needs for themselves. They grew much of their own food, spun and wove the linen and woollen fabrics for clothes and household equipment, kept a pig and chickens for meat or a cow for dairy produce and relied on the few village craftsmen – the blacksmith, the thatcher, and the tanner, for example – for the jobs that required special skills. For the little luxuries or the bits of finery they had to wait for the travelling packmen who went from village to village or for the infrequent fairs at the nearest market town. Most people were born, lived, and died without moving more than a few miles from the same parish.

The one industry of any size was the making of woollen cloth, due to the fine pastures for sheep for which this country had long been famous; but even this was not carried on in factories but in the homes of villagers to whom the raw material was taken. Few such workers depended entirely on the wages they received for this work, for most families had a bit of land on which to grow vegetables and many had more than this. Farms were not compact and hedged as they are now but the village was divided into strips and most of the people living in the village owned at least a few of these strips and were therefore also entitled to put sheep or cattle to graze on the common fields.

Life was hard for most people; food was often scarce especially during the winter and there was very little variety. But on the whole one could be fairly sure of the basic essentials and in a neighbourhood where the same families had lived for generations there were usually kinsfolk and neighbours to help one over a crisis.

But during the end of the eighteenth century and the first half of the nineteenth there were a group of related developments which brought profound changes into ways of living. The growth of good communications – first well-made roads, then canals which allowed easy transport of bulky goods such as coal and iron, or clay for potteries, then railways which opened up every region – made it no longer necessary for each small locality to depend solely on its own immediate resources, whether of materials or labour, for daily needs. With the possibility of quick delivery of things from one area to another specialization was developed. Goods could be made on a large scale in one place, to which raw materials could be brought and from which the finished product could be distributed : so it was worth while to develop methods of working machinery by other means than human muscle. At first water power was harnessed and later the steam engine was invented and this in its turn gave opportunities for invention of more and more sophisticated machinery made of steel and using coal to provide the motor force. Thus grew up the great industrial areas with large factories, foundries and mills, and a network of distributive and commercial institutions to gather together the tools and raw materials and to sell the products.

Agriculture, too, changed greatly. Efficient methods were not possible as long as the open-field system existed, for no improvement was possible without the agreement of every individual involved; so the introduction of better methods was preceded by enclosure. This meant that the owners of strips in the open fields gave them up, as also the accompanying right to put sheep and cattle on the common pastures, and received in return a compact holding which had to be fenced. This undoubtedly led to better farming and allowed experiment in both the arable and stockbreeding branches of the industry but it spelled ruin for many small farmers whose holdings were not worth the expense of fencing. These were forced to leave the land and seek work in the towns and they became the labour force of the developing factories.

There is no doubt that the application of continually expanding new knowledge to industrial techniques and the new structure of production greatly raised standards of living. The United Kingdom was the first country to establish machine industry and so the markets of the world were open to her without any fear of competition. As she became the 'workshop of the world' she found it more economical to concentrate on manufacture and shipping and buy her food and raw materials from other countries that were eager for her manufactured goods. In consequence our food became more varied and less dependent on the seasons. Not only was it important that harvest times vary from one country to another so that food was available from somewhere throughout the year, but many foods which could not be grown in England at all, such as tea and sugar and many fruits, could be bought cheaply in return for British manufactures and transported in British ships.

Clothing too changed. Cotton spinning and weaving were new to this country and so were not as bound by traditional ideas as the woollen industry, and it is not surprising therefore that the cotton industry was the first to be rapidly and extensively mechanized. Though all the raw cotton had to be brought 3,000 miles the large supplies of coal and iron close to the convenient port of Liverpool, and the quickly developed skills of engineers and cotton workers, enabled cotton cloths to be produced at low cost both for home use and for export all over the world. As cotton materials can be washed so much more easily than woollen the substitution of cotton for wool in making a good deal of our underwear improved health by raising the standard of cleanliness. It was easier also for towns to be kept cleaner when road surfaces were improved and the use of iron pipes instead of wooden ones allowed supplies of piped water to be available to larger numbers of households and for sewerage to be removed instead of remaining in the streets to breed disease.

But there was a price to be paid for all these improvements in the profound social changes that resulted from them.

(1) For the first time there was a large wage-earning class. There had, of course, always been hundreds of thousands who depended on getting paid for a job in order to maintain themselves but only a small proportion depended on this and nothing else. In that mixture of town and country in which so many people lived most could grow a bit of their own food so that even when work was hard to find they did not starve. But in the tightly packed factory towns it was wages or nothing.

(2) There came to be a clear distinction between the breadwinner and his dependants. In both agriculture and domestic industry (that is, when spinning and weaving, for

example, were carried on in the home with simple hand tools) all the family helped to produce the income which supported them all. Even small children had their duties which were an essential part of the ways in which the family earned its living. But as factory production developed, social legislation restricted the use of child labour and to an increasing extent the wives and mothers of families found it impossible to combine earning with their domestic responsibilities. When work is done in the home it is not too difficult to cook the dinner, look after the children and yet be able to give a hand with the family's productive work whether industrial or agricultural. But it is quite a different matter to leave the house to work in a factory for ten or twelve hours a day, particularly when the children are young; and with the large families that were customary in the last century, there always *were* young children to be looked after until the wife reached an age when she would find it almost impossible to get a factory job.

The change did not come about all at once and, indeed, there were some industries in which it was never fully established. When, for instance, the textile industry left the home for the factory it seemed natural to take on women because they had been traditionally associated with it for so long; but this was not true of the metal industries and engineering which soon became the dominant occupations, nor of building and furniture-making which expanded enormously as a result of the growing population; and by the end of the nineteenth century only one in ten of married women worked for pay.

(3) Though the new methods were so much more efficient they contained a new element of risk. The small farmer producing food for his own family or selling a part to neighbours, or the craftsman making clothes or furniture or shoes for sale in the nearest market town could not produce much in a week, but unless there was a very bad season or a great calamity he was fairly sure of his living. But the wage-earner in the new industries had no such security. The de-

mand for his labour, and, therefore, his income depended on circumstances that were beyond his control or even his knowledge. The invention of a new machine might make redundant thousands who had taken years to develop their skill. Or storms at sea might delay raw materials from reaching their destination or finished goods from getting to their markets. Changes in national boundaries with resulting changes in tariff policies of their countries might completely alter the demands for the goods that the factory was geared to make. And all this meant that just at the time that families became completely dependent on the wage of the father the insecurity of any opportunity to gain it became much more pronounced.

(4) Increase in communications meant more personal mobility : and this also brought its problems. When generation after generation remained in the same village there was almost always somebody to help at a time of crisis. If the mother of a family fell sick there was usually a sister or aunt or grandmother to come in to nurse her and to cook the meals. But when a man left the village to find work in the town he did not take with him all his sisters and cousins and aunts and if he was in trouble he was a stranger with neither kin nor familiar neighbours to whom to turn. Of course, as time went on new social patterns were formed, but this does not happen quickly as we realize now from the difficulties that so many people find when they move from over-crowded slums to the greater amenities of the New Towns. It is usually the young family that moves to better surroundings and wider opportunities of earning. The older members of the family are left behind and this means that as they get older and less capable of looking after themselves it is much more difficult for their children to help them however affectionate and willing they may be; and at the same time the young family has no close relatives to whom to turn during illness or other domestic crisis.

All these changes in ways of living gradually forced upon the attention of compassionate people the realization that the assumptions of the past were no longer valid and that new arrangements had to be made. I use the word 'assumptions' because there was very little accurate knowledge about social and economic conditions and it would be true to say that the one biggest factor in changing men's minds about the needs of society was the building up of accurate information against which these assumptions could be tested. A few illustrations will show what is meant.

(1) It was taken for granted that in a country of rapidly growing wealth the majority of the population lived lives of modest comfort and that, therefore, those who were poverty-stricken were so because of some defect of character. They were work-shy or spendthrift or drank too much or were guilty of other social misdemeanours. But during the end of the nineteenth century Charles Booth and his collaborators carried out a series of detailed investigations which showed how false this idea was. Booth was a Liverpool ship-owner with a serious concern for the welfare of the common man. In a series of seventeen volumes published between 1886 and 1903 and called the *Life and Labour of the People of London* he gave the results of painstaking inquiries into the actual conditions of thousands of people living in the working-class areas of London – the wages they earned, what they worked at, the number of children they had, the rents they paid for their accommodation and what they got for it, their habits of life, and social and religious conditions. The effect of this sober investigation was to explode forever the bland assumption that had been uncritically accepted. Far from poverty being confined to a tiny fringe and due to laziness and intemperance Booth showed that, in the richest city in the world, no less than 35.2 per cent of the working class were living in abject poverty and that, whilst it was certainly true that a small part of this poverty was caused by drink and idleness, over two-thirds of it was directly due to low wages and the irregularity of employment.

These revelations proved so devastating that many argued

that they must be the result of London's special position as a large port and the biggest urban concentration. But an inquiry made by Seebohm Rowntree in 1899 soon killed this optimism. For York, which was an old settled country town with a few well established industries and not a metropolis likely to attract the derelicts from other regions, showed practically the same picture. The conclusion was inescapable – that probably the same characteristics would be found all over the country.

(2) Another surprising source of information was the newly established trade unions, almost entirely amongst the skilled workers. Several of them started a system of friendly benefits, that is, out of the contributions of their members they built up funds from which to pay small sums to help out those who were unable to earn through illness or difficulty in finding a job. The unemployment benefit was especially important in the revelations it brought because it had been assumed that any man willing to work could always get work and that, therefore, the unemployed were a special class who needed to have their moral fibre strengthened. But the unions which paid benefits had to keep records and these showed that far from those out of work belonging to a special category, practically everybody had short bouts of unemployment. The number of men on the books in receipt of unemployment benefit might be the same from week to week, but the names showed that they were not the same men. There was a constant movement in and out of work. Sometimes the periods out of work were quite prolonged, when there was a general depression in industrial activity, sometimes they were regular every season as, for example, in the building trades. But in neither case was the possibility of getting a job within the control of the man who was out of work.

This was more than confirmed by Beveridge's great work called *Unemployment: a Problem of Industry*, published in 1909. The title is significant because it called attention to the fact that unemployment is much more a function of the structure of industry than of the moral character of the workman.

(3) Before 1890 there was no distinction made of the ages of those in receipt of Poor Relief (the assistance given to the destitute) for although the Boards of Guardians (the local bodies responsible for the administration of Poor Relief) were not permitted to give help except in the workhouse to any but the non-able-bodied, there was no definition of when a man or woman could expect to be admitted to this category on account of age. But an inquiry was then made to try to find out to what extent poverty was an effect of age – 'try to find out' because the compulsory registration of births did not begin until the forties so there was a good deal of confusion about the exact age of those in the older groups. But even allowing for inaccuracies the picture that emerged was startling. In a year when the amount of pauperism for the whole population was less than 5 per cent it was 20 per cent for the 65–70 age group, about 30 per cent for those between 70 and 75 and nearly 40 per cent for those over 75. In fact, it was simply old age which was a major factor in poverty.

This gradual accumulation of knowledge did not change men's minds overnight for few people are as rational as that. But it did mean that there gradually came to be more readiness to accept that there might be circumstances in which it would be right for the community to organize help for those in distress without the fear of undermining the spirit of independence; and as one small experiment after another was made without disaster familiarity itself made people more ready to extend them. Bit by bit people began to realize that the problems to be dealt with were not simply those of men and women living on the edge of an abyss but that the miseries that came with the illness or unemployment of the breadwinner, the extreme poverty which almost always came with old age, the bad housing and lack of educational opportunity which stunted the physical and mental growth of the new generation were the conditions that coloured the lives, not of a submerged few, but of the general mass of the population. This was the really big change in ideas; the realization that the normal conditions of life required something more than individual effort and courage. It was this that began to make men believe that organized society should do for its members what they are unable to do for themselves either as separate individuals or as members of voluntary societies. The idea that some conditions are intolerable in a civilized community thus came to be part of the political and psychological atmosphere and it is this belief which is the basis of the Welfare State.

But this does not mean that there is no controversy about how far the State should take responsibility for ensuring the welfare of its citizens nor about the methods by which it should seek to attain its ends.

In a short chapter it is not possible to deal with all the varied services comprised in the Welfare State but only certain important strands can be disentangled in an effort to see what have been the main lines of development and what are now the chief issues.

(1) This country, in common with most other industrialized communities, is primarily composed of people who work for pay. Whether it is as a managing director of a huge business or as an unskilled labourer, 95 per cent of us get our living through paid employment. (The remainder live on past earnings or get their living from the profits of a business, shop, or farm.) How much we get is, as has been shown in Chapter 9, the result of bargaining between our employers and the organizations that represent us, but unless we are employed we do not get the pay. One big section of our social provision, therefore, is to ensure that we have an income even when we are not able to earn, through the common vicissitudes of life : sickness, failure to find a suitable job, injury, and old age. The original social security schemes which were started in 1911 took their shape from the voluntary schemes which had been introduced by the Friendly Societies and the Trade Unions for their own members. These had shown that a comparatively small

weekly contribution built up sufficient funds to enable a weekly sum to be paid to those members who incurred the risk insured against – sickness and unemployment for the most part; and that this was generally enough to enable those benefiting to get through a bad period without recourse to the hated Poor Law. The State schemes differed from these both in being compulsory and in involving both the employers and the community in the provision of the funds; but they followed their example in one respect : there was no idea of giving a sum that would provide basic subsistence needs; the aim was to give a sum which, though small, would be a firm foundation for one's own savings and would therefore give an incentive to people to think of future needs and put aside part of their earnings to meet them. Nor was any account taken of dependants. Wages are paid for the work done and a man with children does not receive more from his employer than a bachelor doing the same job. As insurance benefits were thought of as an alternative to wages there was similarly no idea of providing more for the family man than for the bachelor.

It was not until the chronic mass unemployment which characterized the twenties and thirties that this aim was seriously challenged. It was one thing to assume that men could save enough to help themselves if they were out of a job for two or three weeks; one can cut down purchases to the bare essentials and postpone the buying of, say, new shoes, or pots and pans, until better times. But this was not possible when people were without work for months and even years at a time as happened to hundreds of thousands of those who had been employed in the great industries – mining, shipbuilding and textiles – which were declining.

It was this more than anything else which altered the whole conception of social security schemes. At first, when it was hoped that the difficulties would be short-lived, all sorts of temporary supplements were introduced; allowances for dependants, larger benefits to approximate more closely to costs of living, longer-term benefits even after the period for which one had an insured right had been completed and so on. And for well over a decade it was assumed that, as soon as the severe industrial depression was over, the schemes would revert to their original design. But the 'temporary' crisis went on for so long that new ideas and expectations were created. What now began to be accepted as the right and proper aim of insurance was a payment that would provide a basic subsistence and not simply a jumping-off ground for private saving, and this meant that it must inevitably take account of the number of people, including wives and children, who had to be maintained.

It was primarily the problems posed by long-term unemployment that led to these developments, but it was soon seen that the difficulties caused by lack of earnings due to sickness or industrial accident were just as serious, and must be provided for in the same way. Moreover thirty years of development of schemes each with its own funds and its own administration had led to all sorts of anomalies which could not be rationally justified. It was decided, therefore, to have a thorough inquiry into the whole system of income maintenance during periods when normal earnings were not forthcoming and this was the famous investigation made by Sir William Beveridge (later Lord Beveridge), whose main recommendations became the basis of the comprehensive scheme of social security embodied in the Act of 1946.

Beveridge started from the point that it is the duty of a civilized community to ensure that all its citizens have a minimum income to live on, and a minimum provision of medical service, education, and housing, and that all social policy should be designed with this as its objective. In so far as an adequate income is concerned this must take account of the fact that the needs of a family vary with the numbers of which it consists and as the price of necessities is the same whether one's income has disappeared because of sickness or of unemployment there is no reason to have varying benefits. So one weekly contribution during the earning period should be made enough to cover all benefits, at one standard rate, during non-earning times.

There were two important innovations in this scheme. (a) The provision for old age had formerly been made by a pension paid out of State funds; now it became part of the general contributory system. (b) The new system applied to everybody and not simply to wage-earners. The long-term depression of the twenties and thirties showed that large sections of the non-manual and 'middle-class' employees might be as insecure as weekly workers; and perhaps equally strong in its effect was the sense of community of all classes which had grown up during the trials of the Second World War.

The new National Insurance scheme was designed to maintain a standard of living during periods when the bread-winner was unable to earn; but inquiries made during the thirties showed that a very large number of people were dangerously near or even below the poverty line even when in full work. Most families go through a cycle of good and bad times. The newly married man generally earns enough for himself and his wife but as each child arrives it gets more and more difficult to stretch the same wage to cover the requirements of the added numbers. If there are several children and the father is earning only a modest wage there is likely to be severe poverty when all the children are below earning age; then as each child begins to earn the pressure eases until once again the wage is sufficient to meet the needs of the earner and his wife. During the difficult thirties when wages were low and often irregular Mr Colin Clark, who made a careful investigation of income distribution, came to the conclusion that more than half the dependent children in the community at any one time were living in families whose income per head brought them very close to the danger line. Later on as the children grew older and began to earn these families would not be in poverty but the undernourishment, bad housing, and narrow experience of these children during their most formative years would have a lasting effect on their health and ability. No amount of good food later on could possibly compensate for extreme deprivation during childhood.

The way out of this dilemma was pointed out by Miss Eleanor Rathbone in a book called *The Disinherited Family* in which she urged the State to accept responsibility for the welfare of its future citizens and help to support children when their father was in work just as it had agreed to do when he was unemployed. This led to the Family Allowances Act and a payment, made out of taxation funds, to the parents of dependent children; it was one further strand in society's method of ensuring a minimum standard of living.

A national scheme must treat alike all citizens in the same or similar circumstances. But human beings are so infinitely variable that, however carefully categories are defined, it is impossible to fit everybody neatly into them. The insurance and family allowance systems provided an income as a matter of civic right; there was no requirement to prove that the recipient was in need through lack of his own resources, as had been necessary under the Poor Law. But an amount that is sufficient for the majority of people may fall badly below what is needed by those in special difficulties. And so there is always a need for a residual service, a net put to catch those who for one reason or another are not adequately provided for by the ordinary system. This was the National Assistance Scheme, now renamed and reorganized as the Supplementary Benefits Commission. The money for this does not come from insurance contributions but out of national taxation and is intended to provide for the special needs which may not be covered by insurance benefits or retirement and widows' pensions. To qualify for this, need must be shown but the changed temper of the community in this respect is well illustrated by the difference in this kind of means test from that associated with the old Poor Law. The inquisition of those administering the Poor Law means test and the social stigma attached to being 'on relief' were so great that thousands suffered dreadful deprivation rather than submit to them. Nowadays people are *urged* to ask for supplementary benefits and a considerable amount of expense is incurred by the authorities in bringing their rights to the notice of those who might be in need of them. The Supplementary Benefits Commission lays down – and varies with changes in prices – what might be called a minimum income to which everybody has a right, and those whose resources fall below this amount are entitled to receive a sum which makes up the difference.

Before the National Insurance Act 1946 those who reached a certain age could claim an Old Age Pension provided their own resources fell below a certain amount and even today there are still a number of elderly men and women who are not entitled to the contributory Retirement Pension because they were too old when the Act was passed to be able to establish a claim. In 1970 special provision was made for them by an additional grant, as a statutory right. Since 5 July 1970 a man who on that day was aged 87 or more and a woman aged 82 or over can now claim a pension of £7.90 a week without any means test.

More will be said about this in the chapter on poverty.

Two of the problems of trying to maintain a minimum standard of living are that (a) when prices rise the cost of the main elements in the cost of living are the first to be affected and (b) the concept of what constitutes a minimum standard does not remain the same. The first is easy enough to understand though not so easy to deal with. If the weekly benefit paid out in the national insurance scheme is raised as prices go up this involves a proportionate rise in the contributions paid by workers and their employers. Neither group welcomes such a rise. The worker who is not immediately in need of benefit because he is young, healthy, and in employment resents the further erosion of his pay packet; and the employer finds that his costs of employing people go up even though wage rates remain the same. There is also an administrative difficulty. Twenty-five million people are in the occupied population and all of them must be informed in good time of the changes, and similarly all the local offices responsible for actually handing over the money must know the new details. It is inevitable, therefore, that there must always be a time gap between changes in the cost of living and the consequential changes in rates of benefit. The administrative problems are the same even when no contributory factor is involved, but a benefit paid from State funds has the additional problem that it must make adequate provision for collecting the money through the taxation system and most people resent an increase in taxes just as much as an increase in the direct contribution to insurance benefits.

But the second problem is rather more difficult because it is less obvious. How far should the standard rates of benefit and retirement pension and the standard rates calculated for supplementary benefits reflect a general change in the wealth of the country as a whole? Even though the annual rate of growth in this country has been considerably less than that of many of its industrial competitors, it has nevertheless been positive; that is, the country as a whole is richer than it was, say, a decade ago. Ought we to raise the minimum guaranteed income to individual citizens to take account of this increase in wealth or ought we to continue simply to ensure that each has the opportunity to purchase the essentials, even though he would not, in that case, enjoy the same *proportion* of the wealth of the community as he did before? It depends very much on what we believe to be the aim of the whole system of social provision, and will be more fully discussed in the chapter on poverty.

There is, however, a very much knottier problem to solve. One of the great improvements introduced by the Act of 1948 and based on the Beveridge recommendations was the idea of universality. Every member of the community, it was thought, should have the same rights and the same responsibilities. This view had strong economic and social arguments to support it for the long depression between the two world wars had shown that the insecurities of modern life were not confined to the manual working class. Hundreds of thousands of non-manual employees whose earnings had brought them above the level of the incomes of those insured had found themselves thrown out of work and similarly thousands of small business men saw their profits dwindling to such a degree that they could no longer pay their way as they had been accustomed to do. But probably the most important argument was psychological and sociological. It stemmed from the desire that everybody should be treated as equals and that the maintenance of a minimum standard of living should be accepted as a right for the whole community and paid for by the whole community. Though, as has been shown, it was necessary still to retain a residual service for those whose resources, despite these rights, were not sufficient to keep them on this standard, and therefore there had to be some investigation of the amount of resources they could command, so as to establish their extra needs. There was a determined effort to ensure that this inquiry into the individual's income should be very different in character from the means test associated with the old Poor Law. So much hated had the old means test become that it developed into a kind of myth symbolizing all that was most hated in a less compassionate society. Under the new régime the kind of inquiries that could be made were carefully laid down by the Government and generous allowances were made for the possessions that could be left out of account so that individuals might have the right to additional assistance without giving up their prized possessions or any considerable amount of their savings.

But a problem arises from this effort to treat all alike. The revenue at the disposal of the State is limited. It can only be increased if people are willing to pay higher taxes. If we want to raise sickness and unemployment benefit and retirement and widows' pensions the funds cannot be got in any other way than by higher taxes. The question is asked now, whether we have not, after more than a quarter of a century, wiped out the bitter memory of the means test and so given ourselves the freedom to raise the amounts provided for the more needy without increasing the benefits and pensions for those who do not need the extra amount. This is the question of selectivity; but, of course, it is not only in connection with income maintenance that this problem arises and the discussion of it must be left until the other most important elements in the Welfare State have been mentioned.

(2) The National Health Service is one of the biggest and most constructive factors in social provision. The maintenance of a money income during periods when the breadwinner could not earn was the first national insurance scheme to be introduced (even the unemployment scheme was at first confined to certain industries), for it was recognized that illness might occur to anybody and its financial consequences could be disastrous. And as part of this insurance scheme the insured person had the right to a certain amount of medical attention; but this medical service was confined to the insured person; that is, mainly manual workers. What the National Health Service did was to extend to the whole community the right to medical, hospital, dental and other services. There are many people who believe that this Service is paid for out of insurance contributions but this is not so. It is true that there is a Health Service contribution which is collected, for the sake of convenience, at the same time and through the same means as the national insurance contributions; but the total raised in this way pays for about only 10 per cent of the cost of the Service. The other 90 per cent comes out of national taxation, and the Service is available to all whether they are liable to pay the contribution or not. When the Service first began in 1946 it was over-optimistically hoped that the costs would decline because it would bring about such an improvement in the health of the population. This was a rather absurd idea and was soon proved wrong. The greater facilities available have brought to light all kinds of disability from which people who could not afford treatment were

suffering silently and the whole concept of a Health Service has constantly widened. The annual costs have, therefore, increased enormously quite apart from the fall in the value of money which has bedevilled all social provision for the last thirty years. This has meant that it has proved increasingly difficult to retain the original objective of making all medical attention and its corollaries – medicines, surgical and other appliances, spectacles and dentures, completely free to all who needed them and has led to constant controversy about what charges should be made and at what level. Some payment for spectacles and dentures has long been accepted, however reluctantly; but any suggestion that the amount be raised invariably meets with an outcry. But perhaps the charge which generally raises most discussion is that on prescriptions and during the history of the Health Service such charges have been imposed, removed, reimposed, and altered in amount. What are the arguments to be considered in this matter?

(a) The amount that can be spent by a Government on the Service must inevitably be limited in some way, however generous it may be. It is, then, a question of priorities. Of course, a tax on prescriptions is a tax on sickness but is this particular charge worse than inadequate provision of, say, hospitals? Yet the more that is spent on free medicines the less there is to spend on new buildings and better equipment.

(b) When medicine is free many people make frivolous demands for drugs which they do not take in the prescribed manner and which are therefore wasted.

(c) The more one has to pay for spectacles and similar aids the more careful one is likely to be of them. When spectacles were quite free there was a heavy expense due to careless breakages.

(d) On the other hand the higher the cost the more likely people are to postpone getting both the medical advice and the aids they ought to have and this is likely to be particularly a deterrent to those of low-income ranges.

(e) But are there not other ways of getting the same amount of money without deterring people from getting the help they need? For example, why should not hospital patients be charged something for the food (not the medicines) they eat? They would have to pay for their food if they were out-patients; why not also as in-patients? This is specially to be considered for those patients whose incomes remain unchanged during their hospital stay.

It is mainly a matter of personal opinion rather than statistical fact or logical argument where one puts the emphsis or how one rates the priorities in balancing these arguments.

(3) Education is the other big national system of provision. Since the Education Act 1944 free education has been open to all up to the statutory school-leaving age and later than that for those able and willing to stay on at school. In addition a whole network of further and higher educational institutions has been established with fees paid out of public funds and maintenance allowances made for those taking advantage of them.

Income maintenance, health, and education have been singled out for mention because these three illustrate particularly the objective of making social provision that is 'universal', that is, to which every citizen has a right. Other services such as housing are still concerned primarily with special categories and income ranges and when we consider the rights and wrongs of selectivity it is as well to recall the extent to which it is still embodied in our social legislation. Quite apart from the supplementary benefits the resources that people have at their disposal are taken into account in the amounts they are required to pay for school meals, for rent rebates, for home helps, for higher education, for medical prescriptions and the cost of physical aids for disability, for the charges in old peoples' homes and for children in care, for legal aid, and so on. There are some people who believe that all these tests are wrong and should be abandoned; but for the most part the discussion centres on whether those services which have come to be accepted as universal in their application should have an element of selectivity introduced into them now. What are the arguments for and against this system?

(1) Selectivity necessarily involves an inquiry into means and the term 'means test' has come to be associated with the bitterness and misery of a deterrent Poor Law. Despite the care and even generosity with which most officers now conduct this type of inquiry there are still a considerable number of elderly men and women who would have every right to supplementary benefits but who do not, and cannot be persuaded to, claim them, because they believe them to have the social stigma that used to be associated with 'going on relief'. On the other hand, younger people do not have this feeling and as the very old die (and they are now a comparatively tiny proportion of the total) this difficulty will fade away.

(2) Selectivity is socially divisive. Although most of our social legislation has aimed at providing security against specific and widely encountered difficulties, it has had the secondary objective of creating a sense of community. Instead of 'the rich' paying to help 'the poor' there has been the hope that there would be created the understanding that the whole community makes provision for problems that any member might have to cope with at one or other time in his life. But if benefits are available only to those below a certain income level, once again we create the 'them' and 'us' attitude. In some instances, it is argued, this may lead to real unhappiness; for example, if those children whose school meals or milk are provided free because of the low incomes of their parents are separated from the rest of the class they might feel a degree of humiliation that could leave a scar for the rest of their lives. On the other hand this is an administrative problem that could be overcome with very little difficulty if those in charge of the arrangements at school gave a little thought to it. It is doubtful whether the fact that a parent's income is taken into account when calculating the amount of maintenance allowance for a uni-

versity student has any socially divisive effect at all, so the two are not inevitably connected.

(3) Nobody, probably, would argue that every inquiry into income is wrong or has anti-social consequences. The assessment of the amount of income tax due from an individual requires a most meticulous and comprehensive investigation into his resources and a justification of any expense that he claims he must incur in getting it. Everybody accepts that this is essential and that details of his family and similar commitments must be forthcoming if he is to avoid paying an excessive amount. Why is this different from the similar inquiry needed to claim a social payment? There *is* a difference and this must be admitted. Filling in an income tax form is certainly a formidable undertaking for most people but it is, after all, something that everybody must do. Filling in the appropriate forms to claim free school meals, or a children's clothing allowance or a rent rebate, etc., is an admission of poverty and separates one from the rest of the community. Many of those who would have a rightful claim to welfare benefits are unwilling to make it because they are ashamed to let others (and as these are local inquiries, that means usually their neighbours) know the extent of their poverty.

There is a growing school of thought that proposes that the best way out of the difficulty is to substitute a negative income tax for all social payments. This would do away with the multiplicity of different forms for different benefits as well as the variations made by different local authorities. In this system there would be one inquiry and one only and moreover one which already has wide acceptance – and just as those whose resources are above certain levels have to pay so much to the Inland Revenue, those with less would be credited with a suitable amount to bring them up to the required matching level of income and needs. This is so simple-seeming and so straightforward that it is very attractive; but there are enormous administrative difficulties in its implementation.

(a) How should income be defined? Simply that of one individual or of the whole family? And if not the latter how can needs be made to match resources?

(b) What period of time should be taken as the unit for income? a month? a year? or more? The earnings of those likely to receive negative income tax are notoriously irregular, as indeed, also are their needs.

(c) What would be the effect on the incentive to earn more? or to try harder to find a job? or to be more regular? Already voluntary absenteeism is one of the serious problems in many industries.

(d) Income deficiency is only one of the problems with which a family that falls below the accepted standard of living has to cope. When a claim is made for a particular purpose it is possible for personal help to be given. A negative income tax is inevitably impersonal; indeed that is one of its main attractions to its supporters. But the factors which cause a family to be in special need are so infinitely variable that often a more individual and personal kind of assistance is required as much as the money.

(4) Selectivity throws more responsibility on the individual himself. When the greater part of the working populations lived close to poverty, it is argued, it was undoubtedly essential for the community to come in to organize schemes and build up funds to ensure the prevention of hardship. But is this still true in the 'affluent society'? Should not people who earn good and regular wages (for the percentage of unemployment has been low since 1940, until the mid seventies) be expected to make provision for themselves? Is not such a voluntary provision, which leaves the choice to the individual, an element in a free society? But on the other hand the experience of the past has shown that people are not as rational as this supposes. They do not envisage their lives as a whole, calculate the amounts they are likely to require in the distant future and make prudent provision accordingly. It is an inescapable fact that whilst we are all liable to suffer misfortune – sick-

ness, injury, loss of earning capacity from one cause or another – we do not, in fact, each have the same amount during our lives. And it is part of the optimism of most of us to think that troubles will happen to the other fellow but not to us. If, in fact, we have *not* made adequate provision what is to be done? and how do we justify the misery of the innocent dependants who had no part in making the choice?

(5) The problem finally centres round the funds at our (i.e. the State's) disposal. If benefits are universal we are forced to spread them rather thinly. Many sections of the community receive amounts they do not need and thus deplete the funds which could be provided for those who are in real need. Raising, for example, retirement pensions for everybody or family allowances for all families increases the incomes of hundreds of thousands who are well able to meet their requirements from their own resources but makes it more difficult to provide adequately for old people who have no other income and no family to help them, or families with many children and low earning capacity. Yet it must be remembered that both retirement pensions and family allowances enter into the recipients' income tax returns and that, therefore, part of the amount is clawed back in taxes. To this degree there is already a certain amount of selectivity. Indeed, in so far as family allowances are concerned a deliberate amount of selectivity was introduced in 1967–8. In that year the allowances, which were then nil for the first child, £46 per annum for the second and £52 for the third, were increased by 50p per week. But at the same time this extra amount was 'clawed back' from those paying income tax at standard rate so that the increased allowance was concentrated entirely on those too poor to pay income tax at all, that is, those with an income of £894 provided there were two dependent children. In this way selectivity was introduced without a means test. But on the other hand it must be remembered that income tax payers received, in a sense, selective advantages through the rebates they could claim if they had dependent children. £115 was

deducted from taxable income for every child under 11, £140 for children between 11 and 16 and £165 for those over 16 if still dependent on the taxpayer. The lowest amount was worth £45 a year for those paying tax at standard rate.

Whatever the basis on which services are provided they must be paid for, and even those which have a contributory element, such as insurance benefits and retirement pensions, depend to quite a large extent on public funds; whilst others, such as supplementary benefits, education, and ninety per cent of the Health Service are paid for entirely by rates and taxes. As everybody has to pay these, for even those with very low incomes buy some goods of which the price includes an indirect tax, the question must be asked, 'How much do we gain by these services?' It is a question that is much easier to ask than to answer.

Obviously the person who has no children to take advantage of educational provision, who lives in a house he owns himself so cannot possibly be subsidized in his rent, and who chooses to be a private patient instead of using the National Health Service will not have much advantage from the most important services. On the other hand a family with several children of school age, living in a council house with a subsidized rent and getting medical attention free and welfare foods at low cost, will have a considerable addition to the income. But this addition will not be the same throughout the family's life. When the children grow up they will no longer be taking advantage of educational facilities nor will they need welfare foods; and most people are likely to need more medical attention when they are elderly than when they are in the prime of life. So there is no typical family or household whose gains we can accurately measure.

Again it is extremely difficult to assess exactly how much people of different income ranges pay in taxation. As far as income tax is concerned we can get a pretty good idea because this is a direct tax and most of us pay it through P.A.Y.E. according to a definite code which takes into account the amount of the income and the number of dependants as well as many other factors. But indirect taxation, and this provides just about half of the total revenue, is another matter. Unless we buy the goods on which taxes are levied we don't, of course, pay the tax and whether we buy or not is a matter of personal choice. The taxes on tobacco, petrol, and alcohol between them account for about 40 per cent of the total raised by indirect taxation and a man who does not smoke or drink or drive a car and rarely uses buses contributes nothing to this amount.

All we can do, therefore, is to try and calculate the probable situation for families consisting of differing numbers of men, women, and children, enjoying incomes of different sizes.

This kind of calculation is made periodically by the Central Statistical Office. As was pointed out in the chapter on incomes we know how much is raised by a particular tax, for example, that on tobacco, and though we do not know how much each family spends on smoking we can calculate and make a fairly good estimate of how much is probably spent by a family of a certain size. In this way we can relate taxes and benefits but it must always be remembered that this does not refer to any particular family but is simply an assessment of how a family with a certain income and consisting of such and such a number of adults and children is *likely* to be affected. The latest such calculation published refers to 1973.

Average household income by household composition[1], United Kingdom

£ per year

Household composition	Code[2] 1964[3] A	B	1969 A	B	1973 A	B
1 adult –non-pensioner	655	642	769	805	1,149	1,254
1 adult – pensioner[4]	13	263	24	415	32	620
2 adults – non pensioner	1,104	1,050	1,156	1,441	2,366	2,295
2 adults – pensioner	39	444	52	651	80	1,035
2 adults 1 child	1,112	1,117	1,586	1,559	2,673	2,564
2 adults 2 children	1,213	1,299	1,762	1,818	2,755	2,784
2 adults 3 children	1,164	1,386	1,705	1,971	2,890	3,188
2 adults 4 children	1,136	1,453	1,638	2,121	2,652	3,372
3 adults	1,473	1,442	2,140	2,065	3,366	3,274
3 adults 1 child	1,543	1,581	2,123	2,195	3,506	3,641
3 adults 2 children	1,657	1,829	2,232	2,491	3,412	3,885
4 adults	2,039	1,944	2,789	2,698	4,520	4,426
All households in the sample	1,129	1,188	1,519	1,600	2,309	2,443

1. Source: Family Expenditure Survey.
2. Code: A Original income
       B Income after direct taxes and benefits
3. In 1964 original income included employers' contributions to national insurance, etc.: from 1969 these contributions have been excluded. Income after direct taxes and benefits is unaffected.
4. A pensioner household is one which derives at least three-quarters of its income from national insurance retirement and similar pensions and/or supplementary benefit.

Chapter 12

THE MEANING AND EXTENT
OF POVERTY

WHAT do we mean when we say that, despite all the developments of the Welfare State mentioned in the last chapter,
poverty has not been abolished? How do we define poverty
and is it possible to measure it? These are questions which
have aroused a great deal of discussion in recent years.
When the Welfare State was coming into being as a result
of the many Acts developing the social services, it was
hoped, and even categorically stated, that poverty would be
abolished; but within the last decade serious doubts have
arisen. It must be said at once that these questions are not
easy to answer. If we could define precisely what we mean
by poverty we could fairly easily decide on means of measuring its extent. The difficulty is to define.

When Charles Booth wrote his monumental series of
books on the *Life and Labour of the People of London* he
had to make some rough assessment of the amount needed
to keep families of varying sizes; but the first attempt at a
precise definition was made by Seebohm Rowntree for the
book he published in 1899. He calculated the exact amounts
of essentials required – food, accommodation, clothing, etc. –
and at what prices such things could be bought in the area
he was studying, and thus arrived at a figure showing the
money needed to keep a household in a state of bare physical efficiency (that is, not ill through malnutrition). This
amount of money assumed that no member of the family
ever spent a penny on anything not absolutely essential; not
a pipe of tobacco or a glass of beer or any other small luxury,
no newspapers, no leisure-time occupation, or anything else.
It also assumed that the housewife had enough knowledge
and intelligence, as well as the opportunity, to make her

purchases in the cheapest market and to lay out the funds available to her in the best possible way from the point of view of value for money. None of these assumptions was, of course, warrantable. The poorest people of necessity buy in small quantities and therefore at higher average cost than those with more margin in their incomes; they have no storage space nor the kitchen equipment to make good use of foodstuffs that need careful cooking to make them palatable. Nor have most of them the knowledge of food values to guide them or the means to reach shops which might sell at lower prices than the one nearest to them. But this calculation allowed Rowntree to concoct a basic 'poverty line'. Anyone with less income to dispose of could quite certainly be said to be existing below the subsistence level.

His second calculation was rather less austere. It took into account the facts of ignorance and narrow opportunity and allowed some very small expense on such elements in living as the odd smoke or drink, some small variations in diet, a newspaper or a bus ride and so on; and thus constructed another poverty line. The first gave the line of demarcation between those living as it was called in 'primary poverty' and the second those in 'secondary poverty'.

This type of calculation has since become the recognized method of trying to define poverty; but that has not solved the problem, for the idea of what we mean by 'essentials' has undergone a transformation and there is always a good deal of difference of opinion as to what should be included. The decision of what is acceptable as a basic standard depends very largely on what is customary in a country. The daily handful of rice, the sleeping mat spread on the mud floor of a small hut and the slight amount of clothing that are all that the millions of Indian peasants take for granted as their lot would not be acceptable in the United Kingdom even allowing for the necessary items that would have to be changed or included on account of climate. They would not have been acceptable even in the more austere situation of late-nineteenth-century British life. But as the general wealth of a country grows, as industry develops, as communications improve, as more and more members of a community get some idea of how others live, a more and more sophisticated kind of housing and its material equipment come to be regarded as elements in a standard below which nobody could be expected to live and, therefore, as the new 'poverty line'. Since Rowntree made his calculations many kinds of food that could then either not be bought at all or by only the richest people have become generally available, and have thus come to be part of the varied and more palatable diet that is assumed to be necessary. Such amenities as radio and television did not exist then for even the richest people but nowadays radio, at least, is no longer thought of as even a modest luxury, and over ninety per cent of households own a TV set.

The amount that is now accepted as representing this poverty line is the rate of supplementary benefit laid down by the Supplementary Benefits Commission. This takes into account the numbers in the household dependent on the person to whom the benefit is paid as well as changes in the prices of the goods and services included in the estimate. And because of the great degree of variation in the rents paid and the practical difficulties (if not impossibility) of people being able to move to accommodation that might be more within the scope of their resources, an extra allowance is made for the actual rent unless this can be shown to be more extravagant than the circumstances warrant. It is the amount of this benefit which is the constant subject of discussion; some arguing that it is grossly inadequate and that it does not permit of a standard of life that should be accepted as tolerable in a civilized society and others that it is dangerous to raise the amount too easily lest it destroys the incentive to make provision for oneself when one would be capable of doing it. Obviously the level of benefit determines the extent of acknowledged poverty. The higher the level is put the larger proportion of people whose resources fall below it; the lower, the more we can believe that poverty is to be found only in very small sections of the community.

This is the problem to which reference was made in the last chapter. If one were to consider simply the amounts needed to keep people physically healthy one would reach a very different estimate from one which accepted that as wealth increases and the kinds of food, accommodation, clothing, and amenities of the mass of the population become more varied and of better quality, so should the concept of the socially acceptable minimum for those in need be altered. If not, those in need of benefits from the State, such as the aged or handicapped or widows with children to support are compelled to live on standards which fall farther and farther below the level of the rest of the community, and the gap in life experience widens between those who are able to fend for themselves and those who, for whatever reason, are unable to do so. It must be noted that this is not a discussion of whether social provision should be deliberately made in such a way as to bring about a more equitable general distribution of wealth; it is simply a question of whether those whose needs are catered for from public funds should have a share as a matter of course in the greater productivity of the community even though this leaves them in the same relative position as before to other sections of the community.

But perhaps an even more serious problem is the decision of how to make a compromise between the two types of poverty line demonstrated by Rowntree in his delineation of primary and secondary poverty. Whatever one agrees to consider as basic essentials, however much one decides to include varieties of foodstuffs and home equipment that have come to be accepted as common to every household, there is still the difficulty of the extent to which one can assume that the person spending the amount of money thus judged to be needed knows how to lay it out to the best advantage. Spending habits are not rational but are part of a social context. We buy various things because we have been used to them and all the other people we know have similar meals, clothes, etc., and not because we have made a careful estimate of, for example, the dietetic value of meals. And thus it might well happen that a family which has what seems sufficient income to keep adults and children from hunger is still suffering from malnutrition. It cannot be too often emphasized that what we take to be necessaries is determined primarily by convention and not by a calculation of the amount needed to keep life in the body or at a prescribed level of physical health. A modest quantity of cosmetics, if only a lipstick and a box of powder may be as much a 'necessity' to a woman as the food she eats. Of course, in the last analysis though she could not do without any food at all she would not die if she had no lipstick; but she would almost certainly prefer to forgo part of her food in order to look as nearly like all her neighbours as possible rather than feel ashamed to take part in any social intercourse because of her dowdy appearance. The difficulty is that once one departs from the fairly objective calculation that can be made of subsistence needs of food and accommodation one enters something of a no-man's-land. The austere person who never smokes or drinks and who feels no need to go to a cinema or other form of public entertainment would see no necessity for including any such expenses in a basic income. On the other hand, the man who takes pleasure in such things would be likely to judge that some expenditure on these things must be considered as essential unless people are to feel themselves entirely cut off from the social groups amongst which they live.

For practical purposes there is no alternative but to use the level of rates fixed by the Supplementary Benefits Commission. How their figures are reached is never revealed; there is, for example, no list of quantities and prices of foodstuffs, clothing, etc., that could be presumed to be purchased by households of varying sizes such as formed the basis of the Rowntree poverty line but the rates are constantly adjusted as prices change so presumably there is some departmental scale as a guide. But nowadays a great many refinements are introduced in the effort to ensure that all identifiable needs are taken into account. For example, there is a 'long-term' addition to the basic rates – at present 50p – because it is realized that there are certain types of expenditure which become important as time goes on although they could not be considered essentials for a short period. Naturally it is those on retirement pensions who are most likely to qualify for these because if they are in receipt of supplementary benefit the need is likely to continue for the remainder of their lives. In fact, in the latest year for which figures are available, 1969, ninety-eight per cent of those receiving supplementary pensions were also in receipt of the 'long-term' allowance. In addition quite a large proportion can, and do, claim a special payment to meet an exceptional need, for example, the replacement of clothing and bedding, and those entitled to benefit, as also those whose resources are only slightly above the level of the benefit, can receive refunds of payments made for drugs, dental treatment, and glasses, obtained through the National Health Service.

In the previous chapter mention was made of one of the difficulties of a negative income tax that it is impersonal and cannot take account of the enormous amount of variation in individual people. The Supplementary Benefits Commission is responsible for providing this individual care. It has a duty to exercise its functions 'in such manner as shall best promote the welfare of the persons affected by the exercise thereof' and one of its jobs under this heading is to tailor the award to the particular circumstances of the person concerned. There may be a need for special increases over the statutory level on account of special diets due to sickness or infirmity, or extra fuel where a person is housebound, or special footwear for a disabled person or help in replacing curtains or cooking utensils when the recipient has been a long time on benefit. And in the necessary investigation required to identify such needs the officer of the Commission has an opportunity to assess whether other welfare services may be required.

Though the rates of benefit are nationally standardized there are considerable variations in the income and resources of individual recipients quite apart from the allowances for special circumstances because certain possessions are ignored in the calculation of entitlement. For example, any earnings which a person may receive provided they do not exceed £2 (after allowing for reasonable expenses) are not taken into account and this applies not only to a claimant but also to his wife or any dependent children for whom he may be responsible. Again capital assets up to £300 are ignored and any other capital up to £800 is presumed to bring in only a fairly small weekly income; and the Commission has discretionary powers to leave out of account other resources such as the provision, from some other source, of a holiday or a television set.*

A real difficulty is that, although the Commission lays down guidelines, the actual assessment of special needs depends on the official dealing with a particular client and, naturally enough, different officials take different views of a situation. For example, during the seventies there have been many criticisms of officials who assume, without careful inquiries, that a woman who had a male lodger was likely to be partially supported by him though there was often no evidence of a special relationship between them.

Of those receiving supplementary benefits in 1969, 70 per cent were old, 12 per cent were sick, and 8 per cent were unemployed. The remaining 10 per cent were mainly those who were employed but whose earning capacity was so low that their wages were less than the level of the benefit rates. This last group always presents a serious problem. Ever since the days of Speenhamland in the early part of the nineteenth century it has been generally accepted that it is unsafe to give allowances from public funds to those with low wages be-

---

* During the present inflationary period these figures are often altered. For example, the earnings figure has been increased but of necessity changes are made so frequently that it is not useful to give details.

cause this probably leads to the wages sinking even lower as unscrupulous employers rely on getting their work done by men who are being partially supported by the State. Thus there has always been a 'wages stop' on allowances. When first dependants' allowances were introduced into unemployment insurance benefit during the period of the chronic mass unemployment of the late twenties and thirties it was decreed that no amount could be paid to an unemployed man which brought his income from this source within so many shillings (usually four) of his normal weekly earnings; and a similar bar has been placed on supplementary benefit. This raises a difficulty in respect of those families where the father is in a low-paid occupation – either because of his lack of any skill or because of his shiftlessness or other characteristic – and there are several young children to be supported. There is felt to be some danger in making as full provision for the family as he would have got in work. There is now little apprehension that this will lead employers to reduce wages still further, for trade unions now cover a very wide range of occupations and are certainly strong enough to prevent any such erosion; and Wages Councils covering about three million of what used to be the least protected occupations are some shield in the trades that are still unorganized. But the danger is felt rather in the possible effect on the father and his willingness to work and earn as much as he could if he knows that in any case neither he nor his children will suffer. On the other hand poverty during childhood has consequences that remain throughout the adult life and it is questioned whether those unfortunate enough to be born into such households should be left to be the victims of circumstances which are obviously not in their control. In the effort to overcome this difficulty the Government has introduced a measure to provide a Family Income Supplement for such families. The proposal is to add an amount to the income of every family which falls below the poverty line whether the father is in full-time work or not. It is based on a scale of £15 a week for a family with one child plus £2 for each additional child. The actual sum to be paid is half the amount by which the family income (including family allowances) falls short of this scale, with a possible maximum of £3 and a minimum of 20p. This F.I.S. will be paid only to families with children and is estimated to cost £8 million a year to be distributed between 160,000 families. This is intended to overcome the problem of the 'wage stopped' benefit.*

There are other factors which create very different standards of living for those in receipt of supplementary benefit quite apart from the variations in their own resources. These depend on the area where one lives and the kind of amenities available, whether they are provided by the local authority or by voluntary agencies. For example elderly men and women living on retirement pensions in one locality may receive regular nourishing 'meals on wheels', have transport provided to enable them to attend Darby and Joan Clubs or Day Centres, be able, if they wish, to live in sheltered housing (that is, in flats or houses grouped in such a way that help is easily available during illness or any other period of stress), have a regular chiropody service, and be in touch with a well-run voluntary agency which takes care that those who want companionship and friendly visits can get them, all of which enables them to remain happily independent. Others with exactly the same money income may live in an entirely different locality where none or few of these amenities are available to them.

Again, two fatherless families with identical incomes might similarly have very different standards of living if one lives in an area, say a New Town, where a council house or flat can be procured at a modest rent and where the children attend a new school with the latest equipment and good teachers and where there are good medical facilities; whereas the other might be in a run-down slum housing area, paying for poor accommodation at a higher price, with

* Again, the amounts have been changed because of inflation.

schools built in the Victorian period and where there are fewer teachers and doctors because of the unpleasantness of living in such an area for those who can make a choice for themselves.

With all these various provisions for low-income groups why is there still poverty? or is there? The answer to the second question depends on how one defines poverty and how far one accepts that the Supplementary Benefit Commission calculates accurately what is required in different circumstances. If one were to compare standards of living in this country with those in a great part of the rest of the world, particularly in the East, in many parts of South America, and in the less developed lands of Africa, one would be compelled to admit that poverty here is non-existent. If, however, one defines poverty relatively to the accepted ways of living in the community the answer would be different and this is now coming to be the more widely accepted definition. People are said to be in poverty if their resources, whether provided by themselves or by public funds, do not allow them to have the kind of diet, the living accommodation and amenities, and to take part in the general activities, customary in the society in which they live. It is this 'relative deprivation' which is coming to be taken as the new Poverty Line.

If this definition of poverty is accepted it can be readily understood why there are still groups of people in poverty though the numbers would depend on the scale on which one expects everybody to be able to 'have the kind of diet, living accommodation and amenities and take part in the general activities customary to the community', that is, how one defines 'relative deprivation'. Half the households in Great Britain now own a car but there would be few who would say that the ownership of a car is necessary to take one above the poverty line; hundreds of thousands of families now go abroad for an annual holiday but one would not include a visit to the Costa Brava as an essential to bring one above the poverty line; nor would the variety and quantity of food and drinks usual to an affluent wage-earner in, say, the motor industry, be considered as basic essentials. But it can easily be seen that people will differ quite a lot in what they believe to be 'relative deprivation'.

Whatever the level, however, there is little doubt as to which households are likely to fall below the poverty line, though the numbers would vary. Where the father of a family with several young children is in a low-paid occupation there will fairly certainly be deprivation even if the mother is a paragon of a housewife and can make every 10p go as far as other people do with 20p; an old person living alone entirely on pension or supplementary benefit and with no family or kind neighbours near at hand to help out; the families with chronically disabled or mentally handicapped members to whom constant attention must be given; fatherless families where the mother, either because she is unmarried or widowed, must earn to support the children as well as look after domestic affairs : it is fairly certain that most of these would be considered to fall below the poverty line if it is defined as 'relative deprivation'. And it is largely because of this new definition that the question of selectivity has become so important. Poverty amongst children is probably the most serious of all because it cramps the health and mental and emotional development for the rest of life and this is a kind of poverty that could be most easily dealt with. Family allowances already exist; a really steep increase in the amounts would lift all families with young children out of poverty but unless those with adequate means of their own were excluded the cost to the taxpayer would be enormous. To raise the allowance to £1.75 per child and also include the first child (who at present is excluded) would cost £250 million a year, and that figure takes into account that richer householders would pay some part of the allowance back in the higher income tax to which they would be liable.

But even higher family allowances would not provide adequately for fatherless families. If the mother is widowed and the father had paid his national insurance contributions regularly she is entitled to a widow's pension if she has dependent children, and a rise in this pension as well as the increase in the allowance for the children would bring her out of poverty; but when the mother is alone because she has been divorced or abandoned or if she has never had a husband the position is more difficult. To provide a universal state income for all those in these categories might be considered too strong an inducement to less responsible men to shove their legal obligations on to the taxpayer so that any estimate of the cost involved depends on one's view of human nature. Already despite the legal obligation to pay separation and maintenance allowances to a former wife or the mother of one's child, it is extremely difficult to devise sanctions to enforce the law.

If 'relative deprivation' is taken as the definition it is obvious that, whether universal or selective allowances were to be made available, they would have to be constantly reviewed to determine what is needed, not simply because of changes in prices but on account of changes in customary diets, living accommodation, and amenities. One could imagine that if it comes to be as common for every household to possess colour TV as it is now for it to have a radio, this might be included as an essential in the same way that we now include some modern method of cooking and lighting. But a quite different calculation would be needed if poverty were defined as suggested on page 309 as inequality. There are many people who consider our present social stratification to be as great an element in poverty as the difficulty in acquiring food, clothing and house room that are now thought of as basic essentials. They argue that the wide divergence in habits of living between, say, the top 20 per cent of income ranges and the bottom 20 per cent is so great that it develops or preserves such a difference in social status as to make people 'feel' poor and others take them as being poor even though they have enough to live on in the ordinary manner of speaking. How far one accepts this view depends on the extent to which one believes in an egalitarian society. To a great extent the development of social provision has stemmed from a desire to lessen inequalities almost as much as to reduce poverty; and this is particularly true of expanding educational facilities and the National Health Service and of a progressive income and surtax and increased capital taxes. It is not certain how far these developments have, in fact, lessened inequalities between differing income ranges. There is no doubt that there is considerable reallocation of resources between sections of the same income group. For example, a man with no children pays very much more tax than he can possibly gain from social provision whilst one earning the same income but with children may get more than he gives. But it is not so certain that the gap between richer and poorer is narrower than it used to be. The general impression is that it is so. There are certainly less obvious differences in ways of living between the fairly well paid wage-earner and the main body of the middle classes than there used to be. The equipment of homes, food, and clothing approximate to an increasing extent. In a sense, that is, the middle of the community has become very much larger and now includes a large proportion of the manual wage-earners as well as the white-collar worker and manager. But the extremes remain. Despite high surtax there are still some very rich people, mainly because of the tremendous inequality in the possession of capital wealth. How far this should be considered to be an element in the extent of poverty is a matter of opinion. It is part of social philosophy rather than of economics.

But there is still one other cause of poverty to be mentioned. Legislation can provide entitlement to various kinds of provision from public funds; it cannot ensure that everybody with the right to them actually gets them. This depends on whether or not those entitled make their claims. During the last ten or twenty years a very determined effort has been made by public authorities to publicize the rights to which different categories of people are entitled and to urge them to claim them. But it is quite certain that there is still a large number of people who are living more poverty-stricken lives than they need to because they have not made a claim. There are a number of reasons to account for this anomaly.

(1) There are still those who cannot realize that the stigma which used to be associated with receiving Poor Relief is a thing of the past and who therefore obstinately refuse to accept what they persist in looking on as charity. This is true much more of the very elderly than of the younger age groups because they retain such bitter memories of their earlier years; but there are also some amongst the younger generation who have the same feeling. This is specially so when there is a possibility that the receipt of special help might be made in such a way as to be obvious to others who are not in the same predicament. For example, in some schools, probably through inadvertence or the lack of imagination of those in control, the children who get free meals (because of their home circumstances) have a different coloured ticket from those who pay the price demanded.

(2) The various types of help are conditioned by so many different regulations that those who are entitled and who would be ready and glad to make a claim remain ignorant of their rights. It is one of the problems of a system which tries really hard to temper the wind to the shorn lamb that the various elements in social provision must have different qualifying rules because they attempt to meet such a wide variety of circumstances; but there is no doubt that these variations are very bewildering to those they are meant to help. Much is already done by public announcements, by the Citizens' Advice Bureaux, by the visits of social workers, and by both the statutory and the voluntary agencies to discover those in need of help and assist them to make their claims, but there are unfortunately still a considerable number who live narrow and difficult lives quite unnecessarily simply because they do not know that there is an alternative. It is difficult to know how to get over this problem. A

Citizens' Advice Bureau can help provided a person comes and asks for information or advice but nobody can force anybody to do so; and no amount of publicity will reach those who do not read it or have it brought to their attention by others.

(3) Some people will not take the slight amount of trouble necessary to make a claim even when no means test of any sort is involved. For example when the right to welfare foods for children was available during the Second World War (when severe food rationing was in force and the authorities tried to make special provision for small children) many mothers were too indolent or too ignorant to collect them.

Chapter 13

CONFLICTING VALUES

THE great eighteenth-century wit, Sydney Smith, was once walking along a narrow street when he heard two women, each leaning out of a bedroom window on opposite sides of the street, and quarrelling at the tops of their voices. 'Those two will never agree,' said Smith to his companion, 'they are arguing from different premises.' It is a pity we do not keep this in mind when 'the premises' are mental rather than geographical. Many of the most heated arguments that take place can never be resolved because the disputants have not made clear to themselves or to the other party exactly what it is they are discussing. Only very foolish persons argue about facts which can be verified; the argument centres on the interpretation or the assessment, and that means that, whether explicit or not, it is being measured against some criterion. It is here precisely that the trouble arises because the criteria are rarely explicit. People judge certain policies to be 'good' or 'bad' without thinking out, much less making clear to others, what is the scale of values by which their judgement is formed. Yet it is obvious that a thing must be 'good' for something or 'bad' for something and it depends on whether one wants the objective, that is, the end for which it is good or bad, before one can decide if one agrees or not with the assessment. This chapter is about these conflicts of value.

Economics is, at present, the most precise of the group of social sciences of which it forms a part, because the object of economic action is measurable. It is to maximize the output with the minimum of effort and resources. I don't say that we always know how to do this and particularly not when we are trying to peer into the crystal ball and decide what the result of future actions is likely to be. But we can certainly measure what has already happened and get a fair degree of accuracy in determining both the quantity of the product and the cost in labour and resources that have been involved.

We are not, however, economic robots and the maximization of wealth is not our sole aim in life. There are a great many other facets to our nature and therefore many other things that we want as part of our life; art and nature and the leisure to enjoy them, happy companionship, hobbies and general interests and the time to develop them and so on. In recent years so much has been said and written about Gross National Product – G.N.P. as it is familiarly called – and we have become so used to the tables showing how each country rates in this respect, that there is danger of forgetting that increased production is not the only thing in the world that matters. Of course, it never was. But rising standards of material living now play such a big part in our thinking that there is a danger in overlooking that different aims must be reconciled with one another.

The greatest difficulty comes from the fact that we can measure the economic results of our actions much more easily than the other consequences. Indeed, it is doubtful whether we can actually *measure* the other results at all; all we can really do is to decide whether we like them or not and whether we are, therefore, prepared to forgo a measurable amount of economic wealth in order to achieve them. What we are, in fact, doing is trying to measure against one another things which are not really comparable because they exist in different worlds of value.

The constantly increasing complexity of modern life confronts us with a bewildering number of such issues but they are an inevitable part of social life and always have been; it is only when the greater extent to which our life as members of a community has to be subject to some form of deliberate control that we become aware of the number of such conflicts and the problems involved in attempting to reconcile different aims. In the early years of the last century when modern industry was first establishing itself the conditions of employment in the factories were extremely bad. Unfenced machinery was a danger to life and limb, the buildings were often dirty and insanitary, and the hours of work, even of children of five or six years of age, were intolerably long. When the idea was first mooted that there must be some legislative control to limit the hours of work of, at least, young children, there were heated debates in Parliament and a deep division of opinion in the country. One set of people – and these were not confined to hard-hearted owners of factories – argued that any such control would do irreparable damage because it would so raise costs of production as to prevent the expansion of the markets on which the employment of hundreds of thousands of people depended for their livelihood. The others argued that, even if it did raise costs, the conditions in which those workers were compelled to work could not be tolerated in a civilized society and that, therefore, the risk must be taken in the name of humanity. We know now, from experience, that most of the fears of the first school of thought were unfounded. In actual fact, the control did the opposite of what had been feared because workers who were not dropping with fatigue and ill health could and did work so much better that output increased with fewer hours of work. But this could not have been foretold and those who worked so hard for the legal limitation of hours of work and the improvement of hygienic conditions did so because they believed that the lives of the workers were more important than the expansion of industry.

Unfortunately this does not mean that one can argue for a constant reduction of hours in order to increase output. If so, one could take this to the extreme and propose that no hours at all should be worked if one wanted to maximize output! But the more highly mechanized the work is, the less effect can there be from the better health, etc., of the worker because the pace is set by the machine and not by the worker. It would be possible, by a controlled experiment, to find out just what number of hours worked would lead to maximum output in each occupation; that is, the point at which the decrease in fatigue of the worker ceased to have any effect on production, but that would not mean that that working day should necessarily be the one worked. Suppose, as it might well be in a very highly mechanized occupation, that eleven hours a day brought maximum output, it is very unlikely that anybody would now argue that this is the ideal day. The worker is also an ordinary human being who wants to spend time with his family and to have leisure to take part in social or political activities, to read and develop his hobbies and do all the other things which make life worth living; and it is recognized that his needs as a human being must be reconciled with the demands of industry.

One of the best examples of this conflict of aims is to be seen in the long and bitter fight about tariffs and free trade which was discussed in the chapter on imports and exports. A great deal of the rancour that characterized that debate was due to the fact that the different sections did not realize that 'they were arguing from different premises' as Sydney Smith put it. One school of thought was concerned to show that the retention of completely free trade would lead to greater economic wealth than the imposition of tariffs; another argued that it was politically dangerous to be too dependent on other countries for essential foodstuffs and raw materials in case we were cut off from supplies in time of war; a third group were anxious to protect the agricultural industry because they believed that a very highly urbanized society would be a less valuable type of community than one which is more diversified. The great bitterness of the dispute arose primarily because people did not realize they were arguing about different things – wealth, political safety, the good society – and there is no reason to assume that a course of action which promotes one will inevitably also lead to the others. Hence the need to decide what you value most – a higher standard of material living, more security, a more diverse community, or what?

The part played by Government in our activities is so much more than it used to be that we are now confronted by issues which are increasingly complex. It would be less difficult to make up our minds between things which we recognize that we value for different reasons if we could know with greater accuracy just how much economic wealth we should have to sacrifice for non-economic objectives; but we have to admit that, whilst economics is more capable of measurement than the other social sciences, we can never be certain what will be the future effects of the action we take and this means that there is a considerable area of guesswork in even this side of the question.

(1) Consider the policies we have pursued with regard to the siting of industry. During the last century most of the new industries employed steam power produced from coal and as coal is a heavy and bulky article to carry it was more economical to bring labour and the raw materials required to the coalfields rather than take loads of coal to centres of population. So there were large shifts of population from rural areas to the towns and from the South to the North. The decision where to set up one's firm was left entirely to the owner who naturally judged according to what he believed would prove most profitable, and it did not occur to anybody that any other factor should be taken into account. It was not until the earlier years of this century that Professor Pigou pointed out that the decisions of firms might also have social consequences which are of importance to the country as a whole. The most obvious one – though not necessarily the most important – was the changed character of the locality as it became industrialized : the destruction of natural beauty, the smoke-grimed buildings and smoke-laden air with its consequent danger to health, the lack of open spaces and the greater and greater estrangement between town and country, the increased time taken getting to and from work, and so on. Gradually the idea came to be accepted that a business man could not be a law unto himself but that the wider repercussions of his actions were a legitimate concern of the community as a whole.

After the First World War the decline in the major industries and the rise of others which before had been of less importance brought this problem to the fore. The new industries were not dependent on steam power because electricity had taken place as the chief motor force so there was no necessity to settle on the coalfields and the new industries developed in the Midlands and the South-East. As a result hundreds of thousands of men were out of work in the industrialized areas of the North whilst the younger and more mobile men, with their families, moved away in search of jobs. Whole localities became derelict in one part of the country and new concentrations of population developed elsewhere. Both had a lopsided social structure – one with a preponderance of the old; the other with mainly young families without the support and sense of security of their old social relationships. Thus grew up the idea of deliberately controlling the location of industry with the aim of preserving the fabric of society. 'Take work to the worker instead of the worker to the work' became the slogan. The methods tried to achieve this have been discussed in the chapter on the location of industry; the question here is, 'What are the issues involved?'

First, has it been successful in revitalizing the declining areas? Are the new industries keeping their heads above water? Do they offer enough attractive jobs to dissuade people from moving away? What would have happened had there not been this control? We have to admit that none of these questions can be answered with confidence. Certainly these areas are no longer dependent as most of them were on one single occupation and its ancillaries so that a decline in size of one industry no longer involves the whole area in ruin. But many of the new industries that have established themselves offer much more employment to semi-skilled women than to the highly skilled men thrown out of jobs by the lessening importance of coal mining, and the older industries. Nor do we know how many of the new occupations would have settled in those areas without the large financial inducements (which are provided from public funds and therefore the taxpayer). Nor, even more important, can we know to what extent these firms have been less productive than they would have been if they had sited themselves in the area of their unfettered choice. So that the economic price of the controlled location is largely in the area of guesswork.

But when we come to consider the social consequences which were the principal aim of the policy we are in even greater difficulties. Is it always 'better' to stay put where there is already a developed network of social relationships? Or is it 'better' to move to a new area where all the amenities are likely to have been provided on the higher standards customary in the mid twentieth century, with new houses, pleasantly laid out streets, good shopping precincts, better designed schools and technical colleges, even if one must face feeling strange and isolated until one builds up one's new friendships and contacts? There is no doubt that there has been an enormous amount of movement from choice, not from necessity. Hundreds of thousands of people have deliberately moved to the New Towns away from the congested neighbourhoods of their youth even though they knew this entailed leaving behind loved relations and friends, partly because of the good work opportunities, and partly to give their children fresh air and more space. It has often been difficult for them to feel as much part of the New Town as they did of the old but it is rare for them to move back. On the other hand, there are many who react differently. What appears as a horribly congested, even slum, area to one group may give to another a sense of warmth and cosiness, of 'belonging'. It takes all sorts to make a world. Some people enjoy holidaying on a crowded beach where there is hardly space to move between the deckchairs and the sand castles; others prefer camping in some out-of-the-way spot. How is one to judge whether 'staying put' or 'mobility' brings more happiness and satisfaction to those concerned? And until we can get some idea of this how are we to judge whether, and to what extent, the unknown cost of controlled location has justified itself?

(2) Control of the location of industry is not the only way in which there is conflict of interest between aims which are mainly economic and those which are primarily social. For example, the elevated road built over the Harrow Road in London to enable motor traffic to come into and out of Central London from the West avoids what had before been a narrow bottle-neck which caused great loss of time; but it goes very close to the upper windows of houses along the route. When estimating the cost of making the road and its effect on speeding up important traffic nobody had bothered to take into account the noise, dirt, and misery the inhabitants of these houses would suffer; and it was not until there had been strong protests – accompanied by action to prevent the road being used – that this element began to be fully considered. In this instance the social loss to those living in the houses was so obvious (and incidentally the cost of removing and rehousing them was so small in comparison with the huge bill for making the road) that the decision to do something about it could be quickly reached. But in some other circumstances it is not so easy to determine how to reconcile conflicting interests. For example :

(a) Where should the third London Airport be sited? There are some people who argue, very cogently, that there is no need for a third airport at all; but if we accept that there *should* be one, where should it go? So much discussion has been aroused by this question and there are such violently opposed views that the Roskill Commission was appointed to review the many alternatives. The matter resolved itself into two choices – Cublington in Buckinghamshire and Foulness on the Thames estuary. But by what criteria should the final decision be made?

The cost of building at Foulness would be higher than that at Cublington. Should that factor be given prime consideration? After all, an airport once built lasts a long time and it would need a very big difference in costs, spread over the years, to be really important. What about the convenience to passengers? Here we enter into the realms of speculation because nobody can predict what the nature of the traffic load is likely to be by the time the airport will be in use. Getting from London to Foulness would probably take longer than to Cublington and journeys to and from other towns would be even greater. If the majority of passengers were to be holiday makers, an extra hour or two would not make such a lot of difference; but if the majority were businessmen with urgent appointments to keep, it might.

What about the loss of natural beauty and buildings of historic interest that would be involved? An airport is an enormous complex of buildings, quite apart from the runways: booking halls, waiting rooms, restaurants, shopping areas, freight storage facilities, hotels, housing for workers; and, in addition, main roads which act as feeders from the principal towns. All this necessarily involves the urbanization of large areas. Is it better to destroy the agricultural areas which give a breathing space between London and Birmingham, and all their old villages, and small country towns? or destroy the vast marshlands of the Thames estuary with their wealth of wild life? One has only to ask these questions to realize that the final decision cannot be made on economic grounds alone and that it depends on a personal preference for one kind of world over another rather than a nice calculation of measurable factors. In fact, the differences between the Majority and Minority Reports of the Roskill Commission are an excellent illustration of the conflict of values. As the *Guardian* put it when the Report was published:

The Roskill Report is more than a brief for a third London airport. By implication it raises all the issues of social policy which have led to the establishment of a Department of the Environment. It is about how we mean to live in 1980 and 1990, and at the turn of the century, and more especially, how far we are prepared to go to civilize our runaway world and bring it under control. What are the attitudes that should determine the balance of choice? The Majority believe that Britain's economic difficulties are too great at this moment of time to permit of too much high-mindedness and that, therefore, economic advantages must take precedence over environmental disadvantages. The Minority Report comes to the opposite conclusion and that, despite the extra cost involved, Cublington must be saved so as to prevent the permanent destruction of one of the most charming areas of the country.

There is a third school of thought which, whilst accepting that a third airport is required, thinks that too much fuss is made about the non-economic losses involved. This school insists that the creation of a large number of good jobs for the people living in the locality would be of great value, not only in providing work which is generally much better paid than agriculture, but in offering to young people a wider choice of alternative occupations than is usually available to rural inhabitants.

Indeed, this consideration served to support still further the argument put forward by the writer of the Minority Report, Professor Colin Buchanan, that the choice should fall on Foulness rather than Cublington. His main argument was based on the serious destruction of the environment that would, he believed, be the consequence of placing an airport in Buckinghamshire; but he pointed out that the choice of Foulness would also help alleviate London's complex social problems.

Development of Foulness would play a vital role in reducing the social imbalance between the eastern and western side of London and no other site has the capability to advance any major social objective. So it is my conclusion that Foulness, in spite of certain undoubted environmental disadvantages, is the best site in the interests of the country as a whole.

Since that discussion was at its height the decision has been taken not to build at Foulness and, indeed, general opinion has veered more strongly to the belief that no new airport is needed at all. Instead the extension of facilities at Heathrow and Gatwick has begun to seem more practicable than it was held to be before.

Opinions on all these matters are not only in conflict with one another at any time but change from one time to another and a factor which could be given little weight at one period begins to weigh more and more heavily at another. Until quite recently none but a tiny minority believed that it was a viable policy to curb the amount of transport in the busiest parts of a town; yet now it has become part of 'conventional wisdom' that there should be traffic-free shopping precincts to be used solely by pedestrians; and it is rapidly coming to be accepted, if the method is not yet agreed, that some curtailment of our travelling freedom is required in order to promote a more civilized life. So that to give a higher priority to the non-economic factors in the determination of the site of an airport fits with this kind of concept. But whilst one can quantify – albeit with some difficulty and no complete accuracy – the economic cost of various sites, one cannot similarly quantify what one means by a 'civilized life'.

(b) We do not build a large number of airports so the siting of a new one becomes a topic of national concern; but new roads are constantly needed and these also present problems. Everybody agrees that a good network of roads is an essential from every point of view but how does one decide whether it is worth while to have the increased expense of adding an extra two miles to a particular road in order to avoid cutting through a piece of country which has special beauty – the dispute, for instance, associated with the road scheme across the Chilterns. Again a road which bypasses the High Street in a small village or country town seems good for everybody at first sight; it allows through traffic to move with speed, it reduces accidents to pedestrians in the street, it cuts down the noise and petrol fumes to be endured by those living in the place. But it may spell ruin to the small businesses in the by-passed street. If you want to buy something which is expensive so that you get it only at long intervals, such as a new TV set, the dining-room furniture and so on, you take the trouble to go to the store you think will serve you best. But for such things as tobacco and con-

fectionery, which you buy almost every day and of which
most shops have a similar assortment, you are more likely to
make your purchases at a shop you happen to pass, and if
the traffic is diverted there are fewer passers-by. Recently a
shop of this type calculated that the building of a by-pass
had cost it a drop of £100 a week in its takings.

(c) The closing of many railway lines and stations after
the Beeching Report (see Chapter 2) brought to the front
the serious problem involved in the consequent social isola-
tion of hundreds of thousands of people who were cut off
from shopping areas and the normal opportunities for
friendly intercourse. This led to the decision to subsidize certain lines which could not possibly be made to pay their
economic way but which were thought to be necessary on
other grounds. How much inconvenience and loss to social
life to one group of people must there be to justify an extra
burden on the general taxpayer? This is one example of a
much larger group of problems. In most big cities the press
of motor vehicles is making it almost impossible to move at
all during some parts of the day. The more people who use
private cars the less possible it becomes for public transport
to pay its way and the more inadequate the services it can
afford to offer; and therefore the greater the number who
decide to run their own cars despite the delays, and the
vicious circle becomes more and more vicious. Should com-
muter railways and buses be heavily subsidized so that they
can run a service which would induce more people to leave
their cars at home during working hours? There is an
economic calculation to be made here for the greater the
number of cars the heavier are the charges for road maintenance and, in any case, this charge must be borne on public
funds; so that even on economic grounds it might pay to
cheapen the fares of public transport so as to give a greater
incentive to use it. But the value of the time lost in delayed
journeys, and the secondary social costs in frayed tempers
and frustration of both residents and commuters are more
difficult to evaluate.

(3) It is now fashionable to talk about cost-effectiveness as the criterion by which one should judge different policies. By this is meant the attempt to equate the cost in labour and resources of the implementation of a scheme with its probable result. One could, for example, estimate the cost of building a fleet of Boeing 747s and try to predict the numbers of passengers that could be carried and what fares they would be prepared to pay and so decide whether the project would be worth undertaking. In doing this it would be necessary to estimate the probable charges for maintenance, and the probable life of the aircraft as well as the need to 'keep up with the Joneses' – that is, how much traffic might be lost to other airlines as a whole, if one decided not to build these giants. How can one apply this reasoning to the social services? In the example I have given it is possible to do the sums wrongly, particularly as one half of the calculation has an inevitable element of speculation in it (because we cannot know how potential passengers will react until they have been given the choice) and even the cost of production cannot be known with any certainty (as is well evidenced by the astronomical increase in the cost of the Concorde since its inception); but at least both sides of the calculation are in the same terms. In the social services this is not so, and therefore much of the attempt to measure their cost-effectiveness is nonsense.

Take, for example, the raising of the school-leaving age. We can estimate how many more schools will be needed and the probable cost of their equipment; we can similarly estimate the extra teachers, administrators, school cleaners, doctors, dinner cooks, and so on, and can make a guess at the extra cost involved. We can even make a guess, though not very accurately, at the amount of production for which these young people might have been responsible if they had not spent the extra year at school. But when we come to the other side of the bargain, where are we? How do we put a value on the existence of more educated young people in the community? We might argue that a year of employment in the 'school of life' would do more for their mental development and their character than another year at school. I am not saying this – in fact, I do not believe it – but I *am* saying that we don't know, and therefore any statement, on whichever side it is, is a matter of opinion and not of calculation. Most of us, particularly those who have any connection with the educational system, have strong views about the content and methods of the education of adolescents. Our opinion of the value of the extra year would vary according to whether the schools offered the kind of education we favour or not.

We have a similar problem when we consider the expansion of the universities. Should everybody who wants it – and who can show the minimum educational capacity – have the right to go to a university or a comparable form of higher education? and how do we judge whether the cost to the taxpayer is justified? We might possibly make a rough guess if every student studied some form of discipline which could be applied to increased productivity in industry – technicians, technologists, applied scientists, managers, and so on; though the validity of even this is doubtful: but how do we measure the value of those who devote themselves to metaphysics, or the social structure of a little-known tribe in Polynesia, or theological doctrine or literature or any other subject of study which has no obvious practical application? And what about the thorny problem of the higher education of women? With the present pattern of early marriage most women do not work for pay for more than a few years after qualifying and even if they return to work ten or fifteen years after marriage when their children are older it is more likely to be part-time work because of their family commitments.

The plain fact is that we make our judgements on social and not on economic grounds. We choose because we believe in justice or equality or the inalienable right of the individual to develop his potentialities to the full, or any other element we think to be an essential of a 'good society'.

The effectiveness of the equation cannot be measured because it is a quality and not a quantity.

I used education as an illustration but exactly the same reasoning can be applied to any other social service. Indeed, this is why we call them 'social services' and not 'nationalized industries'. Let us be quite clear about this. This is not to say that a healthier and better-educated community will not be more productive than its opposite. Of course it will; anything which reduces sickness and helps to develop mental ability is fairly certain to have economic advantages; but we cannot measure them. And the real point of the argument is that the possible economic advantages are not the main reason for providing the facilities to bring about a healthier and better-educated population. We don't, for example, make provision for the mentally and physically handicapped in order to increase our economic wealth. We do it for moral reasons; because we have faith that this is the 'right' thing to do and that the quality of life in a community which shows compassion and generosity is better than its opposite.

(4) The dangers to our environment resulting from new developments in ways of living have now become a matter of widespread concern. Plastic goods, cheaper to produce than those made from the conventional raw materials, are now employed in almost every part of our material equipment; but the trouble is that they are not subject to natural disintegration. So the world is cluttered up with articles no longer in use but which seem to be indestructible. Detergents, cheaper and often more effective than soaps, pollute rivers and lakes. Only collective action can counter these effects of individual activity.

But there is a more difficult conflict to resolve. When earnings were lower and communications more difficult, most manual workers tried to live as near to their work as possible. This was cheaper and cut down the length of the working day. So in most industrial towns you had a welter of streets full of small houses with few open spaces, mixed up with factory and commercial premises. Those with higher incomes moved out to pleasant spacious suburbs or country villages because they could afford both time and transport to get to their offices. Or they went a step further; they lived in the town during the week and moved out to the country house for weekends.

All this has now changed. Wages are higher and a great many wage-earners have cars so that they, too, move from the towns to the suburbs; so more and more of the country is swallowed up by housing estates. But the changes are not confined to the siting of homes. At the weekends – and with the five-day week this means two days – crowds drive out to the beauty spots for sport, walking, and picnics, and places whose main attraction was their peace and tranquillity are now invaded, every fine weekend, by thousands of cars seeking parking space and hundreds of thousands of people looking for food, drink and other entertainment. The very natural desire to find the beauty and quiet of the countryside destroys what it seeks. How does one reconcile the wish for better housing and more recreation with the preservation of the amenities they tend to destroy?

Suppose you restrict building in special areas so as to preserve old villages or historic country towns, you are in danger of leaving these as museum pieces. And it is possible that their inhabitants may resent the fact that restrictions lower the value of the land they might want to sell if new houses and roads were to be built. If the State imposes restrictions for social purposes should it compensate the losses it thus enforces?

It is sometimes said that there tends to be class bias (even though this is generally unconscious) in much of the desire to preserve rural amenities. Most of the strongest opponents of the developments which ruin country tranquillity – or perhaps most of those who are articulate – are middle-class people who have long enjoyed the peace and natural life of their surroundings and forget that eighty per cent of their fellow citizens live in towns and long for some respite from narrow horizons and crowded conditions. Of course rural life was pleasanter and more serene before demands for lower housing densities began to pour the urban masses into the countryside; and it is easy to forget – or more likely not even to know – that areas with more than average unemployment may need industrial developments even though they will destroy some of the natural beauty. Ordinary people want better standards of living, including less congested housing areas and more washing machines and refrigerators and TV sets and all the other things that go with higher standards; and this means that some environmental beauties must be destroyed to make this possible. This is a social need as well as an economic one and makes it more difficult to decide just where the priorities lie.

One of the most difficult of these conflicts centres on the question of whether the mining of what are thought to be extensive deposits of copper and zinc in the neighbourhood of Snowdon should be permitted. The Snowdonia National Park is considered one of the most outstanding beauty spots in Great Britain and it attracts a large number of holiday-makers, hikers, mountain climbers, and those who go simply to wander round this exceptionally lovely locality. But the district is one of the poorest in the country with few opportunities for even modestly paid employment for those who live there. How extensive the deposits of minerals are cannot be known for certain until drilling starts but it is believed that 1,000 people could be employed directly apart from all the ancillary and consequential developments. It is calculated that if you take into account the increased jobs in shops, bus routes, and all the other service trades that are needed to serve a well-paid community, the number of new jobs created would be nearer to three times those directly employed in the mines. A large proportion of these could be recruited locally and there is little doubt that many Welsh expatriates in professional jobs who have been compelled to go elsewhere to earn a living would jump at the chance to come back to their own country. But even with the most careful safeguards to try to prevent more destruction of the natural beauty than is absolutely essential, some urbanization must result and some reduction in the present attractiveness of the area must take place. Which interest should predominate?

(5) There is a conflict of a different nature when one thinks of the character of our taxation system. It is generally agreed that a fiscal system should be just, though there are many different opinions about the best way to achieve this. In this country about half our national revenue is raised by direct taxation (that is, taxes levied on the actual income or capital wealth of the taxpayer) and half by indirect means (that is, the tax is paid as part of the price of goods or services bought, as for instance, taxes on tobacco and alcohol). Direct taxes can be carefully designed so as to ensure the taxpayer contributes whatever amount has been decreed as right; and this, of course, is where differences of opinion arise : but whatever the amount, this is what must be paid. But indirect taxes are paid only by those who buy the goods on which they are levied. The things chosen are those which enter in the budgets of the majority of households but they are by no means universally bought. This means that some sections of the population pay less in tax than the proportion of their income that has been judged the right and just contribution to national expenditure, simply because they happen not to be consumers of these goods. There is no way out of this dilemma unless we decide to get rid of all indirect taxation and collect the total by a straight tax on income. Hence there is always a conflict about the proportion that should be raised by indirect taxes and the particular products on which the taxes should be put.

But there is another and less obvious area of conflict; between justice, however we define it, and simplicity. Income tax is not paid on every penny we receive; there is an effort to temper the wind to the shorn lamb. So there are all sorts of deductions made before our 'taxable income' is calculated : so much because it is earned rather than proceeds from investment, so much for a personal allowance to meet basic needs, and so much for the maintenance of a wife and children and, in certain circumstances, other dependants, so much for premiums on life insurance, and so on. The purpose of all these deductions is the effort to get some degree of justice between one citizen's obligations and another's. But every additional refinement makes the whole thing more difficult to administer (as well as more costly and more difficult for the ordinary man to understand). Would it be better to sacrifice some part of the justice to a larger degree of simplicity? How do we decide such a question? It is fairly easy to agree to exclude some details if one can show that the cost of collection is more than they bring in; but beyond that it becomes solely a matter of personal values.

What has economics to say about all these conflicts of values? Very little it must be admitted. One of the most heated controversies of recent years centres on the degree of priority we give to national economic growth. Some noted economists – J. K. Galbraith for one – have argued that in the richest country in the world, the U.S.A., the enormous increase in wealth has not benefited groups at the lower end of the scale, and there are many in this country, too, who maintain that the more modest British achievement in production has been made at the expense of making the poor relatively poorer than before. There are others, equally noted, who argue that no reallocation of resources will appreciably benefit the standard of living of the poorest unless we produce more as a whole. Which view we take must inevitably be a gamble because it is a speculation about the future and the extent to which on the one hand we believe that unless people have the hope of reaping the rewards of their work and initiative there will be less for everybody to share and on the other hand the belief that a more equal society is so important that it is worth while making a sacrifice for it.

But while economics cannot give us the answers it can help us to clear our minds about the issues. It is something gained to realize that we are generally arguing about things which are not really comparable because they are subject to different criteria. As free individuals we have the right to give a high priority to justice, or equality, or compasssion, or art, or pleasant surroundings, or a different pattern of living, or anything else we favour. What we have not the right to do is to assume that whatever it is to which we give precedence will also automatically raise the material standard of living. To quite a marked extent we can estimate the cost of pursuing any of the objectives we prefer because there is often some experience of the past to guide us, though there must always be also an element of speculation about the future. What we have to consider is how much of this cost we are prepared to pay in order to bring nearer the particular aim we think supremely important. Mankind has always been searching for the philosopher's stone that will resolve all problems. Alas! this is an illusion. Economic analysis, like science, is a tool; it has no moral direction inherent in it. The decision what to do rests, as always, on men and women.

INDEX

Advertising, cost of, 122, 124
  faults of, 125ff.
  forms of, 105–6
  value of, 121–5
  virtues of, 105
'Affluent society', 137
African labour, 15
Agrarian revolution, 160
Agricultural Marketing Acts
    (1931, 1933), 68
Agricultural subsidies, 180–81
Agriculture, 54, 181ff.
  effects of tariffs, 173–6
American loan, 162–3

Balance of trade, 166
Bank deposits, 141ff.
Bank of England, 141–3
Bank rate, see Interest rate
Bankers' Clearing House, 142
Banking, 158
Barlow Report (1940), 95
Basic standards, 32–3
Beeching, Dr, 37, 38, 39, 203
Beeching Report, 38, 347
Beveridge, Sir William (later
    Lord), 301, 305, 309
Board of Trade, 71, 96, 181
Bookselling, and Restrictive
    Trade Practices Act, 74–5
Booth, Charles, 49, 300, 321
Boots, 119
Bretton Woods Conference, 169
British Broadcasting
    Corporation, 35–6, 61

British Electricity Authority, 61
British Home Stores, 119
British Medical Association
    (B.M.A.), 214
British Transport Commission,
    37, 38, 61, 203
Buchanan, Prof. Colin, 345
Budgeting, national, 133, 135,
    147
  personal, 21–2, 23, 34, 35
Building industry, 29, 77, 96, 279
Bulk buying (grocers' groups),
    113

Capital, accumulation of, 254–5
  amount required, 47
  export of, 158–9, 166, 167
  industrial, 87
  investment, 277
  mobilization of, 59–60
  private, 56–9
  provision of, 269–71
  social, 88–9
Capital goods, 270ff.
Catering Wages Act, 222
Central Statistical Office, 261,
    319
Chancellor of the Exchequer,
    144, 199, 219, 227, 275ff.
Cheap labour, 241
Child labour, 298
Church of England, 233
Citizen's Advice Bureau, 334,
    335
Citizens, welfare of, 31–2

Civil Service Clerical Officers
Association, 214
Civilization, growth of, 20, 23
Clark, Colin, 43, 219, 255, 306
Coal, 11, 153
deposits in Britain, 44
exports, 156, 159, 163
minimum prices fixed, 68
nationalization of, 65
output, 163
Coal Mines Act (1930), 68
Coal mining,
unemployment in, 87
Coal and Steel Community, 184
Choice of goods, 72
Commissioners of Inland
Revenue, 200
Common Market, *see* European
Economic Community
Commonwealth, position of in
relation to Common
Market, 187–91
Communications, affecting
expansion of markets,
54, 78
Consumer research, 110
Contracts of Employment Act
(1963), 287
Co-operative Societies, 51, 61,
107, 116–17, 118–19
Co-operative Wholesale
Societies, 118
Corn Laws, repeal of, 177
Cost effectiveness, definition,
348
Cost of labour, effects of, 219
Cost of Living Index, 132, 133,
134, 135, 137, 259, 261
Interim Index of Retail Prices
(1947), 135, 136, 138, 259

Cotton, 10, 11, 156, 159
Cripps, Sir Stafford, 165, 207
Crops (food), 10
Currency, 164ff., 179–80. *See
also* Money

Death duties, 254–7
Debentures, 58
Defence services, 36
Deflation, 134, 145ff.
De Gaulle, President, 194
Department stores, 73, 107
average turnover, 108
variety of choice, 113
Depressed areas, 84, 97, 98
Depression (1931), 158
Devaluation, 165–7
Development areas, *see*
Depressed areas
Diamond, Lord, 199
Diet, diversity of, 154–5
Distribution of goods, 29ff.
Distribution of Industry Act
(1945), 95, 97
Domestic service, 226
Donovan Report (1968), 229

Economic behaviour, 15
Economic laws, 14, 15
Economics, definition of, 13
personal application, 9, 12,
13, 14
Economists, 15, 16, 17
Economy, method of
maintaining, 275–7
Education, 27, 28, 31, 34,
208–9, 247, 248–9. *See also*
Welfare State
Education Act (1944), 208, 313

'Elastic' demands, 22, 23, 25, 215
Elections, 12
Electricity, 11, 79, 159, 176
Empire, preferential treatment of, 178–9
Employees, privileges of, 206
Employment, Dept. of, 230, 290, 291
Employment, fluctuation in, 264ff.
 policy, 272ff.
 sex differentiation in, 232ff.
 social distinctions in, 210, 211
 White Papers on, 95, 267
Environmental pollution, 350
Equal Opportunities Commission, 244
Equal pay, 232–44
 Royal Commission on, 233, 235
Equal Pay Act (1970), 244
Eurodollar, 170
European Economic Community, 148, 182, 183ff., 188–98, 276
 arguments for and against joining, 187–93
European Free Trade Association, 183, 186–7
European Monetary Agreement, 168–9
European Payments Union, 168–9
Exchange Equalization Accounts, 168
Expenditure, Government, 250, 277
Exports, 148ff.
 expansion of, 163, 223

invisible, 157ff., 166

Factory legislation, 94
Family allowances, *see* Welfare State
Family Expenditure Survey, 137, 261
Fashion, in relation to industry, 53, 54
 influence on mass production, 80–81
Fishing industry, 197–8
'Five Towns', 50
Food production, 9, 10
Foreign exchange, 164ff.
 chaos in, 173
 competition of, 152, 177–8
 control of, 179ff.
Free trade, 52, 173ff.

Galbraith, J. K., 354
General Agreement on Tariffs and Trade (G.A.T.T.), 182–3, 194
General Index of Retail Prices (1969), 137
General Post Office, 60–61
Gold standard, 167, 169, 178
Government control, 143, 180
Government Training Centres, 98, 288
Gross National Product, 122, 337
'Guiding light' principle, 227

Health services, 31, 35, 206, 247, 248, 249, 261
Holiday camps, 54
Holidays with pay, 55, 206
Hospitals, 28

Household equipment, 9, 54
Household expenditure, inquiry into, 136–7

Impact of Press, 69
Import Duties Act (1932), 178
Import Duties, allocation of, 181
Imports, 148ff.
  classes of, 152ff.
  food, 148, 155
  raw materials, 155
  restriction of, 177, 178, 179, 180, 181
Income, national, 158, 159, 161, 250
  annual estimate, 199–200
  distribution of, 49
  maintenance, 303–311, 313
  White Paper (1967), 258
Incomes Census, 200
Incomes, personal, addition to, 109
  distribution of, 199
  effect on markets, 55
  fixed, 146
  from 'civic rights', 246ff.
  from property, 244–6
  from work, 203ff. 232–43
  increase in, 55, 138–9, 166, 240, 241
  inequality of, 29, 31, 32
  purchasing power, 42
  redistribution of, 260–62
  White Paper (1948), 128
Incomes, 'social', 205, 261
Industrial estate companies, *see* Trading estates
Industrial Relations Act (1971), 230

Industrialized building, 77
Industries, British, reduced market for, 159–60
  control of, 90ff.
  export, 80, 84
  nationalization of, 55, 65
  subsidiary, 92–3
  See also Location of industry; New industries
Industry, amalgamation in, 65–7
  capital for development, 255
  dependence on foreign supplies, 155
  incentive, 48, 276–7
  instability of conditions, 53, 54
  mechanization in, 45–6
  negotiating bodies in, 66–7
  problem of redundancy in, 284
  revision of methods, 47–8, 99
  seasonal changes, 279–81
  structure of, 51ff., 281
  subsidies in, 180–81
  See also Location of industry; New industries
'Inelastic' demands, 22, 24, 25, 160–61, 252
Inflation, 128, 139, 145ff., 224, 232
Inland Revenue, 245
  commissioners of, 200
Interest rate, 275, 276
International Monetary Fund, 169
International Trade Organization, 182
Investments, overseas, 161
Iron, deposits in Britain, 44

Joint stock companies, 56, 57;
58, 59, 60, 209, 255

Labour, affected by mass
production, 80–81
availability of, 28, 47, 48, 99,
223, 237-8, 264
distribution of, 14, 15, 279
migration of, 85–6
Ministry of, 135, 136
shortage of, 223
Labour Party, 217–18
Land, reclamation of, 95–6
Leisure, value of, 225
Lend-Lease, 162
Local Employment Act (1960),
97
Location of industry, 76ff., 341
control in, 85, 90ff., 343
effect on distribution of
population, 80–81
growth of subsidiaries, 83
influence on employment, 96,
99
light, 3
statistics, 97
See also Industries; New
industries
London Passenger Transport
Board, 240
Longevity, 285
Lord Chancellor, 231
Luxuries, definition of, 23, 24,
31, 109, 135, 154, 252

McKenna Duties (1915), 177
Mail-order buying, increase in,
121
Manufactured goods, 153ff.,
282

distribution of, 78, 101–2
estimate of markets, 26, 27,
29, 52, 84–5
growth of, 176
limitation of design, 67
Manufacturers, and the
wholesaler, 119
Marketing, 120
Markets, 11, 26, 29, 52, 53,
84–5, 101ff., 267ff.
control of, 267
extension of, 54, 55, 78, 271
shrinking, 70
world, 274
Marks and Spencer, 116, 119
Marshall Aid, 156, 157, 163,
164
Mass production, 53, 134, 187,
239
effect on prices, 23, 134
effect on standard of life, 79,
134
technical improvements in,
79
Mechanization, 160, 239
Money, *see also* Currency
cheques, 141ff.
coins and notes, 140ff.
functions of, 128–32
government control of, 143,
180
value of, 131ff.
values, 40–43
Monopolies, 12, 64–7, 70, 127
Monopolies Commission, 70–71;
75
Monopoly (Inquiry and
Control) Act (1948), 70
Multiple stores, 73, 107, 114
Munitions, 28, 96, 161

National Assistance Scheme, 307
  (reorganized as) National
    Supplementary Benefits
    Commission, 307, 308,
    323, 325, 326, 330
National Association of Local
    Government Officers
    (NALGO), 214
National Coal Board, 61
National economy, 10–12
National Health Service, *see*
    Welfare State
National Industrial Relations
    Commission, 230
National Industrial Relations
    Court, 231
National Insurance, 246
National Insurance Act (1946),
    305, 308
National Insurance Act (1948),
    247
National resources, 153, 154,
    352
National Union of Teachers
    (N.U.T.), 214
National Wages Policy, 223
Nationalized industries,
    statutory obligation of,
    219
Natural gas, North Sea, 11
Necessities, definition of, 23–4,
    31–2, 49, 54, 55, 252
New industries, 270
    development of, 80
    growth of, 94–5
    protection of, 176–7
    See also Industries; Location
    of industry
New Towns Act (1946), 97
Non-manual unionism, 214

British Medical Association,
    214
Civil Service Clerical Officers
    Association, 214
National Association of Local
    Government Officers, 214
National Union of Teachers,
    214

Occupation, choice of, 203–7
Organization for European
    Economic Cooperation,
    168–9
Ottawa Agreement Act, 179,
    186

'Package holiday', 55
Parks, public, 28, 262
Parliament, responsibility for
    public corporations, 61
Pay differentials, 207, 224ff.
P.A.Y.E., 286, 318
Pay Pause (1962), 144, 207
Personal savings, 269ff.
Personal tastes, 20, 21, 22, 23,
    48, 135, 138
Pigau, Prof., 340
Planned economy, 16, 18ff.
Planning authorities, duty of,
    95–6
Plastics, 10, 350
Politics, in foreign trade, 151,
    152
Pollution, 350
Poor Law, 246, 302, 304, 307,
    310, 314, 333
    Boards of Guardians, 302
Population, effect on imports,
    154
    increase in, 85–6, 284

industrial, 95
of Britain, 80
transfer of, 85–6, 89–90
Poverty, definition of, 49–50
  resulting from industrial
    depression, 84
  statistics, 50
Prefabricated houses, 77
Price associations, 267
Price enonomy, 18ff., 174
Price system, as a measure of
    relative values, 33, 34
Prices, 164, 165, 166
  fall in, 160
  fixing, 72–4
  fluctuation of, 9, 11, 22, 23,
    25, 28, 66, 139–40, 166,
    167
  inflation of, 42, 128
  settlement of, 12, 65
  significance, 25
Prices Commission, 139
Primitive tools, 44–5
Private enterprise, 16, 60, 61,
    183
  legislation concerning, 94
  See also Joint stock
    companies; Private
    ownership
Private ownership, 56–60
Production, 9, 10, 11, 12
  competitive, 12, 25
  costs of, 165, 214, 224
  economy in, 67
  efficiency of, 12
  factors affecting, 25–7, 137
  fluctuations in, 264ff.
  foreign, 12
  home, 12
  instability in, 124

specialization, 149, 150,
    153–4
Productive resources, 18ff.
Productivity, 160
Products, classification of, 120
  variety of, 102–3
  wholesale distribution of,
    120
Property, 244ff.
Public authorities, expenditure,
    262, 272ff.
Public corporations, 61, 209
  Boards of Governors, 219–20
Public enterprise, 61
Public Health, 247
Public libraries, 28, 262
Public ownership, policy, 36–7,
    255
Public services, 28, 64, 65, 95
Purchase tax, 252

Quotas, allocation of, 181

Railways, economics of, 37ff.,
    282–3
Rates, 28, 85
Rathbone, Eleanor, 307
'Rationalization', 70
Rationing, 19, 28, 30, 31, 66
Raw materials, development of,
    19, 20, 45
  export of, 155–6
  fall in price, 160
  importation of, 154, 156
  natural resources of, 19, 20,
    44
  purchase of, 147
  rationing of, 66
  transport of, 79

Redundancy Pay Acts (1965, 1969), 287
Refrigeration, 154
Refrigerators, 10, 352
Resale Price Maintenance, 71–3
Restrictive Trade Practices Act (1956), 73–5
Retail Prices Index, *see* Cost of Living Index
Retraining of adult workers union attitude to, 288
special register, 288
Rome Treaty, 185, 189
Roosevelt, Franklin D., 161
Roshill Commission, 343
Majority and Minority Reports of, 344–5
Rowntree, Seebohm, 49, 301, 321, 323, 324, 325
Royal Commission on the Distribution of Income and Wealth (1975), 199, 201
Royal Commission on Equal Pay, 233, 235
Royal Commission on Trade Unions and Employers Associations, 229
Donovan Report, 229
Royal Mint, 141

Sainsburys, 119
Safeguarding of Industries Acts (1921–6), 178
Scarcity of supplies, 9, 18
Science, effect on domestic economy, 11, 18–19, 48
Secretary of State for Employment, 221, 230, 231
Security, importance of, 15, 256, 266, 282–8

Self-service stores, 104, 110, 116
Self-sufficiency, 9, 16, 18, 154
Sex Discrimination Act, 243–4
Equal Opportunities Commission, 244
Shareholders, 57, 58, 59, 60
Shipping, 157, 161, 274
Ships, 41, 92
Shopkeeper, problems of the, 103–4
Shops, cash and carry system, 106–7
credit system, 107
retail, 102ff.
Skilled work, 238
Smith, Sidney, 336, 339
Social forces, 13
Social services, 246, 248–9, 262
Social values, 13–14, 46, 208
Special areas, *see* Depressed areas
Specialization, 10, 83, 84, 101, 153, 278, 283
Standard of living, 24, 48, 49, 50, 54, 55, 99, 190, 284, 352
Staple foods, 23
State 'benefits', 146, 202, 246–7, 249
State control, 28, 29, 33, 34, 35, 62, 95, 96, 227–8, 277
State schools, 28
Sterling Area, definition of, 170–72
Stock Exchange, 59, 233
Subsidies, 180–81, 182, 192, 193, 219, 247, 248
Supermarkets, 73, 108, 110–11, 116
Superstore, 112

Supplementary Benefits
  Commission, 307-8, 323,
  325, 326-7, 330
Supplies, 9, 10, 53, 55
Supply and demand, 10, 11,
  18ff., 54, 55, 67, 267, 268ff.

Tariffs, 16, 52, 152, 169ff.,
  173ff., 182ff.
Taxation, method of, 250-54,
  276
Taxes, 250ff., 276-7, 353
  direct, 251, 258, 260, 353
  indirect, 251ff., 259, 260,
  261, 353
  payment of, 28, 61, 144, 202,
  219, 353
Technical equipment, 47
Technical institutes, 83
Techniques, 36, 52, 53, 160,
  215, 270, 283, 284
Technological experiment, 47
Textiles, 11, 41, 53, 54, 155,
  156, 157, 159
Third World, 9-10
Timber, 155
Tobacco, 32, 108, 165, 319,
  346
Tourist trade, 44, 157
Town and Country Planning
  Act (1947), 96, 97
Town planning, 88
Trade, 40, 41, 173ff.
  British policy, 153-4, 177ff.
  by barter, 129, 130, 131
  competition in, 62, 67, 148ff.
  currency problems, 150
  domestic, 149ff.
  effect of war on, 151
  international, 149, 150ff.

monopoly in, 62, 63, 65
multilateral, 166, 167-8
political aspects, 151-2
rise of new markets, 80-81
Trade Boards, *see* Wages
  Councils
Trade 'cycles', 265
Trade unions, 66, 146, 208,
  209ff., 220, 222, 286
  influence of women in, 212
  non-manual, 214
  organized workers, 213,
  220-22
  policy, 266
  structure, 208ff.
Trades Union Congress, 231-2
Trading estates (industrial
  estates), 98
Training centres, provision of,
  288
Transport, 36, 37, 52, 63,
  64, 77, 147, 154, 176, 220

Unemployment, 12, 50, 81, 84,
  85, 86-7, 97, 98, 135, 160,
  216, 223, 225, 264, 265,
  267, 274, 287
Unemployment insurance, 216
Unit shops, 73, 107, 108ff.
United States of America, 10,
  42, 164, 166, 168, 170,
  172, 178, 180
  cost of living, 42
  establishment of industries, 47
  incomes, personal, 42
  industrial output, 45
  industrialists, 47
  manufacturers, 52
  social forces, 13
  'trustbusting' legislation, 69

United States of America —
(*contd.*)
war materials supplied by, 162
See also Lend-Lease; Marshall
Aid
Urban Land Institute (U.S.A.),
111

Wage demands, 223
Wage rates, 138, 203–7
disputes over, 214–15
increase in, 99, 223–4
in industry, 241
in relation to productivity,
227
influences on, 134
methods of settling, 209ff.
overtime, 253
statutory fixing, 220ff.
where Government is the
employer, 242
Wages, determination of, 237
fluctuation in, 11, 14
increases in, 128, 134
national, 222ff.
Wages Councils (Trade Boards),
220ff., 328
Wages Councils Act, 222
War, effects of, 9, 28, 47, 66,
149, 150, 159
manpower problems, 240
materials from U.S.A., 162
transition to peace economy,
162–3

War factories, 96
Wealth, effect on imports, 154,
155
inheritance of, 245–6, 254
national, 40ff.
world, distribution of, 42–4
Wedgwood, Josiah, 256
Welfare State, 263, 290–319,
321
education, 248–9, 261, 291,
313, 318, 348–9. *See also*
Education
family allowances, 286, 291,
307, 317, 329, 331
Family Income Supplement,
328–9
National Health Service, 247,
248, 261, 292, 311–13,
318, 326, 329, 333
retirement pensions, 291, 308,
310, 317, 318, 326, 329
331
school meals, 263, 291, 313,
314, 315
sickness benefit, 310
unemployment benefit, 310,
311, 316, 327
widows' pensions, 310, 332
Woolworths, 112, 116

Youth Employment Service,
291
York, conditions of poverty in,
49

MORE ABOUT PENGUINS
AND PELICANS

Penguinews, which appears every month, contains details of all the new books issued by Penguins as they are published. From time to time it is supplemented by *Penguins in Print*, which is our complete list of almost 5,000 titles.

A specimen copy of *Penguinews* will be sent to you free on request. Please write to Dept EP, Penguin Books Ltd, Harmondsworth, Middlesex, for your copy.

In the U.S.A.: For a complete list of books available from Penguins in the United States write to Dept CS, Penguin Books, 625 Madison Avenue, New York, New York 10022.

In Canada: For a complete list of books available from Penguins in Canada write to Penguin Books Canada Ltd, 2801 John Street, Markham, Ontario L3R 1B4.

GUIDE TO THE BRITISH ECONOMY

Peter Donaldson

Fourth Edition

Guide to the British Economy is intended for the general reader who would like to have some grasp of what economics is about and what makes the economy tick, but who may find the textbook approach unpalatably abstract. Economic ideas, therefore, are presented here within the real context of the British economy. The aim is both to give an impression of the working of the different elements in the economy, and to illustrate the extent to which economic analysis can be helpful in solving the problems which face policy-makers.

In the first part of this introductory guide Peter Donaldson (who has revised and updated this edition) is mainly concerned with matters of finance, including the stockmarket. After a full examination of industry, labour, and trade, he goes on, in the final section of the book, to a general discussion of economic theories, their scope and limitations.

'This highly readable text raises and discusses sensibly and constructively the large and controversial economic arguments that rumble on day after day in our newspapers and in front of the television cameras' – *The Times Educational Supplement*

'An excellent little book. It provides a most lucid and absorbing survey of the British Economy for the intelligent layman or for the beginning student of economics. It really cannot be faulted in either its scope or its exposition' – Professor Lomax in the *Economic Journal*